THE PROBLEMS

Each volume in this series is devoted to the exploration of a single philosophical problem or group of problems. The books are large enough to allow adequate space to all major viewpoints. Selections are from contemporary as well as from classical philosophers, and whenever the issues under discussion involve ideas of other disciplines, extracts from scholars in these fields have also been included. Thus, several of the volumes will contain selections from physicists, mathematicians, psychologists, theologians, historians, and others. Each volume is edited by a specialist who has written a detailed introduction and supplied an annotated bibliography. If there is a sufficient public response, it is our aim to revise the volumes periodically and bring the bibliographies up to date.

We hope that these books will prove useful to readers of very different backgrounds. Teachers of philosophy who wish to discuss a given topic in depth have been handicapped by the absence of anthologies of this kind and by the inaccessibility of much of the material now made easily available. Scholars in related fields who wish to acquaint themselves with what philosophers have said on a given topic should also find these volumes very helpful. Above all, it is hoped that this series will be of value to the constantly growing "lay public" interested in serious subjects. The reader who wants to understand the rival philosophical positions can learn far more from studying the philosophers themselves than from the colorless and frequently inaccurate summaries contained in general histories of philosophy. The aim throughout has been to present only material distinguished for its clarity and intelligibility. If there is any presupposition shared by all the editors, it is the conviction that in order to be profound it is not necessary to be obscure.

PAUL EDWARDS, *General Editor*

The
Existence
of
God

READINGS SELECTED, EDITED, AND
FURNISHED WITH AN
INTRODUCTORY ESSAY BY

John Hick

UNIVERSITY OF BIRMINGHAM

PROBLEMS OF PHILOSOPHY SERIES
Paul Edwards, GENERAL EDITOR

MACMILLAN PUBLISHING CO., INC.
NEW YORK
COLLIER MACMILLAN PUBLISHERS
LONDON

Nineteenth Printing 1979
Macmillan Publishing Co., Inc.
866 Third Avenue, New York, N.Y. 10022
Collier Macmillan Canada, Ltd.
Library of Congress Catalog Card Number: 64-15840
Printed in the United States of America

Acknowledgments

Grateful acknowledgment is hereby made to the following for
permission to use material reprinted in this volume:

Student Christian Movement Press Limited, London, for material
from *Metaphysical Beliefs,* ed. by Alasdair MacIntyre; United
States distributor, Alec R. Allenson, Inc., Naperville, Ill.

The University of Chicago Press, for material from *Systematic
Theology,* Vol. I, by Paul Tillich, copyright 1951 by the University
of Chicago.

Encyclopædia Britannica, for material from "Theism," Vol. 22
(1962).

The Clarendon Press, Oxford, for material from *Statement and
Inference,* Vol. 2, by Cook Wilson; *Laws,* Book 10, "The Dialogues
of Plato," tr. by B. Jowett (1953); *The Theory of Good and Evil,*
Vol. 2, by Hastings Rashdall.

The Westminster Press, Philadelphia, for material from *A
Scholastic Miscellany: Anselm to Ockham.* Ed., tr. Eugene R.
Fairweather. Published 1956, The Westminster Press. Also by
permission of the Student Christian Movement Press Limited,
London, from the Library of Christian Classics, Vol. 10.

Random House, Inc., New York, for material from *Basic Writings of St. Thomas Aquinas,* ed. by Anton C. Pegis. Copyright 1945
by Random House, Inc. Reprinted by permission. Also by permission of Burns & Oates Ltd.

Cambridge University Press, New York, for material from
"Meditation V," *The Philosophical Works of Descartes,* Vol. I,

tr. by Elizabeth S. Haldane and G. R. T. Ross; from *Philosophical Theology*, Vol. II, by F. R. Tennant; *An Empiricist's View of the Nature of Religious Belief*, by R. B. Braithwaite [reprinted in full].

Macmillan & Company Ltd., London, and St. Martin's Press, Inc., New York, and the Macmillan Company of Canada Ltd., Toronto, for material from *Critique of Pure Reason*, by Immanuel Kant, tr. by Norman Kemp Smith.

Norman Malcolm, for permission to reprint his article "Anselm's Ontological Arguments," which first appeared in *The Philosophical Review* (January 1960).

Penguin Books Ltd., for material from *Aquinas*, by F. C. Copleston.

The Society for Promoting Christian Knowledge, publishers of *Essays Catholic and Critical*, ed. by E. G. Selwyn (1926), for material from "The Vindication of Religion," by A. E. Taylor.

Lord Russell and Father F. C. Copleston, for permission to reprint "The Existence of God, A Debate Between Bertrand Russell and Father F. C. Copleston," copyright © 1957, by George Allen & Unwin Ltd.

Charles Scribner's Sons, New York, for material from *Our Knowledge of God*, pp. 119–126, by John Baillie. Copyright © 1959 John Baillie. Reprinted with the permission of Charles Scribner's Sons and of Oxford University Press.

Material from *Philosophical Fragments*, by Sören Kierkegaard, copyright © 1962 by Princeton University Press.

Dover Publications, Inc., New York, and Victor Gollancz, Ltd., London, for material from *Language, Truth and Logic*, by A. J. Ayer, second edition.

Antony Flew, for permission to reprint his article "Theology and Falsification," which first appeared in *University*, published by Basil Blackwell, Oxford; reprinted with permission of The Macmillan Company, New York, from *New Essays in Philosophical Theology*, ed. by Antony Flew and Alasdair MacIntyre. First published in 1955. Also by permission of the Student Christian Movement Press Limited, London.

Theology Today, Vol. XVII, No. 1 (April, 1960), for permission to reprint "Theology and Verification," by John Hick.

John Wisdom, for permission to print his article "The Modes of Thought and the Logic of God," which first appeared in a broadcast on the British Broadcasting Company Third Programme.

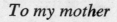

To my mother

CONTENTS

PART II

Discussions and Questionings

PART III

Contemporary Problems

PREFACE

This book is designed for two main classes of readers. It is intended for use in connection with college, university, and seminary courses in the philosophy of religion; and it is also addressed to that apparently increasing group of intelligent nonstudent readers who are concerned with this subject because of its intrinsic interest and importance, quite apart from any formal educational purpose.

The volume brings together basic philosophical writings, both affirmative and negative, both classical and contemporary, dealing with the problem of the existence of God. In some cases new translations which are superior to long-used versions have recently become available and are used—for example, Anton C. Pegis's revision of the English Dominican translation of Aquinas and Eugene R. Fairweather's version of Anselm. Many readers will, I think, welcome in Part III the full text of R. B. Braithwaite's lecture, "An Empiricist's View of the Nature of Religious Belief," and many will be eager to see John Wisdom's "The Modes of Thought and the Logic of God," a paper which has been widely discussed as it has circulated in mimeographed form but which now appears in public print for the first time.

In preparing this book I have sought and received the advice of a number of friends who are teaching either the philosophy of religion or philosophy in general; and without naming them here I should like to thank all who so generously helped in this way. I have gratefully adopted many of their suggestions. I have however had regretfully to pass by others. This was almost invariably due to limitations of space. If everything had been included that was recommended on good grounds the book would have been twice as long, costing twice as much, and would no longer have met the specifications of a series which has, I think, its own proper and distinctive usefulness.

Various considerations caused the notes to each article to

be grouped at the end of the article instead of being placed on the pages on which the references occur.

At the end of the book there is a classified and annotated bibliography through which it is possible to follow further any or all of the topics treated in the readings.

As editor I have not sought to propagate directly or indirectly my own personal conviction as to the reality of God. However it has not been difficult to follow a policy of editorial impartiality since religious faith is not, in my view, dependent upon philosophical arguments. Its sources lie outside the range of such a book as this, although a section of the bibliography (on pp. 304-305) is devoted to works which develop the kind of apologetic that is not based upon the theistic "proofs."

JOHN HICK

June, 1963
Princeton, New Jersey

INTRODUCTION

I

The subject of the existence of God, as a problem in philosophy, revolves around the "theistic proofs" which have been a center of debate since the time of Plato. Whether or not these arguments succeed in establishing their conclusion and whether or not, supposing that they do succeed, they are of any positive religious value, are disputed questions. But that the proofs themselves are classic exercises of philosophical reasoning is not in dispute. Accordingly Parts I and II of this volume are devoted to these proofs, and the greater part of the present Introduction will discuss their status from the points of view both of philosophy and of religion.

Something should perhaps be said at the outset about the phrase "God exists," the propriety of which has been challenged on both philosophical and theological grounds. We are not at the moment concerned with the question *whether* God exists, but with the suitability of the locution "God exists" used either in affirmation or denial. The philosophical objection is that "*x* exists" is a logically misleading way of saying something else, namely that the description or definition indicated by the term *x* applies to some reality. Thus the correct question is not whether a being called God does or does not have the property of existence, but whether the definition of "God" has or lacks an instance. This well-known Russellian analysis of "exists"[1] entails that "God exists" and "the existence (or the reality) of God" are solecisms. They remain however very convenient solecisms, and they can be rendered harmless by stipulating that "God exists" is to be construed as shorthand for "There is an individual, and only one, who is omniscient, omnipotent, etc." With this understanding it is perhaps permissible to retain the traditional phrase even whilst acknowledging its logical impropriety.

The religious objection to speaking of the existence of God

is of a quite different kind and is formulated as follows by Paul Tillich: "Thus the question of the existence of God can be neither asked nor answered. If asked, it is a question about that which by its very nature is above existence, and therefore the answer—whether negative or affirmative—implicitly denies the nature of God. It is as atheistic to affirm the existence of God as it is to deny it. God is being-itself, not *a* being."[2] This is in effect a theological-semantic recommendation that the term "existence" be applied only to entities within the created realm, with the result that it becomes improper to assert of a postulated creator of this realm that he *exists*. The recommendation operates as an emphatic rejection of any notion of God as a finite object alongside others in the universe. But we still want to be able to distinguish between there being and there not being an ultimate reality which is not a part of the universe and to which we may properly direct our "ultimate concern"; and the term "the existence of God" enables us to do this. Once again, then, it seems on the whole preferable to retain the traditional phrase than to risk concealing important issues by rejecting it.

In our own time, whilst the theistic proofs have continued to call forth a steady stream of chapters in philosophical works and articles in the philosophical journals, another aspect of the "problem of God" has also come to the fore. This is the question, logically prior to that of arguments for God's existence, as to what it *means* to assert that God exists. The readings in Part III are concerned with this latter question and will I think be found to define the issues involved without the need for any further introduction.

Except for the last paper, by John Wisdom, all the discussions in this book presuppose a fairly well-defined and agreed conception of God. They presuppose what can be called the Judaic-Christian idea of God. Some argue that there is such a being; others that there is not; and others again hold that there is, but that this or that argument for his existence is not valid, or even that the whole program of the theistic proofs is mistaken and that religious belief properly rests upon quite other grounds. This broadly agreed Judaic-Christian understanding of God may be briefly described as follows. God is the unique infinite personal Spirit who has created out of nothing everything other than himself; he is eternal and uncreated; omnipotent and omniscient; and his attitude towards his human creatures, whom he has made for eventual fellowship with himself, is one of grace and love. This is the kind of being with whose existence or non-existence the thinkers represented in this book are concerned.[3]

The theistic arguments are commonly distinguished as being either *a priori* or *a posteriori*. An *a posteriori* argument is one which relies on a premise derived from (hence after, or posterior to) experience. Accordingly *a posteriori* arguments for the existence of God infer a deity from evidences within our human experience. An *a priori* argument on the other hand operates from a basis which is logically prior to and independent of experience. It rests upon purely logical considerations and (if it succeeds) achieves the kind of certainty exhibited by mathematical truths.

In point of fact only one strictly *a priori* theistic proof has been offered—the ontological argument of Anselm, Descartes, and others (*see* pp. 23f). This claims on *a priori* grounds that the idea of "the most perfect and real conceivable being" is the idea of a being which must and therefore does exist; for a Nonexistent could never be the most perfect and real conceivable being.

The basic philosophical objection to this reasoning is well-developed and widely agreed. The objection is that one is never entitled to deduce from a concept that anything exists which corresponds to that concept. The nature of thought on the one hand and of extra-mental reality on the other, and of the distinction between them, is such that there can be no valid inference from the thought of a given kind of being to the conclusion that there is in fact a being of this kind. The mind is free to form concepts of various species of beings which do not exist, and it is impossible to tell from inspection of a concept alone whether or not there is an extra-mental entity answering to it. Only experience can determine this. This objection is most powerfully stated by Kant in the selection on pp. 39f.

Turning now to the *a posteriori* theistic proofs, it is necessary to distinguish between, on the one hand, those which profess to constitute strict apodictic demonstrations or "knock-down arguments" and those, on the other hand, which are of the nature of probability arguments, seeking to persuade us that theism is the most reasonable of the available alternatives.

In the following two sections I shall discuss each of these two kinds of *a posteriori* argument and shall argue in each case that a philosophical proof of God's existence is impossible. I shall argue not only that no successful argument of this kind has yet been produced, but that it is in principle impossible that such ever should be produced—and equally impossible irrespective of whether or not God does in fact exist. Many philosophers today, perhaps the majority, would agree with this position, although there are others who would emphatically disagree, and it should be emphasized at the outset that virtually all the questions involved fall well within the area of the debatable.

II

Consider first the attempt to demonstrate the reality of God in strict logical fashion from *a posteriori* premises.

In order to define the question at issue it is necessary to distinguish several different senses of "prove." For there are two senses in which we may speak of something being proved in which it is a noncontroversial statement that the existence of God can be proved, and these need to be mentioned and set aside in order to isolate our central problem, which concerns a third sense of "prove."

The existence of God can undoubtedly be proved if a proof is equated with a formally valid argument. For it is a familiar logical truism that a valid argument can be constructed with *any* proposition as its conclusion. Given any proposition, *q*, it is possible to supply other propositions such that it would be inconsistent to affirm these and to deny *q*. The propositions thus supplied constitute premises from which *q* follows as a conclusion. One can easily construct a proof in this sense for the existence of God. For example: If Princeton exists, God exists; Princeton exists; therefore God exists. The argument is formally impeccable—one cannot rationally affirm the premises and deny the conclusion.

This first sense of "prove" is referred to here only to be dismissed as an inconvenient and confusing usage. It is much better to follow the more normal practice and to distinguish between an argument being valid and its conclusion being true. The validity of an argument is a purely formal characteristic of the relation between its constituent propositions, and does not guarantee the truth of any of them. It guarantees that *if* the premises are true the conclusion is true also; but it cannot guarantee that the premises, and therefore the conclusion, *are* true.

A second sense of "prove" is that in which a conclusion is said to be proved, not merely if it follows from premises, but only if it follows from *true* premises. We may consider this second sense in relation to and in distinction from a third in which these logical conditions are supplemented by the yet further requirement that the premises are *known* or acknowledged to be true. There might, in sense number two, be all manner of valid arguments in which true premises lead to true conclusions but which do not prove anything to anyone because no one acknowledges their premises as being true. In this sense, all that can be said is that there is a proof of God's existence *if* God exists but not if he does not! But this is so neutral and noncommittal a point that the atheist will not be concerned to dispute it. It is surely the third sense, in which to prove something means to prove it *to* someone, that is really in question when we ask whether the existence of God can be proved.

The sense of "prove" then which most concerns us is that in which we speak of proving a certain conclusion to an individual or a group. Here it is required not only that the conclusion follows from the premises, and not only that the premises from which it follows are true, but also that they are acknowledged to be true by those to whom we are seeking to prove the conclusion. It is at this point that a basic philosophical objection emerges to all strict theistic proofs of the *a posteriori* type—namely that they necessarily beg the question, in that a person who accepts their premises already acknowledges the reality of God. For theistic arguments of this type rely upon some connection between God and the world. In order to provide a basis for a strict proof of God's existence—and we are at the moment discussing strict proofs —the connection must be such as to warrant the proposition, "If the world (or some particular aspect of it) exists, God exists." But clearly anyone who accepts this premise already either acknowledges the existence of God or else is unable to reason at all. And it is idle to offer a demonstration to one who does not need it or is incapable of using it.

Might not someone however who had not previously accepted a premise of this kind be brought by a process of philosophical reasoning to accept it? This is of course possible, and does in fact happen. Indeed many presentations of the cosmological type of theistic proof include such a prolegomenon as their first stage; and the additional premise which they use is that the world is ultimately explicable by reference to some reality beyond itself and is not a sheer inexplicable "brute fact" which can only be accepted as such. As Father Copleston says in the course of his debate with Bertrand Russell, "my point is that what we call the world is intrinsically unintelligible, apart from the existence of God" (page 174). The first cause argument and the argument from contingency both employ this principle either explicitly or implicitly. Their logical form is that of a dilemma: either there is a God or the world is ultimately unintelligible. The one argument urges that either there is an endless and therefore meaningless regress of causes or else the causal series must finally be anchored in an uncaused first cause which is God. The other argument claims that each item in nature points beyond itself for its sufficient explanation, and urges that either the regress of explanations runs out to infinity, with the result that nothing is ever finally explained, or else that it must terminate in a self-existent being which neither needs nor is capable of further explanation, and which is God. Clearly the force of these arguments depends upon the decisive ruling out of one alternative, namely the conclusion that the world is ultimately inexplicable, so that we may be driven by force of logic to the other conclusion, that God exists. But it is precisely this excluding of the nontheistic alternative that is not and cannot be accomplished by logical considerations alone. For it rests upon a fundamental act of faith, faith in the ultimate "rationality" of existence; and this is part of the larger faith which the atheist refuses. He believes on the contrary that the universe is devoid of ultimate purpose and that the question as to why there is anything at all has no meaning and therefore no answer. Faced with this absence of metaphysical faith the theistic arguer is disarmed. As Father Copleston acknowledges at the end of his explanation of the Five Ways of Thomas Aquinas, "If one does not wish to embark on the path which leads to the affirmation of transcendent being, however the latter may be described (if it is described at all), one has to deny the reality of the problem, assert that things 'just are' and that the existential question is a pseudo-question. And if one refuses even to sit down at the chess board and make a move, one cannot, of course, be checkmated" (p. 93). The same point is made from the other side in the Russell-Copleston debate when Russell remarks, "I should say that the universe is just there, and that's all" (p. 175). Since the cosmological argument thus requires a premise which is not granted by those to whom the argument is primarily directed, it follows that from their point of view it begs the question. And this, I suggest, is the basic philosophical objection to this group of arguments. They can only be probative to those who need no proof.

Perhaps, however, arguments of this cosmological type might be put to a more modest use. Perhaps instead of being offered as strict demonstrations they can be presented as providing significant pointers, suggestive clues, probable arguments appealing not to the principle of logical entailment but to a less rigorous and more informal kind of reasonableness. This leads us to the subject of probability arguments for the existence of God.

III

Whilst the first cause argument and the argument from the contingency of the world profess to be strictly demonstrative, the other arguments of the cosmological type—the design and moral arguments, and those based upon religious experience, miracles, and universal consent—attempt to establish a high probability rather than a logical certainty. They direct attention to some aspect of the world or of human experience—for example, the order and beauty of nature and its apparently purposive character, or man's religious experience and appreciation of values—and conclude that this is most adequately explained by postulating a divine creator, an object of religious experience, or a transcendent ground of value. It is not claimed that the intellectual move from these starting points to God proceeds on the ironclad rails of logical entailment. There can be no strict deduction of an infinite deity from the character of finite things. Rather these function as significant signs and clues, pointing with varying degrees of particularity and force to the reality of God. Formulated as arguments directed to the nonbeliever such inferences accordingly center upon the notion of probability Their general form is: in view of this or that characteristic of the world it is more probable that there is a God than that there is not. Correlatively, it is more rational in the

light of these same considerations to believe in God than to
disbelieve in him or to remain agnostic.

It is clear that the "probability" invoked here is not the
strict mathematical concept employed in the physical and
behavioral sciences. To claim that the probability of the
universe being God-produced is represented by some particular mathematical ratio, $1/n$, would (according to the widely
used frequency theory) presuppose it to be known (a) that
there is a certain determinate number of universes and (b)
that a certain definite proportion of these, namely $1/n$, are
God-produced. Not knowing whether our own universe falls
within the God-produced or the non-God-produced fraction
we should nevertheless know that the probability of its being
God-produced is $1/n$. Clearly, however, any such use of
statistical probability is ruled out by the fact that there is by
definition only one universe. For by "the universe" in this
context is meant "the totality of all that is, excluding any possible creator of everything other than himself." On the basis
of this definition it is a necessary truth that there is but one
universe, and there can accordingly be no ground for judgments to the effect that a certain proportion of universes
exhibit a certain characteristic. This point was first made by
David Hume in his *Dialogues Concerning Natural Religion:*
"When two *species* of objects have always been observed to
be conjoined together, I can *infer*, by custom, the existence
of one wherever I *see* the existence of the other; and this I
call an argument from experience. But how this argument
can have place, where the objects, as in the present case, are
single, individual, without parallel, or specific resemblance,
may be difficult to explain. And will any man tell me with a
serious countenance, that an orderly universe must arise
from some thought and art, like the human; because we have
experience of it? To ascertain this reasoning, it were requisite,
that we had experience of the origin of worlds; and it is not
sufficient surely, that we have seen ships and cities arise from
human art and contrivance . . ."[4]

The concept of probability that operates in the theistic
arguments must clearly be nonmathematical. Stated in terms
of the operations of the judging mind it must be a matter of
more reasonable and less reasonable acts of assent; or in
terms of the subject matter itself, of the relative antecedent
or intrinsic probabilities of different types of hypothesis. It
must, in other words, be claimed that it is more reasonable

or rational to interpret the universe theistically than to interpret it naturalistically; or formulating the same claim from
the other end, that a theistic interpretation of nature is
intrinsically more probable than a naturalistic one.

But the question still has to be raised whether even this
nonmathematical or "alogical" concept of probability is applicable to the theistic problem. It is of course a fact that as
men have looked at the world and have been especially struck
by this or that aspect of it they have concluded that there
is (or that there is not) a God, or have found in the world
confirmation of an already formed conviction as to the existence (or nonexistence) of God in terms varying in degree
from "it seems on the whole more likely than not" to "it is
overwhelmingly more probable." But the question remains
whether the notion of probability or likelihood is being used
in such judgments to express more than a purely personal
and imponderable "hunch" or feeling.

The situation seems to be this. Of the immense number
and variety of apparently relevant considerations some, taken
by themselves, seem to point in one direction and some in the
other. One group can fairly be said to count as at least prima
facie evidence for the existence of God. For not only do
believers urge these particular considerations as supporting
their own position, but disbelievers concurringly treat them
as points requiring special explanation. And likewise there
are other considerations which taken by themselves constitute at least prima facie antitheistic evidences. These are
matters which nonbelievers emphasize but in which the believer on the other hand sees a challenge to his faith which
he must try to meet.

As examples of prima facie theistic evidence, man's distinctively religious experience and the reports of miracles
would never be pointed out by an atheist as tending positively
to support his own position; they are items for which he feels
obliged to seek an explanation other than the one which
the facts themselves, when taken at their face value, suggest.
It is agreed for example that there is such a thing as "religious experience" and this very name embodies a religious
interpretation of the experiences in question as being in some
way cognitive of the divine. Accordingly it is incumbent upon
the disbeliever to respond by offering a naturalistic interpretation of these same experiences. Such reinterpretations have
been offered and have followed the path marked out by

Thomas Hobbes in his paradigmatic remark that when a man says that God has spoken to him in a dream, this "is no more than to say he dreamed that God spake to him."[5]

On the other side, as examples of prima facie antitheistic evidence, human wickedness and the suffering of all sentient creatures including man are not facts which would be selected by the theist as favorable premises from which to launch his own argument; they are rather difficulties which he must endeavor to meet from the wider resources of theism, as has been done by a succession of thinkers from Augustine to Austin Farrer.[6]

There are yet other factors which are not so manifestly evidential as those already mentioned but which seem nevertheless to fit rather more readily into one conception than the other. For example, moral experience finds readier hospitality within a religious metaphysic, whilst on the other hand the infinite vastness of the physical universe and the insignificant place occupied in it by man may be more immediately assimilable into a naturalistic world-view.

Now none of these factors, or of the indefinitely many others that could be added to them, points so unequivocally in one particular direction as to admit of only one possible explanation. Although in isolation they each suggest a conclusion, nevertheless each is capable of being fitted into either a religious or a naturalistic context. There is no item offered as either theistic or antitheistic evidence which cannot be absorbed by a mind operating with different presuppositions into the contrary view. The question then is whether one *way* of interpreting them can be said to be more probable than the other or (putting the same query in another way) whether acceptance of one interpretation can be said to be more reasonable or rational than acceptance of the other. For the choice is never between explanation and blank absence of explanation, but always between alternative explanations which employ radically different categories.

From the fact that there are particular considerations which count as prima facie evidence both for and against theism it follows that if we attend only to selected items we may well receive the impression that the evidence as a whole tends in one direction—*which* direction depending upon which items of evidence are in the forefront of our attention. However since theism and naturalism can each alike lay claim to prima facie evidences and must each admit the existence of prima facie difficulties, any fruitful comparison must treat the two alternative interpretations as comprehensive wholes, each with its own distinctive strengths and weaknesses. This has been recognized by a number of religious apologists. Thus W. R. Matthews represents a widely held position when he says, "The central question of constructive philosophy does not present itself to [the post-Kantian Theist] in the form: given the idea of God as a belief, to find some rational proof of His existence. Rather the problem presents itself as analogous to the scientific problem: given the universe as disclosed in experience, to find the most reasonable account of it. Several hypotheses present themselves for consideration, among them theism. The question before the mind of the philosopher, therefore, is to decide which of the possible hypotheses squares most adequately with the whole experience of the universe which is open to us. The Theist maintains that his hypothesis is the most rational in this sense."[7] Again, according to F. R. Tennant the task of philosophical theology is to demonstrate that "there is a theistic world-view commending itself as more reasonable than other interpretations or than the refusal to interpret, and congruent with the knowledge—i.e. the probability—which is the guide of life and of science."[8] (Tennant's own attempt to do this through what he calls cosmic teleology appears on pp. 121f.)

In what sense however, or on what basis, can it be claimed to be established that one such total interpretation is more probable than another? Can we, for example, simply count points for and against? Can we say that there are say ten items of prima facie evidence in favor of theism and eight against; and conversely eight items in favor of atheism and ten against it—so that theism wins by two points? Clearly, no such mechanical procedure will do, for the conflicting considerations do not constitute units of equal weight. Can we perhaps however place each item in its position on an evidential scale in which, without being assigned any numerical value, they are listed in order of importance? To some extent this is feasible as a separate operation on each side of the debate. In many instances we can accord a greater weight to one item of theistic (or of antitheistic) evidence than to another, and can thus begin at least to construct two parallel lists. But we still have no agreed way of weighing an item on one list against its opposite number on the other list nor, therefore, of evaluating one list as a whole in relation to the other. There are no common scales in which to weigh, for example, human wickedness and folly against the fact of man's moral experience, or the phenomenon of Christ against the problem of human and animal suffering. Judgments on such matters are intuitive and personal, and the category of probability, if it is applied, no longer has any objective meaning.

What is sought to be done here is something which no one has ever yet succeeded in doing, namely to show by arguments acceptable to all parties that one comprehensive world-view has superior probability to another. The criteria which have usually been suggested by which to match metaphysical systems against each other are those developed in connection with the coherence theory of truth—the internal logical consistency of each system of thought; their explanatory comprehensiveness (so that if one covers data which the other has to leave out of account the former is to that extent superior); and the "adequacy" with which they illuminate and explain what they profess to explain. The first two of these criteria will not help us at this point, since there are forms both of theism and of naturalism which are internally consistent and which are equally comprehensive in the sense that there are no data which evade their explanatory scope. The issue is once again not between explanation and no explanation but between two radically different kinds of explanation. The crucial question is thus whether one *way* of accounting for the data can be said to be inherently more adequate than the other. This is in effect our original problem as to whether theism or naturalism can meaningfully be said to possess a superior antecedent probability. And it now seems that there is no objective sense in which one consistent and comprehensive world-view can be described as inherently more probable than another. It is of course a truism, if not a tautology, that to the theist theism seems more adequate and that to the naturalist naturalism seems more adequate. But this is because they are judging from importantly different standpoints and with different criteria and presuppositions. And it appears that the issue between them is not one that can be settled by appeal to any agreed procedure or by reference to any objectively ascertainable probabilities.

IV

We turn now from philosophical to theological considerations. A philosopher unacquainted with modern developments in theology might well assume that theologians would, *ex officio*, be supporters of the theistic proofs and would regard as a fatal blow the conclusion that there can be neither a strict demonstration of God's existence nor a valid probability argument for it. In fact however such an assumption would be true only of certain theological schools. It is true of Roman Catholic theology,[9] of sections of conservative Protestantism,[10] and of most of those Protestant apologists who continue to work within the tradition of nineteenth century idealism. It has never been true, on the other hand, of Jewish religious thought,[11] and it is not true of that central stream of contemporary Protestant theology which has been influenced by the "neo-orthodox" movement, the revival of Reformation studies, and the "existentialism" of Kierkegaard and his successors. Accordingly we have now to take note of this latter reaction to the theistic proofs, ranging from a complete lack of concern for them to a positive rejection of them as being religiously irrelevant or even harmful. There are several different considerations to be noticed and evaluated.

(1) It has often been pointed out (as it is by John Baillie in the selection on pp. 204f.) that for the man of faith, as he is depicted in the Bible, no theistic proofs are necessary. Philosophers in the rationalist tradition, holding that to know means to be able to prove, have been shocked to find that in the Bible, which is supposed to be the basis of Western religion, no attempt whatever is made to demonstrate the existence of God. Instead of professing to establish the reality of God by philosophical reasoning the Bible throughout takes his reality for granted. Indeed to the Biblical writers it would have seemed absurd to try to establish by logical argumentation that God exists. For they were convinced that they were already having to do with him and he with them in all the affairs of their lives. God was known to them as a dynamic will interacting with their own wills, a sheer given reality, as inescapably to be reckoned with as destructive storm and life-giving sunshine, or the hatred of their enemies and the friendship of their neighbors. They did not think of God as an inferred entity but as an experienced

reality. Many of the Biblical writers were (sometimes, though doubtless not at all times) as vividly conscious of being in God's presence as they were of living in a material environment. It is impossible to read their pages without realizing that to them God was not a proposition completing a syllogism, or an idea adopted by the mind, but the experiential reality which gave significance to their lives. It would be as sensible for a husband to desire a philosophical proof of the existence of the wife and family who contribute so much of the meaning and value of life for him as for the man of faith to seek a proof of the existence of the God within whose purpose he believes that he lives and moves and has his being. As Cook Wilson wrote:

"If we think of the existence of our friends; it is the 'direct knowledge' that we want: merely inferential knowledge seems a poor affair. To most men it would be as surprising as unwelcome to hear it could not be directly known whether there were such existences as their friends, and that it was only a matter of (probable) empirical argument and inference from facts which are directly known. And even if we convince ourselves on reflection that this is really the case, our actions prove that we have a confidence in the existence of our friends which can't be derived from an empirical argument (which can never be certain)—for a man will risk his life for his friend. We don't want merely inferred friends. Could we possibly be satisfied with an inferred God?"[12]

Given the standpoint of religious conviction, this seems undeniable. The man of faith has no need of theistic proofs; for he has something which is for him much better. However it does not follow from this that there may not be others who *do* need a theistic proof, nor does it follow that there are in fact no such proofs. All that has been said about the irrelevance of proofs to the life of faith may well be true, and yet it might still be the case that there are valid arguments capable of establishing the existence of God to those who stand outside the life of faith.

(2) It has also often been pointed out that the God whose existence each of the traditional theistic proofs professes to establish is only an abstraction from and a pale shadow of the living God who is the putative object of Biblical faith. A First Cause of the Universe might or might not be a deity to whom an unqualified devotion, love, and trust would be appropriate; Aquinas' *Et hoc omnes intelligunt Deum* ("and

this all understand to be God") is not the last step in a logical argument but merely an appeal to the custom of overlooking a gap in the argument at this point. A Necessary Being, and indeed a being who is metaphysically absolute in every respect—omnipotent, omniscient, eternal, uncreated— might be morally good or evil. As Professor H. D. Aiken has recently remarked "Logically, there is no reason why an almighty and omniscient being might not be a perfect stinker."[13] A divine Designer of the world whose nature is read off from the appearances of nature, might, as Hume showed (*Dialogues*, V, pp. 104f. of the present volume), be finite or infinite, perfect or imperfect, omniscient or fallible, and might indeed be not one being but a veritable pantheon. It is only by going beyond what is proved, or claimed to have been proved, and identifying the First Cause, Necessary Being, or Mind behind Nature, with the God of Biblical faith that these proofs could ever properly impel to worship. By themselves, and without supplementation of content and infusion of emotional life from religious traditions and experiences far transcending the boundaries of the proofs themselves, they would never lead to the life of faith.

The ontological argument on the other hand (*see* pp. 23f.) is in this respect in a different category. If it succeeds it establishes the reality of a being so perfect in every respect that no more perfect can be conceived. Clearly if such a being is not worthy of worship none ever could be. It would therefore seem that, unlike the other proofs, the ontological argument, if it were logically sound, would present the relatively few persons who are capable of appreciating such abstract reasoning with a rational ground for worship. On the other hand, however, whilst this is the argument that would accomplish most if it succeeded it is also the argument which is most absolutely incapable of succeeding. For it is inextricably involved in the fallacy of professing to deduce existence from a concept (*see* pp. 40f).

(3) It is argued by some religious writers that a logical demonstration of the existence of God would be a form of coercion, and would as such be incompatible with God's evident intention to treat his human creatures as free and responsible persons. A great deal of twentieth century theology emphasizes that God, as the infinite personal reality, having made man as person in his own image, always treats men as persons, respecting their relative freedom and au-

tonomy. He does not override the human mind and will by
revealing himself in overwhelming majesty and power but
always approaches us in ways which leave room for an
uncompelled response of human faith. Even God's own
entry into our earthly history, it is said, was in an "incognito"
that could be penetrated only by the eyes of faith. As Pascal
put it, "willing to appear openly to those who seek him with
all their heart, and to be hidden from those who flee from
him with all their heart, he so regulates the knowledge of
himself that he has given indications of himself which are
visible to those who seek him and not to those who do not
seek him. There is enough light for those to see who only
desire to see, and enough obscurity for those who have a
contrary disposition."[14] God's self-revealing actions are accordingly always so mediated through the events composing
our temporal experience that men only become aware of the
divine presence by interpreting and responding to these
events in the way which we call religious faith. For if God
were to disclose himself to us in the coercive manner in
which our physical environment obtrudes itself we should
be dwarfed to nothingness by the infinite power thus irresistibly breaking open the privacy of our souls. Further,
we should be spiritually blinded by God's perfect holiness
and paralyzed by his infinite energy; for "human kind cannot bear very much reality."[15] Such a direct, unmediated
confrontation breaking in upon us and shattering the frail
autonomy of our finite nature would leave no ground for a
free human response of trust, self-commitment, and obedience. There could be no call for a man to venture upon a
dawning consciousness of God's reality, and thus receive this
consciousness as an authentic part of his own personal existence precisely because it has not been injected into him or
clamped upon him by magisterial exercise of divine omnipotence.

The basic principle invoked here is that for the sake of
creating a personal relationship of love and trust with his
human creatures God does not force an awareness of himself
upon them. And (according to the view which we are considering) it is only a further application of the same principle to add that a logically compelling demonstration of
God's existence would likewise frustrate this purpose. For
men—or at least those of them capable of following the
proof—could then be forced to know that God is real. Thus

Alasdair MacIntyre has said, "For if we could produce logically cogent arguments we should produce the kind of certitude that leaves no room for decision; where proof is in place, decision is not. We do not decide to accept Euclid's conclusions; we merely look to the rigour of his arguments. If the existence of God were demonstrable we should be as bereft of the possibility of making a free decision to love God as we should be if every utterance of doubt or unbelief was answered by thunder-bolts from heaven."[16] This then is the "religious coercion" objection to theistic proofs.

To what extent is this a sound argument? We may accept the theological doctrine that for God to force men to know him by the coercion of logic would be incompatible with his purpose of winning the voluntary response and worship of free moral beings. But the question still remains whether the theistic proofs could ever do this. Could a verbal proof of God's existence compel a consciousness of God comparable in coerciveness with a direct manifestation of divine majesty and power? Could anyone be moved and shaken in their whole being by the demonstration of a proposition as men have been by a numinous experience of overpowering impressiveness? Would the things that have just been said about an overwhelming display of divine glory really apply to verbal demonstrations—that infinite power would be irresistibly breaking in upon the privacy of our souls and that we should be blinded by God's perfect holiness and paralyzed by his infinite energy? Indeed could a form of words, culminating in the proposition that "God exists," ever have power by itself to produce more than what Newman calls a notional assent in our minds?[17]

It is of course true that the effects of purely rational considerations such as those which are brought to bear in the theistic proofs are much greater in some minds than in others. The more rational the mind the more considerable is the effect to be expected. In many—indeed taking mankind as a whole, in the great majority—of persons the effect of a theistic proof, even when no logical flaw is found in it, would be virtually nil. But in more sophisticated minds the effect must be greater, and it is at least theoretically possible that there are minds so rational that purely logical considerations can move them as effectively as the evidence of their senses. It is therefore conceivable that someone who is initially agnostic might be presented with a philosophical proof of

divine existence—say the ontological argument, with its definition of God as that than which no more perfect can be
conceived—and might as a result be led to worship the being
whose reality has thus been demonstrated to him. This seems
to be possible; but I believe that even in such a case there
must, in addition to an intelligent appreciation of the argument, be a distinctively religious response to the idea of God
which the argument presents. Some propensity to respond to
unlimited perfection as *holy* and as claiming a response of
unqualified worship and devotion must operate, over and
above the purely intellectual capacity for logical calculation.[18]
For we can conceive of a purely or merely logical mind, a
kind of human calculating machine, which is at the same
time devoid of the capacity for numinous feeling and wor-
shiping response. Such a being might infer that God exists
but be no more vitally interested in this conclusion than
many people are in, say, the fact that the Shasta dam is 602
feet high. It therefore seems that when the acceptance of a
theistic proof leads to worship, a religious reaction occurs
which turns what would otherwise be a purely abstract conclusion into an immensely significant and moving experience.
In Newman's terminology, when a notional assent to the fact
that God exists becomes a real assent, equivalent to an actual
living belief and faith in God, there has been a free human
response to an idea which could instead have been rejected
by being held at the notional level. In other words, a verbal
proof of God's existence cannot by itself break down our
human freedom; it can only lead to a notional assent which
has in itself little or no positive religious value or substance.

v

We conclude then that the theological reasons which have
been offered for rejecting the theistic proofs are considerably
less strong than the philosophical reasons. Theologians who
reject natural theology would therefore do well to do so
primarily on philosophical rather than on theological grounds.
For the situation would seem to be that it is impossible to
demonstrate the reality of God by a priori reasoning, since
this is confined to the realm of concepts; and impossible to
demonstrate it by a posteriori reasoning, because this would
have to include a premise which begs the question; and impossible to establish it as in a greater or less degree probable,

since the notion of probability has no clear meaning in this context. These considerations are of course all entirely independent of the question *whether* God exists. They merely show why it is logically inappropriate to seek to settle the question by means of proofs. If there is a God, this is a fact which must be known in some other way than by means of philosophical argumentation.

We have already noted that the Biblical writings express a consciousness of God at work in and through the events of human history and that this consciousness is not the end product of any process of philosophical reasoning. For those religious thinkers—including today probably the majority of Protestant theologians—who stand on the same ground as the Biblical writers and in a continuous community of faith with them, the important question is not whether the existence of God can be demonstrated but whether this faith-awareness of God is a mode of cognition which can properly be trusted and in terms of which it is rational to live. The central issue thus concerns the epistemological status of the claimed awareness of God as acting within the borders of human experience. Some of the recent works dealing with this subject are listed in the last section of the bibliography.

NOTES

[1] *See* Bertrand Russell, "Logical Atomism" (1918) in *Logic and Language,* London: Allen & Unwin, Ltd., 1956, pp. 228f and *Introduction to Mathematical Philosophy,* London: Allen & Unwin, Ltd., 1919, ch. 16.

[2] *Systematic Theology,* I (Chicago: University of Chicago Press, 1951), p. 237.

[3] Contemporary variants of theism which are not represented in this book are the concept of a finite deity advocated, e.g., by E. S. Brightman in *A Philosophy of Religion* (New York: Prentice Hall, Inc., 1940), and the concept of a deity who is perfect and absolute in some respects but imperfect and relative in others, advocated by Charles Hartshorne in *Man's Vision of God* (Chicago: Willett, Clark & Co., 1941) and *The Divine Relativity* (New Haven: Yale University Press, 1948).

[4] *Dialogues Concerning Natural Religion,* Part II (Kemp Smith's edition, p. 185). Also *Enquiry Concerning the Human Understanding,* Section XI (Selby-Bigge's edition, p. 148). Hume's contention is discussed by Thomas McPherson, "The Argument from Design," *Philosophy,* July, 1957. *See also* F. R. Tennant, *Philo-*

sophical Theology, II, 88 (p. 125 in the present volume), and Arthur Pap, *Elements of Analytic Philosophy* (New York: The Macmillan Company, 1949), pp. 197-200.

[5] *Leviathan,* Pt. 3, ch. 32. For a philosophically elaborate contemporary use of this argument, *see* C. B. Martin, *Religious Belief* (Ithaca: Cornell University Press, 1959), ch. 5.

[6] See Bibliography, pp. 301-302.

[7] W. R. Matthews "Theism," *Encyclopaedia Britannica,* 1962, Vol. 22, p. 50 *Cf.* Matthews' *Studies in Christian Philosophy* (2nd edition, 1928), pp. 78f; W. R. Sorley, *Moral Values and the Idea of God* (1918), pp. 307f.

[8] *Philosophical Theology,* II, 245.

[9] For a recent papal reaffirmation of the position that "human reason can, without the help of divine revelation and grace, prove the existence of a personal God by arguments drawn from created things," *see* Pope Pius XII's Encyclical *Humani Generis,* 1940, especially paras. 2, 3, 25, 29.

[10] *See* e.g. J. Oliver Buswell, *What is God?* (1937); Robert E. D. Clark, *The Universe: Plan or Accident?* (1961).

[11] *See* Abraham J. Heschel, *God in Search of Man: A Philosophy of Judaism* (New York: The Jewish Publication Society of America, 1955), pp. 246f. *Cf.* Martin Buber, *Eclipse of God* (New York: Harper and Row, 1952), ch. 8.

[12] *Statement and Inference* (Oxford: Oxford University Press, 1926) II, p. 853.

[13] "God and Evil: a study of some relations between faith and morals," *Ethics,* Vol. LXVIII, No. 2 (January, 1958), p. 82.

[14] *Pensées,* edited by Leon Brunschvicg, 430.

[15] T. S. Eliot, "Burnt Norton," I, *Four Quartets* (London: Faber & Faber, 1944).

[16] *Metaphysical Beliefs* (London: S. C. M. Press, New York: Alec R. Allenson, Inc., 1957), p. 197. MacIntyre has made the same point in his more recent *Difficulties in Christian Belief* (London: Student Christian Movement Press, 1950), p. 77.

[17] *Cf.* J. H. Newman, *The Grammar of Assent* (1870).

[18] The exercise of this capacity is well described by C. S. Peirce as the unfolding of what he calls "the humble argument" for the reality of God. *See* his *Collected Papers* (Harvard University Press, 1934) 6.467 and 6.486.

1

The
Theistic
Arguments

THE ONTOLOGICAL
ARGUMENT

Statement of the Argument

ST. ANSELM

St. Anselm (c. 1033-1109), Abbot of Bec and later Archbishop of Canterbury, shows himself in the opening chapters of his *Proslogion* and in his reply to his critic Gaunilo to be a genuinely original as well as penetrating and exact thinker. His ontological argument for the existence of God[1] is in many ways the most philosophically interesting of the theistic proofs and one that has exercised a perennial fascination which is being felt as strongly today as in almost any previous age.

Anselm's argument hinges upon the definition of God as "something than which nothing greater can be conceived."[2] By "greater" he does not mean spatially larger, but superior or more perfect. (On several occasions he uses "melior," better.)[3] But—we may ask—why should God be conceived as that reality than which no more perfect can be conceived? The question is well answered by a contemporary philosopher, J. N. Findlay. He defines the idea of God as the idea of the "adequate object of religious attitudes," and proceeds: "Thus we might say, for instance, that a religious attitude was one in which we tended to abase ourselves before some object, to defer to it wholly, to devote ourselves to it with unquestioning enthusiasm, to bend the knee before it, whether literally or metaphorically . . . Plainly we shall be following the natural trends of unreflective speech if we say that religious attitudes presume *superiority* in their objects, and such superiority, moreover, as reduces us, who feel the attitudes, to comparative nothingness. For having described

23

a worshipful attitude as one in which we feel disposed to
bend the knee before some object, to defer to it wholly,
and the like, we find it natural to say that such an attitude
can only be fitting where the object reverenced *exceeds*
us very vastly, whether in power or wisdom or in other
valued qualities. And while it is certainly possible to worship stocks and stones and ordinary articles of common
use, one does so usually on the assumption that they
aren't merely stocks and stones and ordinary articles, but
the temporary seats of 'indwelling presences' or centres of
extraordinary powers and virtues. And if one realizes
clearly that such common things *are* merely stocks and
stones or articles of common use, one can't help suffering
a total vanishing or grave abatement of religious ardour.
To feel religiously is therefore to presume surpassing greatness in some object: so much characterizes the attitudes in
which we bow and bend the knee, and enters into the
ordinary meaning of the word 'religious.' But now we advance further—in company with a large number of theologians and philosophers, who have added new touches
to the portrait of deity, pleading various theoretical necessities, but really concerned to make their object worthier
of our worship—and ask whether it isn't wholly anomalous
to worship anything limited in any thinkable manner. For
all limited superiorities are tainted with an obvious relativity, and can be dwarfed in thought by still mightier
superiorities, in which process of being dwarfed they lose
their claim upon our worshipful attitudes. And hence we
are led on irresistibly to demand that our religious object
should have an *unsurpassable* supremacy along all avenues,
that it should tower *infinitely* above all other objects. And
not only are we led to demand for it such merely quantita-
tive superiority: we also ask that it shouldn't stand surrounded by a world of *alien* objects, which owe it no
allegiance, or set limits to its influence. The proper object
of religious reverence must in some manner be *all-compre-
hensive:* there mustn't be anything capable of existing, or
of displaying any virtue, without owing all of these absolutely to this single source . . . But we are also led on
irresistibly to a yet more stringent demand, which raises
difficulties which make the difficulties we have mentioned
seem wholly inconsiderable: we can't help feeling that the
worthy object of our worship can never be a thing that

merely *happens* to exist, nor one on which all other objects merely *happen* to depend. The true object of religious reverence must not be one, merely, to which no *actual* independent realities stand opposed: it must be one to which such opposition is totally *inconceivable*. God mustn't merely cover the territory of the actual, but also, with equal comprehensiveness, the territory of the possible. And not only must the existence of *other* things be unthinkable without him, but his own nonexistence must be wholly unthinkable in any circumstances. There must, in short, be no conceivable alternative to an existence properly termed 'divine': God must be wholly inescapable, as we remarked previously, whether for thought or for reality. And so we are led on insensibly to the barely intelligible notion of a Being in whom Essence and Existence lose their separateness. And all that the great medieval thinkers really did was to carry such a development to its logical limit."[4]

Given this concept of the most adequate possible object of religious attitudes, or of something than which no more perfect can be conceived, Anselm's argument is that it is incoherent and self-contradictory to think of such a Being as not existing; for a nonexistent entity, or a nonentity, would not be the most adequate object of worship, or that than which no more perfect can be conceived.

❊

FROM *Proslogion*[5]

CHAPTER 2: GOD TRULY IS

And so, O Lord, since thou givest understanding to faith, give me to understand—as far as thou knowest it to be good for me—that thou dost exist, as we believe, and that thou art what we believe thee to be. Now we believe that thou are a being than which none greater can be thought [*aliquid quo nihil maius cogitari possit*]. Or can it be that there is no such being, since "the fool hath said in his heart, 'There is no God'"? [Psalms 14:1; 53:1] But when this same fool hears what I am saying—"A being than which none greater can be thought"—he understands what he hears, and what he understands is in his understanding, even if he does not understand that it exists. For it is one thing for an object to be in the understanding, and another thing to understand that it exists. When a painter considers beforehand what he is going to paint, he has it in his understanding, but he does not suppose that what he has not yet painted already exists. But when he has painted it, he both has it in his understanding and understands that what he has now produced exists. Even the fool, then, must be convinced that a being than which none greater can be thought exists at least in his understanding, since when he hears this he understands it, and whatever is understood is in the understanding. But clearly that than which a greater cannot be thought cannot exist in the understanding alone. For if it is actually in the understanding alone, it can be thought of as existing also in reality, and this is greater. Therefore, if that than which a greater cannot be thought is in the understanding alone, this same thing than which a greater cannot be thought is that than which a greater can be thought. But obviously this is impossible. Without doubt, therefore, there exists, both in the understanding and in reality, something than which a greater cannot be thought.

CHAPTER 3: GOD CANNOT BE THOUGHT OF AS NONEXISTENT
And certainly it exists so truly that it cannot be thought of as nonexistent. For something can be thought of as existing, which cannot be thought of as not existing, and this is greater than that which *can* be thought of as not existing. Thus, if that than which a greater cannot be thought can be thought of as not existing, this very thing than which a greater cannot be thought is *not* that than which a greater cannot be thought. But this is contradictory. So, then, there truly is a being than which a greater cannot be thought—so truly that it cannot even be thought of as not existing.

And *thou* art this being, O Lord our God. Thou so truly art, then, O Lord my God, that thou canst not even be thought of as not existing. And this is right. For if some mind could think of something better than thou, the creature would rise above the Creator and judge its Creator: but this is altogether absurd. And indeed, whatever is, except thyself

alone, can be thought of as not existing. Thou alone, therefore, of all beings, hast being in the truest and highest sense,
since no other being so truly exists, and thus every other
being has less being. Why, then, has "the fool said in his
heart, 'There is no God,' " when it is so obvious to the
rational mind that, of all beings, thou dost exist supremely?
Why indeed, unless it is that he is a stupid fool?

CHAPTER 4: HOW THE FOOL HAS SAID IN HIS HEART WHAT CANNOT BE THOUGHT

But how did he manage to say in his heart what he could
not think? Or how is it that he was unable to think what he
said in his heart? After all, to say in one's heart and to think
are the same thing. Now if it is true—or rather, since it is
true—that he thought it, because he said it in his heart, but
did not say it in his heart, since he could not think it, it is
clear that something can be said in one's heart or thought in
more than one way. For we think of a thing, in one sense,
when we think of the word that signifies it, and in another
sense, when we understand the very thing itself. Thus, in the
first sense God can be thought of as nonexistent, but in the
second sense this is quite impossible. For no one who understands what God is can think that God does not exist, even
though he says these words in his heart—perhaps without
any meaning, perhaps with some quite extraneous meaning.
For God is that than which a greater cannot be thought, and
whoever understands this rightly must understand that he
exists in such a way that he cannot be nonexistent even in
thought. He, therefore, who understands that God thus exists
cannot think of him as nonexistent.

Thanks be to thee, good Lord, thanks be to thee, because
I now understand by thy light what I formerly believed by
thy gift, so that even if I were to refuse to believe in thy
existence, I could not fail to understand its truth.

FROM *Reply to Gaunilo*[6]

3. But, you say, suppose that someone imagined an island in
the ocean, surpassing all lands in its fertility. Because of the
difficulty, or rather the impossibility, of finding something

that does not exist, it might well be called "Lost Island." By reasoning like yours, he might then say that we cannot doubt that it truly exists in reality, because anyone can easily conceive it from a verbal description. I state confidently that if anyone discovers something for me, other than that "than which a greater cannot be thought," existing either in reality or in thought alone, to which the logic of my argument can be applied, I shall find his lost island and give it to him, never to be lost again. But it now seems obvious that this being than which a greater cannot be thought cannot be thought of as nonexistent, because it exists by such a sure reason of truth. For otherwise it would not exist at all. In short, if anyone says that he thinks it does not exist, I say that when he thinks this, he either thinks of something than which a greater cannot be thought or he does not think. If he does not think, he does not think of what he is not thinking of as nonexistent. But if he does think, then he thinks of something which cannot be thought of as nonexistent. For if it could be thought of as nonexistent, it could be thought of as having a beginning and an end. But this is impossible. Therefore, if anyone thinks of it, he thinks of something that cannot even be thought of as nonexistent. But he who thinks of this does not think that it does not exist; if he did, he would think what cannot be thought. Therefore, that than which a greater cannot be thought cannot be thought of as nonexistent.

4. You say, moreover, that when it is said that the highest reality cannot be *thought of* as nonexistent, it would perhaps be better to say that it cannot be *understood* as nonexistent, or even as possibly nonexistent. But it is more correct to say, as I said, that it cannot be thought. For if I had said that the reality itself cannot be understood not to exist, perhaps you yourself, who say that according to the very definition of the term what is false cannot be understood, would object that nothing that is can be understood as nonexistent. For it is false to say that what exists does not exist. Therefore it would not be peculiar to God to be unable to be understood as nonexistent. But if some one of the things that most certainly are can be understood as nonexistent, other certain things can similarly be understood as nonexistent. But this

objection cannot be applied to "thinking," if it is rightly considered. For although none of the things that exist can be understood not to exist, still they can all be thought of as nonexistent, except that which most fully is. For all those things—and only those—which have a beginning or end or are composed of parts can be thought of as nonexistent, along with anything that does not exist as a whole anywhere or at any time (as I have already said[7]). But the only being that cannot be thought of as nonexistent is that in which no thought finds beginning or end or composition of parts, but which any thought finds as a whole, always and everywhere.

You must realize, then, that you can think of yourself as nonexistent, even while you know most certainly that you exist. I am surprised that you said you did not know this. For we think of many things as nonexistent when we know that they exist, and of many things as existent when we know that they do not exist—all this not by a real judgment, but by imagining that what we think is so. And indeed, we can think of something as nonexistent, even while we know that it exists, because we are able at the same time to think the one and know the other. And yet we cannot think of it as nonexistent, while we know that it exists, because we cannot think of something as at once existent and nonexistent. Therefore, if anyone distinguishes these two senses of the statement in this way, he will understand that nothing, as long as it is known to exist, can be thought of as nonexistent, and that whatever exists, except that than which a greater cannot be thought, can be thought of as nonexistent, even when it is known to exist. So, then, it is peculiar to God to be unable to be thought of as nonexistent, and nevertheless many things, as long as they exist, cannot be thought of as nonexistent. I think that the way in which it can still be said that God is thought of as nonexistent is stated adequately in the little book itself.

NOTES

[1] *Proslogion*, 1-4. In the *Monologion* Anselm offers three other theistic proofs—a Platonic argument to God as the Good (chs. 1 and 2), a cosmological argument (ch. 3), and an argument (ch. 4) which has affinities with Aquinas's fourth Way (*see* p. 84).

² Anselm uses four different but synonymous formulations: *aliquid quo nihil maius cogitari potest, aliquid quo nihil maius cogitari possit, aliquid quo maius cogitari non valet,* and *aliquid quo maius cogitari nequit.*

³ E.g. *Proslogion,* chs. 14 and 18.

⁴ J. N. Findlay, "Can God's Existence be Disproved?" (*Mind,* April, 1948. Reprinted in *New Essays in Philosophical Theology,* Flew and MacIntyre, editors. Quotation from pp. 49, 51-2). Professor Findlay proceeds to argue that the concept of God which he has thus described is self-contradictory, since there can be no such thing as a necessarily existent being, with the result that the existence of God is open to *a priori* disproof. In his argument he assumes that God is alleged in the religious tradition to be a *logically* necessary being. This assumption is questioned in J. H. Hick, "God as Necessary Being," *The Journal of Philosophy,* (Vol. LVII, Nos. 22 and 23, Oct. 27 and Nov. 10, 1960).

⁵ From *A Scholastic Miscellany: Anselm to Ockham,* edited and translated by E. R. Fairweather (The Library of Christian Classics, Vol. X, Philadelphia: The Westminster Press and London: The Student Christian Movement Press, 1956), pp. 73-75.

⁶ *Ibid.,* pp. 94-96.

⁷ *Responsio,* I.

Rejection of the Argument

ST. THOMAS AQUINAS

St. Thomas Aquinas (1224/5-1274), writing two centuries after Anselm, rejected the ontological argument, which he formulates here in Objection 2 and answers in the paragraph beginning *I answer that* and in his Reply to Objection 2.¹ His own alternative theistic argument, at which he hints at the end of the central paragraph, is presented on pp. 83-85. For an important drawing out of the contrast between the "ontological" approach originated by Anselm and the "cosmological" approach originated by Aquinas, and of their wider implications, *see* Paul Tillich, "The Two Types of Philosophy of Religion"

(*Theology of Culture,* New York, Oxford University Press, 1959).

✳

FROM *Summa Theologica*[2]

FIRST ARTICLE: WHETHER THE EXISTENCE OF GOD IS SELF-EVIDENT?

We proceed thus to the First Article:

OBJECTION 1. It seems that the existence of God is self-evident. For those things are said to be self-evident to us the knowledge of which exists naturally in us, as we can see in regard to first principles. But as Damascene says, the knowledge of God is naturally implanted in all. Therefore the existence of God is self-evident.

OBJ. 2. Further, those things are said to be self-evident which are known as soon as the terms are known, which the Philosopher says is true of the first principles of demonstration. Thus, when the nature of a whole and of a part is known, it is at once recognized that every whole is greater than its part. But as soon as the signification of the name God is understood, it is at once seen that God exists. For by this name is signified that thing than which nothing greater can be conceived. But that which exists actually and mentally is greater than that which exists only mentally. Therefore, since as soon as the name God is understood it exists mentally, it also follows that it exists actually. Therefore the proposition God exists is self-evident.

OBJ. 3. Further, the existence of truth is self-evident. For whoever denies the existence of truth grants that truth does not exist: and, if truth does not exist, then the proposition Truth does not exist is true: and if there is anything true, there must be truth. But God is truth itself: I am the way, the truth, and the life (Jo. xiv. 6). Therefore God exists is self-evident.

On the contrary, No one can mentally admit the opposite of what is self-evident, as the Philosopher states concerning the first principles of demonstration. But the opposite of the proposition God is can be mentally admitted: The fool said in his heart, There is no God (Ps. lii. I). Therefore, that God exists is not self-evident.

I answer that, A thing can be self-evident in either of two ways: on the one hand, self-evident in itself, though not to us; on the other, self-evident in itself and to us. A proposition is self-evident because the predicate is included in the essence of the subject: e.g., Man is an animal, for animal is contained in the essence of man. If, therefore, the essence of the predicate and subject be known to all, the proposition will be self-evident to all; as is clear with regard to the first principles of demonstration, the terms of which are certain common notions that no one is ignorant of, such as being and non-being, whole and part, and the like. If, however, there are some to whom the essence of the predicate and subject is unknown, the proposition will be self-evident in itself, but not to those who do not know the meaning of the predicate and subject of the proposition. Therefore, it happens, as Boethius says, that there are some notions of the mind which are common and self-evident only to the learned, as that incorporeal substances are not in space. Therefore I say that this proposition, God exists, of itself is self-evident, for the predicate is the same as the subject, because God is His own existence as will be hereafter shown. Now because we do not know the essence of God, the proposition is not self-evident to us, but needs to be demonstrated by things that are more known to us, though less known in their nature—namely, by His effects.

REPLY OBJ. 1. To know that God exists in a general and confused way is implanted in us by nature, inasmuch as God is man's beatitude. For man naturally desires happiness, and what is naturally desired by man is naturally known by him. This, however, is not to know absolutely that God exists; just as to know that someone is approaching is not the same as to know that Peter is approaching, even though it is Peter who is approaching; for there are many who imagine that man's perfect good, which is happiness, consists in riches, and others in pleasures, and others in something else.

REPLY OBJ. 2. Perhaps not everyone who hears this name

God understands it to signify something than which nothing greater can be thought, seeing that some have believed God to be a body. Yet, granted that everyone understands that by this name God is signified something than which nothing greater can be thought, nevertheless, it does not therefore follow that he understands that what the name signifies exists actually, but only that it exists mentally. Nor can it be argued that it actually exists, unless it be admitted that there actually exists something than which nothing greater can be thought; and this precisely is not admitted by those who hold that God does not exist.

REPLY OBJ. 3. The existence of truth in general is self-evident, but the existence of a Primal Truth is not self-evident to us.

NOTES

¹ Also *Summa Contra Gentiles,* Book I, chs. 10 and 11.
² From *Basic Writings of St. Thomas Aquinas,* ed. by Anton C. Pegis, *Summa Theologica,* Third Article (New York: Random House, Inc.; London: Burns & Oates, Ltd., 1945). The translation is Pegis' revision of the English Dominican Translation.

Restatement of the Argument

RENÉ DESCARTES

Apparently as a result of the vast respect accorded to Aquinas's criticism of it, the ontological argument dropped out of discussion from the end of the thirteenth century until the middle of the seventeenth. René Descartes (1596-1650), in his *Meditations,* V, provided the new formulation of it upon which most of the discussions in the modern period have centered. (Whether he was aware of Anselm's previous formulation is uncertain.) The ontological argument is not the only theistic proof which Descartes used. In Meditation III he had formulated an argument to God as the cause of our idea of him—an argument which is like the ontological in that it starts from our concept of God as the infinitely perfect being, but like the cosmological argument in that it depends upon the causal principle. The relation between the two arguments has been much discussed.[1] On the one hand it is claimed that the causal argument is a necessary prelude to the ontological proof; for it guarantees that the properties which are necessarily affirmed of anything by our minds must belong to it in reality, a premise which the ontological argument then applies to the theistic concept as one which includes the property of existence. On the other hand, however, it is pointed out that in Descartes' *Principles of Philosophy* the ontological argument is the first of the proofs to be offered and therefore does not seem to presuppose any of the others; and that in Meditation V he says "although all that I concluded in the preceding Meditations were found to be false, the existence of God would pass with me as at least as certain as I have ever held the truths of mathematics (which concern only numbers and figures) to be."

✳

Meditation V

. . . But now, if just because I can draw the idea of something from my thought, it follows that all which I know clearly and distinctly as pertaining to this object does really belong to it, may I not derive from this an argument demonstrating the existence of God? It is certain that I no less find the idea of God, that is to say, the idea of a supremely perfect Being, in me, than that of any figure or number whatever it is; and I do not know any less clearly and distinctly that an [actual and] eternal existence pertains to this nature than I know that all that which I am able to demonstrate of some figure or number truly pertains to the nature of this figure or number, and therefore, although all that I concluded in the preceding Meditations were found to be false, the existence of God would pass with me as at least as certain as I have ever held the truths of mathematics (which concern only numbers and figures) to be.

This indeed is not at first manifest, since it would seem to present some appearance of being a sophism. For being accustomed in all other things to make a distinction between existence and essence, I easily persuade myself that the existence can be separated from the essence of God, and that we can thus conceive God as not actually existing. But, nevertheless, when I think of it with more attention, I clearly see that existence can no more be separated from the essence of God than can its having its three angles equal to two right angles be separated from the essence of a [rectilinear] triangle, or the idea of a mountain from the idea of a valley; and so there is not any less repugnance to our conceiving a God (that is, a Being supremely perfect) to whom existence is lacking (that is to say, to whom a certain perfection is lacking), than to conceive of a mountain which has no valley.

But although I cannot really conceive of a God without existence any more than a mountain without a valley, still from the fact that I conceive of a mountain with a valley, it does not follow that there is such a mountain in the world; similarly although I conceive of God as possessing existence, it would seem that it does not follow that there is a God which exists; for my thought does not impose any necessity upon things, and just as I may imagine a winged horse, although no horse with wings exists, so I could perhaps attribute existence to God, although no God existed.

But a sophism is concealed in this objection; for from the fact that I cannot conceive a mountain without a valley, it does not follow that there is any mountain or any valley in existence, but only that the mountain and the valley, whether they exist or do not exist, cannot in any way be separated one from the other. While from the fact that I cannot conceive God without existence, it follows that existence is inseparable from Him, and hence that He really exists; not that my thought can bring this to pass, or impose any necessity on things, but, on the contrary, because the necessity which lies in the thing itself, i.e. the necessity of the existence of God determines me to think in this way. For it is not within my power to think of God without existence (that is

of a supremely perfect Being devoid of a supreme perfection)
though it is in my power to imagine a horse either with wings
or without wings.

And we must not here object that it is in truth necessary
for me to assert that God exists after having presupposed
that He possesses every sort of perfection, since existence is
one of these, but that as a matter of fact my original supposition was not necessary, just as it is not necessary to
consider that all quadrilateral figures can be inscribed in the
circle, for supposing I thought this, I should be constrained
to admit that the rhombus might be inscribed in the circle
since it is a quadrilateral figure, which, however, is manifestly false. [We must not, I say, make any such allegations
because] although it is not necessary that I should at any
time entertain the notion of God, nevertheless whenever it
happens that I think of a first and a sovereign Being, and, so
to speak, derive the idea of Him from the storehouse of my
mind, it is necessary that I should attribute to Him every
sort of perfection, although I do not get so far as to enumer-
ate them all, or to apply my mind to each one in particular.
And this necessity suffices to make me conclude (after
having recognized that existence is a perfection) that this
first and sovereign Being really exists; just as though it is
not necessary for me ever to imagine any triangle, yet, whenever I wish to consider a rectilinear figure composed only of
three angles, it is absolutely essential that I should attribute
to it all those properties which serve to bring about the conclusion that its three angles are not greater than two right
angles, even although I may not then be considering this
point in particular. But when I consider which figures are
capable of being inscribed in the circle, it is in no wise
necessary that I should think that all quadrilateral figures are
of this number; on the contrary, I cannot even pretend that
this is the case, so long as I do not desire to accept anything
which I cannot conceive clearly and distinctly. And in consequence there is a great difference between the false suppositions such as this, and the true ideas born within me, the
first and principal of which is that of God. For really I
discern in many ways that this idea is not something factitious,

and depending solely on my thought, but that it is the image
of a true and immutable nature; first of all, because I cannot
conceive anything but God himself to whose essence existence
[necessarily] pertains; in the second place because it is not
possible for me to conceive two or more Gods in this same
position; and, granted that there is one such God who now
exists, I see clearly that it is necessary that He should have
existed from all eternity, and that He must exist eternally;
and finally, because I know an infinitude of other properties
in God, none of which I can either diminish or change.

NOTES

[1] *See* e.g. Marthinus Versfeld, *An Essay on the Metaphysics of
Descartes* (London, 1940), p. 55; Norman Kemp Smith, *New
Studies in the Philosophy of Descartes* (London, 1952), p. 304.

Addition to the Argument

G. W. LEIBNIZ

G. W. Leibniz (1646-1716) used the ontological argument[1] and sought to show that the idea of the most perfect
conceivable being, upon which the argument rests, is a
coherent and nonself-contradictory idea. (*See* Norman
Malcolm, pp. 64f.)

❉

That the Most Perfect Being Exists[2]

I call every simple quality which is positive and absolute,
or expresses whatever it expresses without any limits, a
perfection.

But a quality of this sort, because it is simple, is therefore
irresolvable or indefinable, for otherwise, either it will not

be a simple quality but an aggregate of many, or, if it is one, it will be circumscribed by limits and so be known through negations of further progress contrary to the hypothesis, for a purely positive quality was assumed.

From these considerations it is not difficult to show that *all perfections are compatible with each other* or can exist in the same subject.

For let the proposition be of this kind:

A and B are incompatible

(for understanding by A and B two simple forms of this kind of perfections, and it is the same if more are assumed like them), it is evident that it cannot be demonstrated without the resolution of the terms A and B, of each or both; for otherwise their nature would not enter into the ratiocination and the incompatibility could be demonstrated as well from any others as from themselves. But now (by hypothesis) they are irresolvable. Therefore this proposition cannot be demonstrated from these forms.

But it might certainly be demonstrated by these if it were true, because it is not true *per se,* for all propositions necessarily true are either demonstrable or known *per se.* Therefore, this proposition is not necessarily true. Or if it is not necessary that A and B exist in the same subject they cannot therefore exist in the same subject, and since the reasoning is the same as regards any other assumed qualities of this kind, therefore all perfections are compatible.

It is granted, therefore, that either a subject of all perfections or the most perfect being can be known.

Whence it is evident that it also exists, since existence is contained in the number of the perfections.

I showed this reasoning to D. Spinoza when I was in The Hague, who thought it solid; for when at first he opposed it, I put it in writing and read this paper before him.

Schol.

The reasoning of Descartes concerning the existence of the most perfect being assumed that the most perfect being can be known, or is possible. For this being assumed because a notion of this kind is granted, it immediately follows that that being exists, since we framed the notion in such a way that it immediately contains existence. But the question is asked whether it is within our power to conceive such a being, or whether such a notion exists on the side of the thing, and can be clearly and distinctly known without contradiction. For the opponents will say that such a notion of the most perfect being or of a being existing through his essence is a chimera. Nor is it sufficient for Descartes to appeal to experience and to allege that he perceives the same in such a manner in himself clearly and distinctly, for this is to break off, not to complete the demonstration, unless he shows the method through which others also can attain the same experience; for as often as we bring experiences into the midst of the demonstration, we ought to show others also the method of producing the same experience, unless we wish to convince them by our authority alone.

NOTES

[1] *Monadology*, 44-45; *Cf. New Essays Concerning Human Understanding*, Bk. IV, Ch. X.

[2] Translated by Alfred Gideon Langley from C. J. Gerhardt, *Die Philosophischen Schriften von G. W. Leibniz*, Vol. 7, pp. 261-262. Reprinted from *New Essays Concerning Human Understanding* by Gottfried Wilhelm Leibniz, translated by A. G. Langley (New York: The Macmillan Company, 1896), Appendix X, pp. 714-5.

Criticism of the Cartesian Argument

IMMANUEL KANT

Immanuel Kant (1724-1804) is the author of the most thorough and damaging critique of the ontological argument in its Cartesian form. Kant's basic contention, sometimes expressed in the slogan that "existence is not a predicate," has been reformulated in the present century by Bertrand Russell in his well-known analysis of "exists."[1] Russell has showed that the assertion that x exists is not an attribution to a subsisting x of the further characteristic of existence. It is rather the assertion, with regard to a certain description (or name as standing for a description) that this description has a referent. Thus "horses exist" has the logical structure: "there are x's such that 'x is a horse' is true." Existence, then, is not something that horses, or God, might have or lack; rather the definition of "horse" and of "God" applies or does not apply to something. (On the doctrine that existence is a perfection, and that therefore God must possess it, *see* Norman Malcolm.)

❋

FROM *Critique of Pure Reason*[2]

THE IMPOSSIBILITY OF AN ONTOLOGICAL PROOF OF THE EXISTENCE OF GOD

It is evident, from what has been said, that the concept of an absolutely necessary being is a concept of pure reason, that is, a mere idea the objective reality of which is very far from being proved by the fact that reason requires it. For the idea instructs us only in regard to a certain unattainable completeness, and so serves rather to limit the understanding than to extend it to new objects. But we are here faced by what is indeed strange and perplexing, namely, that while the inference from a given existence in general to some absolutely necessary being seems to be both imperative and legitimate, all those conditions under which alone the understanding can form a concept of such a necessity are so many obstacles in the way of our doing so.

In all ages men have spoken of an *absolutely necessary* being, and in so doing have endeavored, not so much to understand whether and how a thing of this kind allows even of being thought, but rather to prove its existence. There is, of course, no difficulty in giving a verbal definition of the concept, namely, that it is something the non-existence of which is impossible. But this yields no insight into the conditions which make it necessary[3] to regard the non-existence of a thing as absolutely unthinkable. It is precisely these conditions that we desire to know, in order that we may determine whether or not, in resorting to this concept, we are thinking anything at all. The expedient of removing all those conditions which the understanding indispensably requires in order to regard something as necessary, simply through the introduction of the word *unconditioned,* is very far from sufficing to show whether I am still thinking anything in the concept of the unconditionally necessary, or perhaps rather nothing at all.

Nay more, this concept, at first ventured upon blindly, and now become so completely familiar, has been supposed to have its meaning exhibited in a number of examples; and on this account all further enquiry into its intelligibility has seemed to be quite needless. Thus the fact that every geometrical proposition, as, for instance, that a triangle has three angles, is absolutely necessary, has been taken as justifying us in speaking of an object which lies entirely outside the sphere of our understanding as if we understood perfectly what it is that we intend to convey by the concept of that object.

All the alleged examples are, without exception, taken from *judgments,* not from *things* and their existence. But the unconditioned necessity of judgments is not the same as an absolute necessity of things. The absolute necessity of the judgment is only a conditioned necessity of the thing, or of the predicate in the judgment. The above proposition does not declare that three angles are absolutely necessary, but that, under the condition that there is a triangle (that is, that a triangle is given), three angles will necessarily be found in it. So great, indeed, is the deluding influence exercised by this logical necessity that, by the simple device of forming an *a priori* concept of a thing in such a manner as to include existence within the scope of its meaning, we have supposed ourselves to have justified the conclusion that because existence necessarily belongs to the object of this concept—always under the condition that we posit the thing as given (as existing)—we are also of necessity, in accordance with the law of identity, required to posit

the existence of its object, and that this being is therefore
itself absolutely necessary—and this, to repeat, for the reason
that the existence of this being has already been thought in
a concept which is assumed arbitrarily and on condition that
we posit its object.

If, in an identical proposition, I reject the predicate while
retaining the subject, contradiction results; and I therefore
say that the former belongs necessarily to the latter. But if
we reject subject and predicate alike, there is no contradiction; for nothing is then left that can be contradicted. To
posit a triangle, and yet to reject its three angles, is self-
contradictory; but there is no contradiction in rejecting the
triangle together with its three angles. The same holds true
of the concept of an absolutely necessary being. If its existence is rejected, we reject the thing itself with all its
predicates; and no question of contradiction can then arise.
There is nothing outside it that would then be contradicted,
since the necessity of the thing is not supposed to be derived
from anything external; nor is there anything internal that
would be contradicted, since in rejecting the thing itself we
have at the same time rejected all its internal properties.
"God is omnipotent" is a necessary judgment. The omnipotence cannot be rejected if we posit a Deity, that is, an
infinite being; for the two concepts are identical. But if we
say, "There is no God," neither the omnipotence nor any
other of its predicates is given; they are one and all rejected
together with the subject, and there is therefore not the least
contradiction in such a judgment.

We have thus seen that if the predicate of a judgment is
rejected together with the subject, no internal contradiction
can result, and that this holds no matter what the predicate
may be. The only way of evading this conclusion is to argue
that there are subjects which cannot be removed, and must
always remain. That, however, would only be another way of
saying that there are absolutely necessary subjects; and that is
the very assumption which I have called in question, and the
possibility of which the above argument professes to establish.
For I cannot form the least concept of a thing which, should
it be rejected with all its predicates, leaves behind a contra-

diction; and in the absence of contradiction I have, through pure *a priori* concepts alone, no criterion of impossibility.

Notwithstanding all these general considerations, in which every one must concur, we may be challenged with a case which is brought forward as proof that in actual fact the contrary holds, namely, that there is one concept, and indeed only one, in reference to which the not-being or rejection of its object is in itself contradictory, namely, the concept of the *ens realissimum*. It is declared that it possesses all reality, and that we are justified in assuming that such a being is possible (the fact that a concept does not contradict itself by no means proves the possibility of its object: but the contrary assertion I am for the moment willing to allow).[4] Now [the argument proceeds] "all reality" includes existence; existence is therefore contained in the concept of a thing that is possible. If, then, this thing is rejected, the internal possibility of the thing is rejected—which is self-contradictory.

My answer is as follows. There is already a contradiction in introducing the concept of existence—no matter under what title it may be disguised—into the concept of a thing which we profess to be thinking solely in reference to its possibility. If that be allowed as legitimate, a seeming victory has been won; but in actual fact nothing at all is said: the assertion is a mere tautology. We must ask: Is the proposition that *this or that thing* (which, whatever it may be, is allowed as possible) *exists,* an analytic or a synthetic proposition? If it is analytic, the assertion of the existence of the thing adds nothing to the thought of the thing; but in that case either the thought, which is in us, is the thing itself, or we have presupposed an existence as belonging to the realm of the possible, and have then, on that pretext, inferred its existence from its internal possibility—which is nothing but a miserable tautology. The word "reality," which in the concept of the thing sounds other than the word "existence" in the concept of the predicate, is of no avail in meeting this objection. For if all positing (no matter what it may be that is posited) is entitled reality, the thing with all its predicates is already posited in the concept of the subject, and is assumed as actual; and in the predicate this is merely repeated. But if, on the other hand, we admit, as every reasonable person must, that all existential propositions are synthetic, how can we profess to maintain that the predicate of existence cannot be rejected without contradiction? This is a feature which is found only in analytic propositions, and is indeed precisely what constitutes their analytic character.

I should have hoped to put an end to these idle and fruitless disputations in a direct manner, by an accurate determination of the concept of existence, had I not found that the illusion which is caused by the confusion of a logical with a real predicate (that is, with a predicate which determines a thing) is almost beyond correction. Anything we please can be made to serve as a logical predicate; the subject can even be predicated of itself; for logic abstracts from all content. But a *determining* predicate is a predicate which is added to the concept of the subject and enlarges it. Consequently, it must not be already contained in the concept.

"Being" is obviously not a real predicate; that is, it is not a concept of something which could[5] be added to the concept of a thing. It is merely the positing of a thing, or of certain determinations, as existing in themselves. Logically, it is merely the copula of a judgment. The proposition, "God is omnipotent," contains two concepts, each of which has its object—God and omnipotence. The small word "is" adds no new predicate, but only serves to posit the predicate *in its relation* to the subject. If, now, we take the subject (God) with all its predicates (among which is omnipotence), and say "God is," or "There is a God," we attach no new predicate to the concept of God, but only posit the subject in itself with all its predicates, and indeed posit it as being an *object* that stands in relation to my *concept*. The content of both must be one and the same; nothing can have been added to the concept, which expresses merely what is possible, by my thinking its object (through the expression "it is") as given absolutely. Otherwise stated, the real contains no more than the merely possible. A hundred real thalers do not contain the least coin more than a hundred possible thalers. For as the latter signify the concept, and the former the object and the positing of the object, should the former

contain more than the latter, my concept would not, in that case, express the whole object, and would not therefore be an adequate concept of it. My financial position is, however, affected very differently by a hundred real thalers than it is by the mere concept of them (that is, of their possibility). For the object, as it actually exists, is not analytically contained in my concept, but is added to my concept (which is a determination of my state) synthetically; and yet the conceived hundred thalers are not themselves in the least increased through thus acquiring existence outside my concept.

By whatever and by however many predicates we may think a thing—even if we completely determine it—we do not make the least addition to the thing which we further declare that this thing *is*. Otherwise, it would not be exactly the same thing that exists, but something more than we had thought in the concept; and we could not, therefore, say that the exact object of my concept exists. If we think in a thing every feature of reality except one,[6] the missing reality is not added by my saying that this defective thing exists. On the contrary, it exists with the same defect with which I have thought it, since otherwise what exists would be something different from what I thought. When, therefore, I think a being as the supreme reality, without any defect, the question still remains whether it exists or not. For though, in my concept, nothing may be lacking of the possible real content of a thing in general, something is still lacking in its relation to my whole state of thought, namely, [in so far as I am unable to assert] that knowledge of this object is also possible *a posteriori*. And here we find the source of our present difficulty. Were we dealing with an object of the senses, we could not confound the existence of the thing with the mere concept of it. For through the concept the object is thought only as conforming to the *universal conditions* of possible empirical knowledge in general, whereas through its existence it is thought as belonging to the context of experience as a whole. In being thus connected with the *content* of experience as a whole, the concept of the object is not, however, in the least enlarged; all that has happened is that our thought has thereby obtained an additional possible perception. It is not, therefore, surprising that, if we attempt to think existence through the pure category alone, we cannot specify a single mark distinguishing it from mere possibility.

Whatever, therefore, and however much, our concept of an object may contain, we must go outside it, if we are to ascribe existence to the object. In the case of objects of the senses, this takes place through their connection with some one of our perceptions, in accordance with empirical laws. But in dealing with objects of pure thought, we have no means whatsoever of knowing their existence, since it would have to be known in a completely *a priori* manner. Our consciousness of all existence (whether immediately through perception, or mediately through inferences which connect something with perception) belongs exclusively to the unity of experience; any [alleged] existence outside this field, while not indeed such as we can declare to be absolutely impossible, is of the nature of an assumption which we can never be in a position to justify.

The concept of a supreme being is in many respects a very useful idea; but just because it is a mere idea, it is altogether incapable, by itself alone, of enlarging our knowledge in regard to what exists. It is not even competent to enlighten us as to the *possibility* of any existence beyond that which is known in and through experience.[7] The analytic criterion of possibility, as consisting in the principle that bare positives (realities) give rise to no contradiction, cannot be denied to it. But since the realities are not given to us in their specific characters; since even if they were, we should still[8] not be in a position to pass judgment; since the criterion of the possibility of synthetic knowledge is never to be looked for save in experience, to which the object of an idea cannot belong,[9] the connection of all real properties in a thing is a synthesis, the possibility of which we are unable to determine *a priori*. And thus the celebrated Leibniz is far from having succeeded in what he plumed himself on achieving—the comprehension *a priori* of the possibility of this sublime ideal being.

The attempt to establish the existence of a supreme being by means of the famous ontological argument of Descartes is therefore merely so much labor and effort lost; we can no more extend our stock of [theoretical] insight by mere ideas, than a merchant can better his position by adding a few noughts to his cash account.

NOTES

[1] *Introduction to Mathematical Philosophy* (London: Allen & Unwin, Ltd., 1919), ch. 16; "Logical Atomism" in *Logic and Language* (London: Allen & Unwin, Ltd., 1956). pp. 228f.

[2] Second ed.

[3] [Reading, with Noiré, *notwendig* for *unmöglich*.]

[4] A concept is always possible if it is not self-contradictory. This is the logical criterion of possibility, and by it the object of the concept is distinguishable from the *nihil negativum*. But it may none the less be an empty concept, unless the objective reality of the synthesis through which the concept is generated has been specifically proved; and such proof, as we have shown above, rests on principles of possible experience, and not on the principle of analysis (the law of contradiction). This is a warning against arguing directly from the logical possibility of concepts to the real possibility of things.—Kant

[5] [Reading, with Erdmann, *könnte* for *könne*.]

[6] [*alle Realität ausser einer*.]

[7] [*in Ansehung der Möglichkeit eines Mehreren*.]

[8] [Reading, with B, *da aber* for *weil aber*.]

[9] [Reading, with Wille, *stattfände* for *stattfinde*.]

A Contemporary Discussion

NORMAN MALCOLM

Norman Malcolm (1911-), professor of philosophy at Cornell University and author of *Ludwig Wittgenstein: A Memoir* (London, 1958), *Dreaming* (London, 1959), *Knowledge and Certainty* (Englewood Cliffs, N. J.; Prentice-

48   THE EXISTENCE OF GOD

Hall, 1963), provides a sympathetic discussion of the ontological argument by a contemporary philosopher of the "analytical" school.

❋

Anselm's Ontological Arguments

I believe that in Anselm's *Proslogion* and *Responsio editoris* there are two different pieces of reasoning which he did not distinguish from one another, and that a good deal of light may be shed on the philosophical problem of "the ontological argument" if we do distinguish them. In Chapter 2 of the *Proslogion*[1] Anselm says that we believe that God is *something a greater than which cannot be conceived*. (The Latin is *aliquid quo nihil maius cogitari possit*. Anselm sometimes uses the alternative expressions *aliquid quo maius nihil cogitari potest, id quo maius cogitari nequit, aliquid quo maius cogitari non valet*.) Even the fool of the Psalm who says in his heart there is no God, when he hears this very thing that Anselm says, namely, "something a greater than which cannot be conceived," understands what he hears, and what he understands is in his understanding though he does not understand that it exists.

Apparently Anselm regards it as tautological to say that whatever is understood is in the understanding (*quidquid intelligitur in intellectu est*): he uses *intelligitur* and *in intellectu est* as interchangeable locutions. The same holds for another formula of his: whatever is thought is in thought (*quidquid cogitatur in cogitatione est*).[2]

Of course many things may exist in the understanding that do not exist in reality; for example, elves. Now, says Anselm, something a greater than which cannot be conceived exists in the understanding. But it cannot exist *only* in the understanding, for to exist in reality is greater. Therefore that thing a greater than which cannot be conceived cannot exist only in the understanding, for then a greater thing could be conceived: namely, one that exists both in the understanding and in reality.[3]

Here I have a question. It is not clear to me whether Anselm means that (a) existence in reality by itself is greater than existence in the understanding, or that (b) existence in reality and existence in the understanding together are greater than existence in the understanding alone. Certainly he accepts (b). But he might also accept (a), as Descartes apparently does in *Meditation III* when he suggests that the mode of being by which a thing is "objectively in the understanding" is *imperfect*.[4] Of course Anselm might accept both (a) and (b). He might hold that in general something is greater if it has both of these "modes of existence" than if it has either one alone, but also that existence in reality is a more perfect mode of existence than existence in the understanding.

In any case, Anselm holds that something is greater if it exists both in the understanding and in reality than if it exists merely in the understanding. An equivalent way of putting this interesting proposition, in a more current terminology, is: something is greater if it is both conceived of and exists than if it is merely conceived of. Anselm's reasoning can be expressed as follows: *id quo maius cogitari nequit* cannot be merely conceived of and not exist, for then it would not be *id quo maius cogitari nequit*. The doctrine that something is greater if it exists in addition to being conceived of, than if it is only conceived of, could be called the doctrine that *existence is a perfection*. Descartes maintained, in so many words, that existence is a perfection,[5] and presumably he was holding Anselm's doctrine, although he does not, in *Meditation V* or elsewhere, argue in the way that Anselm does in *Proslogion* 2.

When Anselm says, "And certainly, that than which nothing greater can be conceived cannot exist merely in the understanding. For suppose it exists merely in the understanding, then it can be conceived to exist in reality, which is greater,"[6] he is claiming that if I conceived of a being of great excellence, that being would be *greater* (more excellent, more perfect) if it existed than if it did not exist. His supposition that "it exists merely in the understanding" is the supposition that it is conceived of but does not exist. Anselm repeated this claim in his reply to the criticism of the monk Gaunilo. Speaking of the being a greater than which cannot be conceived, he says:

I have said that if it exists merely in the understanding it can be conceived to exist in reality, which is greater. Therefore, if it exists merely in the understanding obviously the very being a greater than which cannot be conceived, is one a greater than which can be conceived. What, I ask, can follow better than that? For if it exists merely in the understanding, can it not be conceived to exist in reality? And if it can be so conceived does not he who conceives of this conceive of a thing greater than it, if it does exist merely in the understanding? Can anything follow better than this: that if a being a greater than which cannot be conceived exists merely in the understanding, it is something a greater than which can be conceived? What could be plainer?[7]

He is implying, in the first sentence, that if I conceive of something which does not exist then it is possible for it to exist, and *it will be greater if it exists than if it does not exist.*

The doctrine that existence is a perfection is remarkably queer. It makes sense and is true to say that my future house will be a better one if it is insulated than if it is not insulated; but what could it mean to say that it will be a better house if it exists than if it does not? My future child will be a better man if he is honest than if he is not; but who would understand the saying that he will be a better man if he exists than if he does not? Or who understands the saying that if God exists He is more perfect than if He does not exist? One might say, with some intelligibility, that it would be better (for oneself or for mankind) if God exists than if He does not—but that is a different matter.

A king might desire that his next chancellor should have knowledge, wit, and resolution; but it is ludicrous to add that the king's desire is to have a chancellor who exists. Suppose that two royal councilors, A and B, were asked to draw up separately descriptions of the most perfect chancellor they could conceive, and that the descriptions they produced were identical except that A included existence in his list of attributes of a perfect chancellor and B did not. (I do not mean that B put nonexistence in his list.) One and the same person could satisfy both descriptions. More to the point, any person who satisfied A's description would *necessarily* satisfy B's description and *vice versa*! This is to say that A and B did not produce descriptions that differed in any way but rather one and the same description of necessary and desirable qualities in a chancellor. A only made a show of putting down a desirable quality that B had failed to include.

I believe I am merely restating an observation that Kant made in attacking the notion that "existence" or "being" is a "real predicate." He says:

> By whatever and by however many predicates we may think a thing—even if we completely determine it—we do not make the least addition to the thing when we further declare that this thing *is*. Otherwise, it would not be exactly the same thing that exists, but something more than we had thought in the concept; and we could not, therefore, say that the exact object of my concept exists.[8]

Anselm's ontological proof of *Proslogion* 2 is fallacious because it rests on the false doctrine that existence is a perfection (and therefore that "existence" is a "real predicate"). It would be desirable to have a rigorous refutation of the doctrine but I have not been able to provide one. I am compelled to leave the matter at the more or less intuitive level of Kant's observation. In any case, I believe that the doctrine does not belong to Anselm's other formulation of the ontological argument. It is worth noting that Gassendi anticipated Kant's criticism when he said, against Descartes:

> Existence is a perfection neither in God nor in anything else; it is rather that in the absence of which there is no perfection. . . . Hence neither is existence held to exist in a thing in the way that perfections do, nor if the thing lacks existence is it said to be imperfect (or deprived of a perfection), so much as to be nothing.[9]

II

I take up now the consideration of the second ontological proof, which Anselm presents in the very next chapter of the *Proslogion*. (There is no evidence that he thought of himself

as offering two different proofs.) Speaking of the being a
greater than which cannot be conceived, he says:

> And it so truly exists that it cannot be conceived not to
> exist. For it is possible to conceive of a being which can-
> not be conceived not to exist; and this is greater than one
> which can be conceived not to exist. Hence, if that, than
> which nothing greater can be conceived, can be conceived
> not to exist, it is not that than which nothing greater can
> be conceived. But this is a contradiction. So truly, there-
> fore, is there something than which nothing greater can be
> conceived, that it cannot even be conceived not to exist.
> And this being thou art, O Lord, our God.[10]

Anselm is saying two things: first, that a being whose non-
existence is logically impossible is "greater" than a being
whose nonexistence is logically possible (and therefore that
a being a greater than which cannot be conceived must be
one whose nonexistence is logically impossible); second, that
God is a being than which a greater cannot be conceived.

In regard to the second of these assertions, there certainly
is *a* use of the word "God," and I think far the more common use, in accordance with which the statements "God is
the greatest of all beings," "God is the most perfect being,"
"God is the supreme being," are *logically* necessary truths,
in the same sense that the statement "A square has four
sides" is a logically necessary truth. If there is a man named
"Jones" who is the tallest man in the world, the statement
"Jones is the tallest man in the world" is merely true and is
not a logically necessary truth. It is a virtue of Anselm's
unusual phrase, "a being a greater than which cannot be
conceived,"[11] to make it explicit that the sentence "God is
the greatest of all beings" expresses a logically necessary
truth and not a mere matter of fact such as the one we
imagined about Jones.

With regard to Anselm's first assertion (namely, that a
being whose nonexistence is logically impossible is greater
than a being whose nonexistence is logically possible) perhaps the most puzzling thing about it is the use of the word
"greater." It appears to mean exactly the same as "superior,"

"more excellent," "more perfect." This equivalence by itself is of no help to us, however, since the latter expressions would be equally puzzling here. What is required is some explanation of their use.

We do think of *knowledge*, say, as an excellence, a good thing. If A has more knowledge of algebra than B we express this in common language by saying that A has a *better* knowledge of algebra than B, or that A's knowledge of algebra is *superior* to B's, whereas we should not say that B has a better or superior *ignorance* of algebra than A. We do say "greater ignorance," but here the word "greater" is used purely quantitatively.

Previously I rejected *existence* as a perfection. Anselm is maintaining in the remarks last quoted, not that existence is a perfection, but that *the logical impossibility of nonexistence is a perfection*. In other words, *necessary existence* is a perfection. His first ontological proof uses the principle that a thing is greater if it exists than if it does not exist. His second proof employs the different principle that a thing is greater if it necessarily exists than if it does not necessarily exist.

Some remarks about the notion of *dependence* may help to make this latter principle intelligible. Many things depend for their existence on other things and events. My house was built by a carpenter: its coming into existence was dependent on a certain creative activity. Its continued existence is dependent on many things: that a tree does not crush it, that it is not consumed by fire, and so on. If we reflect on the common meaning of the word "God" (no matter how vague and confused this is), we realize that it is incompatible with this meaning that God's existence should *depend* on anything. Whether we believe in Him or not we must admit that the "almighty and everlasting God" (as several ancient prayers begin), the "Maker of heaven and earth, and of all things visible and invisible" (as is said in the Nicene Creed), cannot be thought of as being brought into existence by anything or as depending for His continued existence on anything. To conceive of anything as dependent upon something else for its existence is to conceive of it as a lesser being than God.

If a housewife has a set of extremely fragile dishes, then as dishes they are *inferior* to those of another set like them in all respects except that they are *not* fragile. Those of the first set are *dependent* for their continued existence on gentle handling; those of the second set are not. There is a definite connection in common language between the notions of dependency and inferiority, and independence and superiority. To say that something which was dependent on nothing whatever was superior to ("greater than") anything that was dependent in any way upon anything is quite in keeping with the everyday use of the terms "superior" and "greater." Correlative with the notions of dependence and independence are the notions of *limited* and *unlimited*. An engine requires fuel and this is a limitation. It is the same thing to say that an engine's operation is *dependent* on as that it is *limited* by its fuel supply. An engine that could accomplish the same work in the same time and was in other respects satisfactory, but did not require fuel, would be a *superior* engine.

God is usually conceived of as an *unlimited* being. He is conceived of as a being who *could not* be limited, that is, as an absolutely unlimited being. This is no less than to conceive of Him as *something a greater than which cannot be conceived.* If God is conceived to be an absolutely unlimited being He must be conceived to be unlimited in regard to His existence as well as His operation. In this conception it will not make sense to say that He depends on anything for coming into or continuing in existence. Nor, as Spinoza observed, will it make sense to say that something could *prevent* Him from existing.[12] Lack of moisture can prevent trees from existing in a certain region of the earth. But it would be contrary to the concept of God as an unlimited being to suppose that anything other than God Himself could prevent Him from existing, and it would be self-contradictory to suppose that He Himself could do it.

Some may be inclined to object that although nothing could prevent God's existence, still it might just *happen* that He did not exist. And if He did exist that too would be by chance. I think, however, that from the supposition that it could happen that God did not exist it would follow that, if He existed, He would have mere duration and not eternity.

It would make sense to ask, "How long has He existed?,"
"Will He still exist next week?," "He was in existence yester-
day but how about today?," and so on. It seems absurd to
make God the subject of such questions. According to our
ordinary conception of Him, He is an eternal being. And
eternity does not mean endless duration, as Spinoza noted.
To ascribe eternity to something is to exclude as senseless
all sentences that imply that it has duration. If a thing has
duration then it would be merely a *contingent* fact, if it was
a fact, that its duration was endless. The moon could have
endless duration but not eternity. If something has endless
duration it will *make sense* (although it will be false) to say
that it will cease to exist, and it will make sense (although
it will be false) to say that something will *cause* it to cease to
exist. A being with endless duration is not, therefore, an
absolutely unlimited being. That God is conceived to be
eternal follows from the fact that He is conceived to be an
absolutely unlimited being.

I have been trying to expand the argument of *Proslogion* 3.
In *Responsio* 1 Anselm adds the following acute point: if
you can conceive of a certain thing and this thing does not
exist then if it *were* to exist its nonexistence would be *possible*. It follows, I believe, that if the thing were to exist it
would depend on other things both for coming into and continuing in existence, and also that it would have duration and
not eternity. Therefore it would not be, either in reality or
in conception, an unlimited being, *aliquid quo nihil maius
cogitari possit*.

Anselm states his argument as follows:

If it [the thing a greater than which cannot be conceived]
can be conceived at all it must exist. For no one who denies
or doubts the existence of a being a greater than which is
inconceivable, denies or doubts that if it did exist its non-
existence, either in reality or in the understanding, would
be impossible. For otherwise it would not be a being a
greater than which cannot be conceived. But as to whatever
can be conceived but does not exist: if it were to exist its
non-existence either in reality or in the understanding
would be possible. Therefore, if a being a greater than

which cannot be conceived, can even be conceived, it must exist.[13]

What Anselm has proved is that the notion of contingent existence or of contingent nonexistence cannot have any application to God. His existence must either be logically necessary or logically impossible. The only intelligible way of rejecting Anselm's claim that God's existence is necessary is to maintain that the concept of God, as a being a greater than which cannot be conceived, is self-contradictory or nonsensical.[14] Supposing that this is false, Anselm is right to deduce God's necessary existence from his characterization of Him as a being a greater than which cannot be conceived.

Let me summarize the proof. If God, a being a greater than which cannot be conceived, does not exist then He cannot *come* into existence. For if He did He would either have been *caused* to come into existence or have *happened* to come into existence, and in either case He would be a limited being, which by our conception of Him He is not. Since He cannot come into existence, if He does not exist His existence is impossible. If He does exist He cannot have come into existence (for the reasons given), nor can He cease to exist, for nothing could cause Him to cease to exist nor could it just happen that He ceased to exist. So if God exists His existence is necessary. Thus God's existence is either impossible or necessary. It can be the former only if the concept of such a being is self-contradictory or in some way logically absurd. Assuming that this is not so, it follows that He necessarily exists.

It may be helpful to express ourselves in the following way: to say, not that *omnipotence* is a property of God, but rather that *necessary omnipotence* is; and to say, not that omniscience is a property of God, but rather that *necessary omniscience* is. We have criteria for determining that a man knows this and that and can do this and that, and for determining that one man has greater knowledge and abilities in a certain subject than another. We could think of various tests to give them. But there is nothing we should wish to describe, seriously and literally, as "testing" God's knowledge and powers. That God is omniscient and omnipotent has not been determined by the application of criteria: rather these are requirements of our conception of Him. They are internal properties of the concept, although they are also rightly said to be properties of God. *Necessary existence* is a property of God in the *same sense* that *necessary omnipotence* and *necessary omniscience* are His properties. And we are not to think that "God necessarily exists" means that it follows necessarily from something that God exists *contingently*. The a priori proposition "God necessarily exists" entails the proposition "God exists," if and only if the latter also is understood as an a priori proposition: in which case the two propositions are equivalent. In this sense Anselm's proof is a proof of God's existence.

Descartes was somewhat hazy on the question of whether existence is a property of things that exist, but at the same time he saw clearly enough that *necessary existence* is a property of God. Both points are illustrated in his reply to Gassendi's remark, which I quoted above:

> I do not see to what class of reality you wish to assign existence, nor do I see why it may not be said to be a property as well as omnipotence, taking the word property as equivalent to any attribute or anything which can be predicated of a thing, as in the present case it should be by all means regarded. Nay, necessary existence in the case of God is also a true property in the strictest sense of the word, because it belongs to Him and forms part of His essence alone.[15]

Elsewhere he speaks of "the necessity of existence" as being "that crown of perfections without which we cannot comprehend God."[16] He is emphatic on the point that necessary existence applies solely to "an absolutely perfect Being."[17]

III

I wish to consider now a part of Kant's criticism of the ontological argument which I believe to be wrong. He says:

If, in an identical proposition, I reject the predicate while retaining the subject, contradiction results; and I therefore say that the former belongs necessarily to the latter. But if we reject subject and predicate alike, there is no contradiction; for nothing is then left that can be contradicted. To posit a triangle, and yet to reject its three angles, is self-contradictory; but there is no contradiction in rejecting the triangle together with its three angles. The same holds true of the concept of an absolutely necessary being. If its existence is rejected, we reject the thing itself with all its predicates; and no question of contradiction can then arise. There is nothing outside it that would then be contradicted, since the necessity of the thing is not supposed to be derived from anything external; nor is there anything internal that would be contradicted, since in rejecting the thing itself we have at the same time rejected all its internal properties. "God is omnipotent" is a necessary judgment. The omnipotence cannot be rejected if we posit a Deity, that is, an infinite being; for the two concepts are identical. But if we say, "There is no God," neither the omnipotence nor any other of its predicates is given; they are one and all rejected together with the subject, and there is therefore not the least contradiction in such a judgment.[18]

To these remarks the reply is that when the concept of God is correctly understood one sees that one cannot "reject the subject." "There is no God" is seen to be a necessarily false statement. Anselm's demonstration proves that the proposition "God exists" has the same a priori footing as the proposition "God is omnipotent."

Many present-day philosophers, in agreement with Kant, declare that existence is not a property and think that this overthrows the ontological argument. Although it is an error to regard existence as a property of things that have contingent existence, it does not follow that it is an error to regard necessary existence as a property of God. A recent writer says, against Anselm, that a proof of God's existence "based on the necessities of thought" is "universally regarded as fallacious: it is not thought possible to build bridges between mere abstractions and concrete existence."[19] But this way of putting the matter obscures the distinction we need to make. Does "concrete existence" mean contingent existence? Then to build bridges between concrete existence and mere abstractions would be like inferring the existence of an island from the concept of a perfect island, which both Anselm and Descartes regarded as absurd. What Anselm did was to give a demonstration that the proposition "God necessarily exists" is entailed by the proposition "God is a being a greater than which cannot be conceived" (which is equivalent to "God is an absolutely unlimited being"). Kant declares that when "I think a being as the supreme reality, without any defect, the question still remains whether it exists or not."[20] But once one has grasped Anselm's proof of the necessary existence of a being a greater than which cannot be conceived, no question remains as to whether it exists or not, just as Euclid's demonstration of the existence of an infinity of prime numbers leaves no question on that issue.

Kant says that "every reasonable person" must admit that "all existential propositions are synthetic."[21] Part of the perplexity one has about the ontological argument is in deciding whether or not the proposition "God necessarily exists" is or is not an "existential proposition." But let us look around. Is the Euclidean theorem in number theory, "There exists an infinite number of prime numbers," an "existential proposition"? Do we not want to say that *in some sense* it asserts the existence of something? Cannot we say, with equal justification, that the proposition "God necessarily exists" asserts the existence of something, *in some sense*? What we need to understand, in each case, is the particular sense of the assertion. Neither proposition has the same sort of sense as do the propositions, "A low pressure area exists over the Great Lakes," "There still exists some possibility that he will survive," "The pain continues to exist in his abdomen." One good way of seeing the difference in sense of these various propositions is to see the variously different ways in which they are proved or supported. It is wrong to think that all assertions of existence have the same kind of meaning. There are as many kinds of existential propositions as there are kinds of subjects of discourse.

Closely related to Kant's view that all existential propositions are "synthetic" is the contemporary dogma that all existential propositions are contingent. Professor Gilbert Ryle tells us that "Any assertion of the existence of something, like any assertion of the occurrence of something, can be denied without logical absurdity."[22] "All existential statements are contingent," says Mr. I. M. Crombie.[23] Professor J. J. C. Smart remarks that "Existence is not a property" and then goes on to assert that "There can never be any *logical contradiction* in denying that God exists."[24] He declares that "The concept of a logically necessary being is a self-contradictory concept, like the concept of a round square. . . . No existential proposition can be logically necessary," he maintains, for "the truth of a logically necessary proposition depends only on our symbolism, or to put the same thing in another way, on the relationship of concepts" (p. 38). Professor K. E. M. Baier says, "It is no longer seriously in dispute that the notion of a logically necessary being is self-contradictory. Whatever can be conceived of as existing can equally be conceived of as not existing."[25] This is a repetition of Hume's assertion, "Whatever we conceive as existent, we can also conceive as non-existent. There is no being, therefore, whose non-existence implies a contradiction."[26]

Professor J. N. Findlay ingeniously constructs an ontological *dis*proof of God's existence, based on a "modern" view of the nature of "necessity in propositions": the view, namely, that necessity in propositions "merely reflects our use of words, the arbitrary conventions of our language."[27] Findlay undertakes to characterize what he calls "religious attitude," and here there is a striking agreement between his observations and some of the things I have said in expounding Anselm's proof. Religious attitude, he says, presumes *superiority* in its object and superiority so great that the worshiper is in comparison as nothing. Religious attitude finds it "anomalous to worship anything *limited* in any thinkable manner. . . . And hence we are led on irresistibly to demand that our religious object should have an *unsurpassable* supremacy along all avenues, that it should tower *infinitely* above all other objects" (p. 51). We cannot help feeling that "the worthy object of our worship can never be a thing that merely *happens* to exist, nor one on which all other objects merely *happen* to depend. The true object of religious reverence must not be one, merely, to which no *actual* independent realities stand opposed: it must be one to which such opposition is totally *inconceivable*. . , . And not only must the existence of *other* things be unthinkable without him, but his own non-existence must be wholly unthinkable in any circumstances" (p. 52). And now, says Findlay, when we add up these various requirements, what they entail is "not only that there isn't a God, but that the Divine Existence is either senseless or impossible" (p. 54). For on the one hand, "If God is to satisfy religious claims and needs, He must be a being in every way inescapable, One whose existence and whose possession of certain excellences we cannot possibly conceive away." On the other hand, "modern views make it self-evidently absurd (if they don't make it ungrammatical) to speak of such a Being and attribute existence to Him. It was indeed an ill day for Anselm when he hit upon his famous proof. For on that day he not only laid bare something that is of the essence of an adequate religious object, but also something that entails its necessary non-existence" (p. 55).

Now I am inclined to hold the "modern" view that logically necessary truth "merely reflects our use of words" (although I do not believe that the conventions of language are always *arbitrary*). But I confess that I am unable to see how that view is supposed to lead to the conclusion that "the Divine existence is either senseless or impossible." Findlay does not explain how this result comes about. Surely he cannot mean that this view entails that nothing can have necessary properties: for this would imply that mathematics is "senseless or impossible," which no one wants to hold. Trying to fill in the argument that is missing from his article, the most plausible conjecture I can make is the following: Findlay thinks that the view that logical necessity "reflects the use of words" implies, not that nothing has necessary properties, but that *existence* cannot be a necessary property of anything. That is to say, every proposition of the form "*x* exists," including the proposition "God exists," must be *contingent*.[28] At the

same time, our concept of God requires that His existence
be *necessary*, that is, that "God exists" be a necessary truth.
Therefore, the modern view of necessity proves that what
the concept of God requires *cannot* be fulfilled. It proves that
God *cannot* exist.

The correct reply is that the view that logical necessity
merely reflects the use of words cannot possibly have the
implication that every existential proposition must be contingent. That view requires us to *look at* the use of words
and not manufacture a priori theses about it. In the Ninetieth
Psalm it is said: "Before the mountains were brought forth,
or ever thou hadst formed the earth and the world, even
from everlasting to everlasting, thou art God." Here is expressed the idea of the necessary existence and eternity of
God, an idea that is essential to the Jewish and Christian
religions. In those complex systems of thought, those "lan-
guages-games," God has the status of a necessary being. Who
can doubt that? Here we must say with Wittgenstein, "This
language-game is played!"[29] I believe we may rightly take
the existence of those religious systems of thought in which
God figures as a necessary being to be a disproof of the
dogma, affirmed by Hume and others, that no existential
proposition can be necessary.

Another way of criticizing the ontological argument is the
following. "Granted that the concept of necessary existence
follows from the concept of a being a greater than which
cannot be conceived, this amounts to no more than granting
the *a priori* truth of the *conditional* proposition, 'If such a
being exists then it necessarily exists.' This proposition, however, does not entail the *existence* of *anything*, and one can
deny its antecedent without contradiction." Kant, for example, compares the proposition (or "judgment," as he calls
it) "A triangle has three angles" with the proposition "God
is a necessary being." He allows that the former is "absolutely
necessary" and goes on to say:

The absolute necessity of the judgment is only a conditional
necessity of the thing, or of the predicate in the judgment.
The above proposition does not declare that three angles

are absolutely necessary, but that, under the condition that there is a triangle (that is, that a triangle is given), three angles will necessarily be found in it.[30]

He is saying, quite correctly, that the proposition about triangles is equivalent to the conditional proposition, "If a triangle exists, it has three angles." He then makes the comment that there is no contradiction "in rejecting the triangle together with its three angles." He proceeds to draw the alleged parallel: "The same holds true of the concept of an absolutely necessary being. If its existence is rejected, we reject the thing itself with all its predicates; and no question of contradiction can then arise."[31] The priest, Caterus, made the same objection to Descartes when he said:

> Though it be conceded that an entity of the highest perfection implies its existence by its very name, yet it does not follow that that very existence is anything actual in the real world, but merely that the concept of existence is inseparably united with the concept of highest being. Hence you cannot infer that the existence of God is anything actual, unless you assume that that highest being actually exists; for then it will actually contain all its perfections, together with this perfection of real existence.[32]

I think that Caterus, Kant, and numerous other philosophers have been mistaken in supposing that the proposition "God is a necessary being" (or "God necessarily exists") is equivalent to the conditional proposition "If God exists then He necessarily exists."[33] For how do they want the antecedent clause, "*If* God exists," to be understood? Clearly they want it to imply that it is *possible* that God does *not* exist.[34] The whole point of Kant's analysis is to try to show that it is possible to "reject the subject." Let us make this implication explicit in the conditional proposition, so that it reads: "If God exists (and it is possible that He does not) then He necessarily exists." But now it is apparent, I think, that these philosophers have arrived at a self-contradictory position. I do not mean that this conditional proposition, taken alone, is self-contradictory. Their position is self-contradictory in the following way. On the one hand, they agree that the proposition "God necessarily exists" is an a priori truth; Kant implies that it is "absolutely necessary," and Caterus says that God's existence is implied by His very name. On the other hand, they think that it is correct to analyze this proposition in such a way that it will entail the proposition "It is possible that God does not exist." But so far from its being the case that the proposition "God necessarily exists" entails the proposition "It is possible that God does not exist," it is rather the case that they are *incompatible* with one another! Can anything be clearer than that the conjunction "God necessarily exists but it is possible that He does not exist" is self-contradictory? Is it not just as plainly self-contradictory as the conjunction "A square necessarily has four sides but it is possible for a square not to have four sides"? In short, this familiar criticism of the ontological argument is self-contradictory, because it accepts *both* of two incompatible propositions.[35]

One conclusion we may draw from our examination of this criticism is that (contrary to Kant) there is a lack of symmetry, in an important respect, between the propositions "A triangle has three angles" and "God has necessary existence," although both are a priori. The former can be expressed in the conditional assertion "If a triangle exists (and it is possible that none does) it has three angles." The latter cannot be expressed in the corresponding conditional assertion without contradiction.

IV

I turn to the question of whether the idea of a being a greater than which cannot be conceived is self-contradictory. Here Leibniz made a contribution to the discussion of the ontological argument. He remarked that the argument of Anselm and Descartes

> is not a paralogism, but it is an imperfect demonstration, which assumes something that must still be proved in order to render it mathematically evident; that is, it is tacitly assumed that this idea of the all-great or all-perfect being

is possible, and implies no contradiction. And it is already something that by this remark it is proved that, assuming that God is possible, he exists, which is the privilege of divinity alone.[36]

Leibniz undertook to give a proof that God is possible. He defined a *perfection* as a simple, positive quality in the highest degree.[37] He argued that since perfections are *simple* qualities they must be compatible with one another. Therefore the concept of a being possessing all perfections is consistent.

I will not review his argument because I do not find his definition of a perfection intelligible. For one thing, it assumes that certain qualities or attributes are "positive" in their intrinsic nature, and others "negative" or "privative," and I have not been able clearly to understand that. For another thing, it assumes that some qualities are intrinsically simple. I believe that Wittgenstein has shown in the *Investigations* that nothing is *intrinsically* simple, but that whatever has the status of a simple, an indefinable, in one system of concepts, may have the status of a complex thing, a definable thing, in another system of concepts.

I do not know how to demonstrate that the concept of God—that is, of a being a greater than which cannot be conceived—is not self-contradictory. But I do not think that it is legitimate to demand such a demonstration. I also do not know how to demonstrate that either the concept of a material thing or the concept of *seeing* a material thing is not self-contradictory, and philosophers have argued that both of them are. With respect to any particular reasoning that is offered for holding that the concept of seeing a material thing, for example, is self-contradictory, one may try to show the invalidity of the reasoning and thus free the concept from the charge of being self-contradictory *on that ground*. But I do not understand what it would mean to demonstrate *in general*, and not in respect to any particular reasoning, that the concept is not self-contradictory. So it is with the concept of God. I should think there is no more of a presumption that it is self-contradictory than is the concept of seeing a material thing. Both concepts have a place in the thinking and the lives of human beings.

But even if one allows that Anselm's phrase may be free of self-contradiction, one wants to know how it can have any *meaning* for anyone. Why is it that human beings have even *formed* the concept of an infinite being, a being a greater than which cannot be conceived? This is a legitimate and important question. I am sure there cannot be a deep understanding of that concept without an understanding of the phenomena of human life that give rise to it. To give an account of the latter is beyond my ability. I wish, however, to make one suggestion (which should not be understood as autobiographical).

There is the phenomenon of feeling guilt for something that one has done or thought or felt or for a disposition that one has. One wants to be free of this guilt. But sometimes the guilt is felt to be so great that one is sure that nothing one could do oneself, nor any forgiveness by another human being, would remove it. One feels a guilt that is beyond all measure, a guilt "a greater than which cannot be conceived." Paradoxically, it would seem, one nevertheless has an intense desire to have this incomparable guilt removed. One requires a forgiveness that is beyond all measure, a forgiveness "a greater than which cannot be conceived." Out of such a storm in the soul, I am suggesting, there arises the conception of a forgiving mercy that is limitless, beyond all measure. This is one important feature of the Jewish and Christian conception of God.

I wish to relate this thought to a remark made by Kierkegaard, who was speaking about belief in Christianity but whose remark may have a wider application. He says:

> There is only one proof of the truth of Christianity and that, quite rightly, is from the emotions, when the dread of sin and a heavy conscience torture a man into crossing the narrow line between despair bordering upon madness —and Christendom.[38]

One may think it absurd for a human being to feel a guilt of such magnitude, and even more absurd that, if he feels it, he should *desire* its removal. I have nothing to say about that. It may also be absurd for people to fall in love, but they do it. I wish only to say that there *is* that human phenomenon of an unbearably heavy conscience and that it is importantly connected with the genesis of the concept of God, that is, with the formation of the "grammar" of the word "God." I am sure that this concept is related to human experience in other ways. If one had the acuteness and depth to perceive these connections one could grasp the *sense* of the concept. When we encounter this concept as a problem in philosophy, we do not consider the human phenomena that lie behind it. It is not surprising that many philosophers believe that the idea of a necessary being is an arbitrary and absurd construction.

What is the relation of Anselm's ontological argument to religious belief? This is a difficult question. I can imagine an atheist going through the argument, becoming convinced of its validity, acutely defending it against objections, yet remaining an atheist. The only effect it could have on the fool of the Psalm would be that he stopped saying in his heart "There is no God," because he would now realize that this is something he cannot meaningfully say or think. It is hardly to be expected that a demonstrative argument should, in addition, produce in him a living faith. Surely there is a level at which one can view the argument as a piece of logic, following the deductive moves but not being touched religiously? I think so. But even at this level the argument may not be without religious value, for it may help to remove some philosophical scruples that stand in the way of faith. At a deeper level, I suspect that the argument can be thoroughly understood only by one who has a view of that human "form of life" that gives rise to the idea of an infinitely great being, who views it from the *inside* not just from the outside and who has, therefore, at least some inclination to *partake* in that religious form of life. This inclination, in Kierkegaard's words, is "from the emotions." This inclination can hardly be an *effect* of Anselm's argument, but is rather presupposed in the fullest understanding of it. It would be unreasonable to require that the recognition of Anselm's demonstration as valid must produce a conversion.

NOTES

[1] I have consulted the Latin text of the *Proslogion,* of *Gaunilonis Pro Insipiente,* and of the *Responsio editoris,* in S. Anselmi, *Opera Omnia,* edited by F. C. Schmitt (Secovii, 1938), vol. I. With numerous modifications, I have used the English translation by S. N. Deane: *St. Anselm* (LaSalle, Illinois, 1948).

[2] *See Proslogion* 1 and *Responsio* 2.

[3] Anselm's actual words are: "Et certe id quo maius cogitari nequit, non potest esse in solo intellectu. Si enim vel in solo intellectu est, potest cogitari esse et in re, quod maius est. Si ergo id quo maius cogitari non potest, est in solo intellectu: id ipsum quo maius cogitari non potest, est quo maius cogitari potest. Sed certe hoc esse non potest." *Proslogion* 2.

[4] Haldane and Ross, *The Philosophical Works of Descartes,* 2 vols. (Cambridge, 1931), I, 163.

[5] *Op. cit.,* p. 182.

[6] *Proslogion* 2; Deane, p. 8.

[7] *Responsio* 2; Deane, pp. 157-158.

[8] *The Critique of Pure Reason,* tr. by Norman Kemp Smith (London, 1929), p. 505.

[9] Haldane and Ross, II, 186.

[10] *Proslogion* 3; Deane, pp. 8-9.

[11] Professor Robert Calhoun has pointed out to me that a similar locution had been used by Augustine. In *De moribus Manichaeorum* (Bk. II, ch. xi, sec. 24), he says that God is a being *quo esse aut cogitari melius nihil possit* (*Patrologiae Patrum Latinorum,* ed. by J. P. Migne, Paris, 1841-1845, vol. 32; *Augustinus,* vol. 1).

[12] *Ethics,* pt. I, prop. 11.

[13] *Responsio* 1; Deane, pp. 154-155.

[14] Gaunilo attacked Anselm's argument on this very point. He would not concede that a being a greater than which cannot be conceived existed in his understanding (*Gaunilonis Pro Insipiente,* secs. 4 and 5; Deane, pp. 148-150). Anselm's reply is: "I call on your faith and conscience to attest that this is most false" (*Responsio* 1; Deane, p. 154). Gaunilo's faith and conscience will attest that it is false that "God is not a being a greater than which is inconceivable," and false that "He is not understood (*intelligitur*) or conceived (*cogitatur*)" (*ibid.*). Descartes also remarks that one would go to "strange extremes" who denied that we understand the words *"that thing which is the most perfect that we conceive;* for that is what all men call God" (Haldane and Ross, II, 129).

¹⁵ Haldane and Ross, II, 228.

¹⁶ *Ibid.*, I, 445.

¹⁷ E.g., *ibid.*, Principle 15, p. 225.

¹⁸ *Op. cit.*, p. 502.

¹⁹ J. N. Findlay, "Can God's Existence Be Disproved?," *New Essays in Philosophical Theology*, ed. by A. N. Flew and A. MacIntyre (London, 1955), p. 47.

²⁰ *Op. cit.*, pp. 505-506.

²¹ *Ibid.*, p. 504.

²² *The Nature of Metaphysics*, ed. by D. F. Pears (New York, 1957), p. 150.

²³ *New Essays in Philosophical Theology*, p. 114.

²⁴ *Ibid.*, p. 34.

²⁵ *The Meaning of Life*, Inaugural Lecture, Canberra University College (Canberra, 1957), p. 8.

²⁶ *Dialogues Concerning Natural Religion*, pt. IX.

²⁷ Findlay, *op. cit.*, p. 154.

²⁸ The other philosophers I have just cited may be led to this opinion by the same thinking. Smart, for example, says that "the truth of a logically necessary proposition depends only on our symbolism, or to put the same thing in another way, on the relationship of concepts" (*supra*). This is very similar to saying that it "reflects our use of words."

²⁹ *Philosophical Investigations* (New York, 1953), sec. 654.

³⁰ *Op. cit.*, pp. 501-502.

³¹ *Ibid.*, p. 502.

³² Haldane and Ross, II, 7.

³³ I have heard it said by more than one person in discussion that Kant's view was that it is really a misuse of language to speak of a "necessary being," on the grounds that necessity is properly predicated only of propositions (judgments) not of *things*. This is not a correct account of Kant. (See his discussion of "The Postulates of Empirical Thought in General," *op. cit.*, pp. 239-256, esp. p. 239 and pp. 247-248.) But if he had held this, as perhaps the above philosophers think he should have, then presumably his view would not have been that the pseudo-proposition "God is a necessary being" is equivalent to the conditional "If God exists then He necessarily exists." Rather his view would have been that the genuine proposition " 'God exists' is necessarily true" is equivalent to the conditional "If God exists then He exists" (*not* "If God exists then He *necessarily* exists," which would be an illegitimate formulation, on the view imaginatively attributed to Kant).

"If God exists then He exists" is a foolish tautology which says nothing different from the tautology "If a new earth satellite exists then it exists." If "If God exists then He exists" were a correct analysis of " 'God exists' is necessarily true," then "If a new earth satellite exists then it exists" would be a correct analysis of " 'A new earth satellite exists' is necessarily true." If the *analysans* is necessarily true then the *analysandum* must be necessarily true, provided the analysis is correct. If this proposed Kantian analysis of " 'God exists' is necessarily true" were correct, we should be presented with the consequence that not only is it necessarily true that God exists, but also it is necessarily true that a new earth satellite exists: which is absurd.

³⁴ When summarizing Anselm's proof (in part II, *supra*) I said: "If God exists He necessarily exists." But there I was merely stating an entailment. "If God exists" did not have the implication that it is possible He does not exist. And of course I was not regarding the conditional as *equivalent* to "God necessarily exists."

³⁵ This fallacious criticism of Anselm is implied in the following remarks by Gilson: "To show that the affirmation of necessary existence is analytically implied in the idea of God, would be . . . to show that God is necessary if He exists, but would not prove that He does exist" (E. Gilson, *The Spirit of Medieval Philosophy*, New York, 1940, p. 62).

³⁶ *New Essays Concerning the Human Understanding*, Bk. IV, ch. 10; ed. by A. G. Langley (LaSalle, Illinois, 1949), p. 504.

³⁷ See *Ibid.*, Appendix X, p. 714.

³⁸ *The Journals*, tr. by A. Dru (Oxford, 1938), sec. 926.

THE COSMOLOGICAL
ARGUMENT

The term "cosmological argument" is used sometimes to refer to the argument from the contingency of the world, sometimes more widely to include also the First Cause argument, and sometimes more widely still to refer to all arguments which proceed from the world to God. It is used here to cover the arguments concerning contingency and a First Cause.

First Form of the Argument

PLATO

Along with several other of the most important strands of Western thought, "natural" or "rational" theology has its origin in the dialogues of Plato (428/7-348/7 B. C.) Here began the still continuing careers of both the cosmological and the teleological arguments. The following selection contains Plato's proof of divine existence in Book X of the *Laws,* a dialogue of the last and most mature period of Plato's thought. He directs attention to the fact of motion, and in the speech immediately preceding this passage he lists eight different kinds of motion or change—movement round an axis, movement from place to place, movement which is both from place to place and round an axis, retardation, acceleration, growth, decay, and destruction. The selection opens as he adds the two further kinds of motion, or capacity for motion, which are most important for his argument—the power of something to move other objects when it is itself moved by something else, and the power of something to move itself as well as to move other objects. Plato's argument is now, in essence, that the power to *produce* movement is logically prior to the power to receive it and pass it on. In order for there to be causes undergoing and transmitting change there must first be an uncaused cause to originate the movement. And the only kind of reality with the power of spontaneous movement is soul. Therefore the ultimate cause of a universe in motion must be a living soul, and one of a higher order than the human soul.

This (apart from an earlier anticipation of it in Plato's *Phaedrus*, 245, C-E) is the genesis of what has come to be called the cosmological argument. Note also in this selection a passage in which the basic principle of the design (or teleological) argument appears: "If, my friend, we say that the whole path and movement of heaven, and of all that is therein, is by nature akin to the movement and revolution and calculation of mind, and proceeds by kindred laws, then, as is plain, we must say that the best soul takes care of the world and guides it along the good path" (p. 77). In an earlier passage in *Laws*, X, we find the design argument linked with the argument from universal consent: "In the first place, the earth and the sun, and the stars and the universe, and the fair order of the seasons, and the division of them into years and months, furnish proofs of [the gods'] existence; and also there is the fact that all Hellenes and barbarians believe in them" (886 A).

❋

FROM *Laws*[1]

Have we not mentioned all motions that there are, and comprehended them under their kinds and numbered them with the exception, my friends, of two?

CLEINIAS. Which are they?

ATHENIAN STRANGER. Just the two with which our present inquiry is concerned.

CLEINIAS. Speak plainer.

ATHENIAN STRANGER. I suppose that our inquiry has reference to the soul?

CLEINIAS. Very true.

ATHENIAN STRANGER. Let us assume that there is a motion able to move other things, but never to move itself;—that is one kind; and there is another kind which can always move itself as well as other things, working in composition and decomposition, by increase and diminution and generation and destruction,—that is also one of the many kinds of motion.

CLEINIAS. Granted.

ATHENIAN STRANGER. And we will assume that which moves other, and is changed by other, to be the ninth, and that which changes itself and others, and is coincident with every action and every passion, and is the true principle of change and motion in all that is,—that we shall be inclined to call the tenth.

CLEINIAS. Certainly.

ATHENIAN STRANGER. And which of these ten motions ought we to prefer as being the mightiest and most efficient?

CLEINIAS. I must say that the motion which is able to move itself is ten thousand times superior to all the others.[2]

ATHENIAN STRANGER. Very good; but may I make one or two corrections in what I have been saying?

CLEINIAS. What are they?

ATHENIAN STRANGER. When I spoke of the tenth sort of motion, that was not quite correct.

CLEINIAS. What was the error?

ATHENIAN STRANGER. According to the true order, the tenth was really the first in generation and power; then follows the second, which was strangely enough termed the ninth by us.

CLEINIAS. What do you mean?

ATHENIAN STRANGER. I mean this: when one thing changes another, and that another, of such will there be any primary changing element? How can a thing which is moved by another ever be the beginning of change? Impossible. But when the self-moved changes other, and that again other, and thus thousands upon tens of thousands of bodies are set in motion, must not the beginning of all this motion be the change of the self-moving principle?[3]

CLEINIAS. Very true, and I quite agree.

ATHENIAN STRANGER. Or, to put the question in another way, making answer to ourselves:—If, as most of these philosophers have the audacity to affirm, all things were at rest in one mass, which of the above-mentioned principles of motion must necessarily be the first to spring up among them? Clearly the self-moving; for there could be no change in them arising out of any external cause; the change must first take place in themselves. Then we must say that self-motion being the origin of all motions, and the first which arises among things at rest as well as among things in motion, is the eldest and mightiest principle of change, and that which is changed by another and yet moves other is second.

CLEINIAS. Quite true.

ATHENIAN STRANGER. At this stage of the argument let us put a question.

CLEINIAS. What question?

ATHENIAN STRANGER. If we were to see this power existing in any earthy, watery, or fiery substance, simple or compound—how should we describe it?

CLEINIAS. You mean to ask whether we should call such a self-moving power life?

ATHENIAN STRANGER. I do.

CLEINIAS. Certainly we should.

ATHENIAN STRANGER. And when we see soul in anything, must we not do the same—must we not admit that this is life?

CLEINIAS. We must.

ATHENIAN STRANGER. And now, I beseech you, reflect;—you would admit that we have a threefold knowledge of things?

CLEINIAS. What do you mean?

ATHENIAN STRANGER. I mean that we know the essence, and that we know the definition of the essence, and the name,—these are the three; and there are two questions which may be raised about anything.

CLEINIAS. How two?

ATHENIAN STRANGER. Sometimes a person may give the name and ask the definition; or he may give the definition and ask the name. I may illustrate what I mean in this way.

CLEINIAS. How?

ATHENIAN STRANGER. Number like some other things is capable of being divided into equal parts; when thus divided, number is named "even," and the definition of the name "even" is "number divisible into two equal parts"?

CLEINIAS. True.

ATHENIAN STRANGER. I mean, that when we are asked about the definition and give the name, or when we are asked about the name and give the definition—in either case, whether we give name or definition, we speak of the same thing, calling "even" the number which is divided into two equal parts.

CLEINIAS. Quite true.

ATHENIAN STRANGER. And what is the definition of that which is named "soul"? Can we conceive of any other than that which has been already given—the motion which can move itself?

CLEINIAS. You mean to say that the essence which is defined as the self-moved is the same with that which has the name soul?

ATHENIAN STRANGER. Yes; and if this is true, do we still maintain that there is anything wanting in the proof that the soul is the first origin and moving power of all that is, or has become, or will be, and their contraries, when she has been clearly shown to be the source of change and motion in all things?

CLEINIAS. Certainly not; the soul as being the source of motion, has been most satisfactorily shown to be the oldest of all things.

ATHENIAN STRANGER. And is not that motion which is produced in another, by reason of another, but never has any self-moving power at all, being in truth the change of an inanimate body, to be reckoned second, or by any lower number which you may prefer?

CLEINIAS. Exactly.

ATHENIAN STRANGER. Then we are right, and speak the most perfect and absolute truth, when we say that soul is prior to body, and that body is second and comes afterwards, and is born to obey soul, which is the ruler?

CLEINIAS. Nothing can be more true.

ATHENIAN STRANGER. Do you remember our old admission,

that if soul was prior to body the things of soul were also prior to those of body?

CLEINIAS. Certainly.

ATHENIAN STRANGER. Then characters and manners, and wishes and reasonings, and true opinions, and foresight, and recollection are prior to length and breadth and depth and strength of bodies, if soul is prior to body.

CLEINIAS. To be sure.

ATHENIAN STRANGER. In the next place, must we not of necessity admit that the soul is the cause of good and evil, base and honorable, just and unjust, and of all other opposites, if we suppose her to be the cause of all things?

CLEINIAS. We must.

ATHENIAN STRANGER. And as soul orders and inhabits all things that move, however moving, must we not say that she orders also the heavens?

CLEINIAS. Of course.

ATHENIAN STRANGER. One soul or more? More than one—I will answer for you; at any rate, we must not suppose that there are less than two—one the author of good, and the other of evil.

CLEINIAS. Very true.

ATHENIAN STRANGER. Yes, very true; soul then directs all things in heaven, and earth, and sea by her movements, and these are described by the terms—will, consideration, attention, deliberation, opinion true and false, joy and sorrow, confidence, fear, hatred, love, and other primary motions akin to these; which again receive the secondary motions of corporeal substances, and guide all things to growth and decay, to composition and decomposition, and to the qualities which accompany them, such as heat and cold, heaviness and lightness, hardness and softness, blackness and whiteness, bitterness and sweetness, and all those other qualities which the soul uses, herself a goddess, when truly receiving the divine mind she disciplines all things rightly to their happiness; but when she is the companion of folly, she does the very contrary of all this. Shall we assume so much, or do we still entertain doubts?

CLEINIAS. There is no room at all for doubt.

ATHENIAN STRANGER. Shall we say then that it is the soul

which controls heaven and earth, and the whole world?—
that it is a principle of wisdom and virtue, or a principle
which has neither wisdom nor virtue? Suppose that we make
answer as follows:—

CLEINIAS. How would you answer?

ATHENIAN STRANGER. If, my friend, we say that the whole
path and movement of heaven, and of all that is therein, is
by nature akin to the movement and revolution and calculation of mind, and proceeds by kindred laws, then, as is plain,
we must say that the best soul takes care of the world and
guides it along the good path.

CLEINIAS. True.

ATHENIAN STRANGER. But if the world moves wildly and ir-
regularly, then the evil soul guides it.

CLEINIAS. True again.

ATHENIAN STRANGER. Of what nature is the movement of
mind?—To this question it is not easy to give an intelligent
answer; and therefore I ought to assist you in framing one.

CLEINIAS. Very good.

ATHENIAN STRANGER. Then let us not answer as if we would
look straight at the sun, making ourselves darkness at mid-
day,—I mean as if we were under the impression that we
could see with mortal eyes, or know adequately the nature of
mind;—it will be safer to look at the image only.

CLEINIAS. What do you mean?

ATHENIAN STRANGER. Let us select of the ten motions the one
which mind chiefly resembles; this I will bring to your recollection, and will then make the answer on behalf of us all.

CLEINIAS. That will be excellent.

ATHENIAN STRANGER. You will surely remember our saying
that all things were either at rest or in motion?

CLEINIAS. I do.

ATHENIAN STRANGER. And that of things in motion some
were moving in one place, and others in more than one?

CLEINIAS. Yes.

ATHENIAN STRANGER. Of these two kinds of motion, that
which moves in one place must move about a centre like
wheels made in a lathe, and is most entirely akin and similar
to the circular movement of mind.

CLEINIAS. What do you mean?

ATHENIAN STRANGER. In saying that both mind and the motion which is in one place move in the same and like manner, in and about the same, and in relation to the same, and according to one proportion and order, and are like the motion of a globe, we invented a fair image, which does no discredit to our ingenuity.

CLEINIAS. It does us great credit.

ATHENIAN STRANGER. And the motion of the other sort which is not after the same manner, nor in the same, nor about the same, nor in relation to the same, nor in one place, nor in order, nor according to any rule or proportion, may be said to be akin to senselessness and folly?

CLEINIAS. That is most true.

ATHENIAN STRANGER. Then, after what has been said, there is no difficulty in distinctly stating, that since soul carries all things round, either the best soul or the contrary must of necessity carry round and order and arrange the revolution of the heaven.

CLEINIAS. And judging from what has been said, stranger, there would be impiety in asserting that any but the most perfect soul or souls carries round the heavens.

ATHENIAN STRANGER. You have understood my meaning right well, Cleinias, and now let me ask you another question.

CLEINIAS. What are you going to ask?

ATHENIAN STRANGER. If the soul carries round the sun and moon, and the other stars, does she not carry round each individual of them?

CLEINIAS. Certainly.

ATHENIAN STRANGER. Then of one of them let us speak, and the same argument will apply to all.

CLEINIAS. Which will you take?

ATHENIAN STRANGER. Everyone sees the body of the sun, but no one sees his soul, nor the soul of any other body living or dead; and yet there is great reason to believe that this nature, unperceived by any of our senses, is circumfused around them all, but is perceived only by mind; and therefore by mind and reflection only let us apprehend the following point.

CLEINIAS. What is that?

ATHENIAN STRANGER. If the soul carries round the sun, we shall not be far wrong in supposing one of three alternatives.

CLEINIAS. What are they?

ATHENIAN STRANGER. Either the soul which moves the sun this way and that, resides within the circular and visible body, like the soul which carries us about every way; or the soul provides herself with a body of fire or air, as some affirm, and from some point without violently propels body by body; or thirdly, she is without such a body, but guides the sun by some extraordinary and wonderful power.

CLEINIAS. Yes, certainly; the soul can only order all things in one of these three ways.

ATHENIAN STRANGER. And this soul of the sun, which is therefore better than the sun, whether riding in the sun as in a chariot to give light to men, or acting from without, or in whatever way, ought by every man to be deemed a god.[4]

CLEINIAS. Yes, by every man who has the least particle of sense.

ATHENIAN STRANGER. And of the stars too, and of the moon, and of the years and months and seasons, must we not say in like manner, that since a soul or souls having every sort of excellence are the causes of all of them, those souls are gods, whether they are living beings and reside in bodies, and in this way order the whole heaven, or whatever be the place and mode of their existence;—and will anyone who admits all this tolerate the denial that all things are full of gods?

NOTES

[1] *The Dialogues of Plato*, trans. by B. Jowett (Oxford: The Clarendon Press, 4th ed., 1953), Vol. IV, pp. 463-69. (Book X, 894A-899C)

[2] Cf. *Tim.* 89 a.

[3] Cf. *Phaedr.* 245 d.

[4] Cf. *Laws*, xii. 966-7.

The Five Ways

ST. THOMAS AQUINAS

St. Thomas Aquinas (1224/5–1274) was one of the most powerful intellects in the history of Christian thought, and remains the theological patron saint of the Roman Catholic Church. (The Encyclical *Aeterni Patris*, 1879, of Pope Leo XIII both rehearses the numerous previous papal tributes to St. Thomas and confirms the papal approval of the Thomist philosophy for the modern period.) In common with the whole Catholic tradition, Aquinas taught that the existence of God can be philosophically demonstrated. In the famous passage reprinted here from his *Summa Theologica* he offers five proofs, the first three of which are forms of the cosmological argument. The background and presupposition of these arguments is the Aristotelian philosophy which had been rediscovered in Europe in the twelfth and thirteenth centuries. In his *Metaphysics* Aristotle had argued that change implies an ultimate unchanging source of movement; for there cannot be an *infinite* regress of causes. "But if there is nothing eternal, then there can be no becoming: for there must be something which undergoes the process of becoming, that is, that from which things come to be; and the last member of this series must be ungenerated, for the series must start with something, since nothing can come from nothing."[1] This principle is employed by Aquinas in his first three Ways, as is also the Aristotelian distinction between potentiality and actuality. The passage from Father F. C. Copleston, S.J.,[2] which follows, provides a sympathetic commentary upon Aquinas's compressed formulations.

An objection that is raised by several contemporary philosophers against the argument from the contingency of the world (Aquinas's third Way) is that, in the words of one such critic, "the argument purports to argue to the existence of a necessary being." And by a necessary being the cosmological argument means "a *logically* necessary being," i.e. "a being whose non-existence is inconceivable in the sort of way that a triangle's having four sides is inconceivable." The trouble is, however, that the concept of a logically necessary being is a self-contradictory concept, like the concept of a round square. For in the first place "necessary" is a predicate of *propositions,* not of things . . . An existential proposition must be very different from any logically necessary one, such as a mathematical one, for example, for the conventions of our symbolism clearly leave it open for us either to affirm or deny an existential proposition; it is not our symbolism but reality which decides whether or not we must affirm or deny it. The demand that the existence of God should be *logically* necessary is thus a self-contradictory one . . . "Logically necessary being" is a self-contradictory expression like "round square" . . . We reject the cosmological argument, then, because it rests on a thorough absurdity."[3]

In the opinion of the present writer this objection, whilst it could apply to some formulations of the cosmological argument, does not apply to Aquinas's third Way. For this does not make use of the notion, which is attacked above, of "logically necessary being." Aquinas stands in a tradition going back to Anselm in which the necessary existence of God is virtually equivalent to his *aseity* —his eternal, independent "self-existence."[4] Accordingly when Aquinas infers the existence of a necessary being, which is God, he means neither that God exists by logical necessity nor that the proposition "God exists" is a logically necessary truth. His distinction between necessary and contingent being is, in the broadest sense, a factual rather than a logical distinction. He equates contingency with transiency, or having a beginning and an end in time, and necessary existence with eternal and uncreated being. A necessary being is thus factually or ontologically rather than logically necessary; its necessity consists in the circumstance that it has an eternal and independent status such that it is not contingent for its existence upon anything outside itself.[5]

The main weakness of the cosmological argument, considered as an instrument for demonstrating the existence of God to an atheist or an agnostic is (in my opinion) that suggested in the Introduction (pp. 6-7), namely that the argument begs the question. This is virtually acknowledged by Father Copleston at the conclusion of the selection below from his book on *Aquinas*. He there admits that it is not possible even to begin to lead a nonbeliever to God by means of this reasoning unless he shares the cosmological arguer's basic conviction that the fact that there is a world at all is a puzzle which demands an explanation. But it is precisely this premise that the atheist or agnostic is likely to reject—as is made clear in the debate between Father Copleston and Bertrand Russell included in this volume.

Finally, it should be noted that Aquinas's fourth Way, while it points back to Plato's conception of the eternal Forms or archetypes, also points forward to the moral argument, or the argument from value in general, which was to be so fully developed in the nineteenth century (*see* pp. 137f.). Aquinas's fifth Way, again, points forward to the teleological or design argument (*see* pp. 99f.).

✳

FROM *Summa Theologica*[6]

THIRD ARTICLE: WHETHER GOD EXISTS?

We proceed thus to the Third Article:

OBJECTION 1. It seems that God does not exist; because if one of two contraries be infinite, the other would be altogether destroyed. But the name God means that He is infinite goodness. If, therefore, God existed, there would be no evil discoverable; but there is evil in the world. Therefore God does not exist.

OBJ. 2. Further, it is superfluous to suppose that what can be accounted for by a few principles has been produced by many. But it seems that everything we see in the world can be accounted for by other principles, supposing God did not exist. For all natural things can be reduced to one principle, which is nature; and all voluntary things can be reduced to one principle, which is human reason, or will. Therefore there is no need to suppose God's existence.

On the contrary, It is said in the person of God: I am Who am [Exod. 3:14].

I answer that, The existence of God can be proved in five ways.

The first and more manifest way is the argument from motion. It is certain, and evident to our senses, that in the world some things are in motion. Now whatever is moved is moved by another, for nothing can be moved except it is in potentiality to that towards which it is moved; whereas a thing moves inasmuch as it is in act. For motion is nothing else than the reduction of something from potentiality to actuality. But nothing can be reduced from potentiality to actuality, except by something in a state of actuality. Thus that which is actually hot, as fire, makes wood, which is potentially hot, to be actually hot, and thereby moves and changes it. Now it is not possible that the same thing should be at once in actuality and potentiality in the same respect, but only in different respects. For what is actually hot cannot simultaneously be potentially hot; but it is simultaneously potentially cold. It is therefore impossible that in the same respect and in the same way a thing should be both mover and moved, i.e., that it should move itself. Therefore, whatever is moved must be moved by another. If that by which it is moved be itself moved, then this also must needs be moved by another, and that by another again. But this cannot go on to infinity, because then there would be no first mover, and, consequently, no other mover, seeing that subsequent movers move only inasmuch as they are moved by the first mover; as the staff moves only because it is moved by the hand. Therefore it is necessary to arrive at a first mover, moved by no other; and this everyone understands to be God.

The second way is from the nature of efficient cause. In the world of sensible things we find there is an order of efficient causes. There is no case known (neither is it, indeed, possible) in which a thing is found to be the efficient cause of itself; for so it would be prior to itself, which is impossible. Now in efficient causes it is not possible to go on to infinity, because in all efficient causes following in order, the first is the cause of the intermediate cause, and the intermediate is the cause of the ultimate cause, whether the intermediate cause be several, or one only. Now to take away the cause is to take away the effect. Therefore, if there be no first cause among efficient causes, there will be no ultimate, nor any intermediate, cause. But if in efficient causes it is possible to go on to infinity, there will be no first efficient cause, neither will there be an ultimate effect, nor any intermediate efficient causes; all of which is plainly false. Therefore it is necessary to admit a first efficient cause, to which everyone gives the name of God.

The third way is taken from possibility and necessity, and runs thus. We find in nature things that are possible to be and not to be, since they are found to be generated, and to be corrupted, and consequently, it is possible for them to be and not to be. But it is impossible for these always to exist, for that which can not-be at some time is not. Therefore, if everything can not-be, then at one time there was nothing in existence. Now if this were true, even now there would be nothing in existence, because that which does not exist begins to exist only through something already existing. Therefore, if at one time nothing was in existence, it would have been impossible for anything to have begun to exist; and thus even now nothing would be in existence—which is absurd. Therefore, not all beings are merely possible, but there must exist something the existence of which is necessary. But every necessary thing either has its necessity caused by another, or not. Now it is impossible to go on to infinity in necessary things which have their necessity caused by another, as has been already proved in regard to efficient causes. Therefore we cannot but admit the existence of some being having of itself its own necessity, and not receiving it from another, but rather causing in others their necessity. This all men speak of as God.

The fourth way is taken from the gradation to be found in things. Among beings there are some more and some less good, true, noble, and the like. But *more* and *less* are predicated of different things according as they resemble in their different ways something which is the maximum, as a thing is said to be hotter according as it more nearly resembles that which is hottest; so that there is something which is truest, something best, something noblest, and, consequently, something which is most being, for those things that are greatest in truth are greatest in being, as it is written in Metaph. ii.

Now the maximum in any genus is the cause of all in that genus, as fire, which is the maximum of heat, is the cause of all hot things, as is said in the same book. Therefore there must also be something which is to all beings the cause of their being, goodness, and every other perfection; and this we call God.

The fifth way is taken from the governance of the world. We see that things which lack knowledge, such as natural bodies, act for an end, and this is evident from their acting always, or nearly always, in the same way, so as to obtain the best result. Hence it is plain that they achieve their end, not fortuitously, but designedly. Now whatever lacks knowledge cannot move towards an end, unless it be directed by some being endowed with knowledge and intelligence; as the arrow is directed by the archer. Therefore some intelligent being exists by whom all natural things are directed to their end; and this being we call God.

REPLY OBJ. 1. As Augustine says: Since God is the highest good, He would not allow any evil to exist in His works, unless His omnipotence and goodness were such as to bring good even out of evil. This is part of the infinite goodness of God, that He should allow evil to exist, and out of it produce good.

REPLY OBJ. 2. Since nature works for a determinate end under the direction of a higher agent, whatever is done by nature must be traced back to God as to its first cause. So likewise whatever is done voluntarily must be traced back to some higher cause other than human reason and will, since these can change and fail; for all things that are changeable and capable of defect must be traced back to an immovable and self-necessary first principle, as has been shown.

NOTES

[1] *Metaphysics*, Beta, 4 (999b). Translated by Richard Hope (Ann Arbor: The University of Michigan Press, 1960), p. 51.

[2] Biographical note on p. 86.

[3] J. J. C. Smart, "The Existence of God," *New Essays in Philosophical Theology*, edited by Flew and MacIntyre, pp. 38-39.

4 *See* the passage from Anselm printed here on pp. 25f. (*Responsio*, ch. 4). *See also Responsio*, ch. 1; *Proslogion*, ch. 22; *Monologion*, ch. 28.

5 *Cf.* John Hick, "Necessary Being," *Scottish Journal of Theology* (December, 1961).

6 *Basic Writings of St. Thomas Aquinas, op. cit.*

Commentary on the Five Ways

F. C. COPLESTON

F. C. Copleston (1907-), Jesuit priest, is professor of the History of Philosophy both at Heythrop College, Oxfordshire, England and at the Gregorian University, Rome. He is the author of *Friedrich Nietzsche* (1942), *Arthur Schopenhauer* (1946), *Medieval Philosophy* (1952), *Aquinas* (1955), *Contemporary Philosophy* (1956), and a multi-volume *A History of Philosophy* (1946-).

❊

God and Creation[1]

I [now] turn to Aquinas' five proofs of the existence of God. In the first proof he argues that "motion" or change means the reduction of a thing from a state of potentiality to one of act, and that a thing cannot be reduced from potentiality to act except under the influence of an agent already in act. In this sense "everything which is moved must be moved by another." He argues finally that in order to avoid an infinite regress in the chain of movers, the existence of a first unmoved mover must be admitted. "And all understand that this is God."

A statement like "all understand that this is God" or "all call this (being) God" occurs at the end of each proof, and I postpone consideration of it for the moment. As for the ruling out of an infinite regress, I shall explain what Aquinas means to reject after outlining the second proof, which is similar in structure to the first.

Whereas in the first proof Aquinas considers things as being acted upon, as being changed or "moved," in the second he considers them as active agents, as efficient causes. He argues that there is a hierarchy of efficient causes, a subordinate cause being dependent on the cause above it in the hierarchy. He then proceeds, after excluding the hypothesis of an infinite regress, to draw the conclusion that there must be a first efficient cause, "which all call God."

Now, it is obviously impossible to discuss these arguments profitably unless they are first understood. And misunderstanding of them is only too easy, since the terms and phrases used are either unfamiliar or liable to be taken in a sense other than the sense intended. In the first place it is essential to understand that in the first argument Aquinas supposes that movement or change is dependent on a "mover" acting here and now, and that in the second argument he supposes that there are efficient causes in the world which even in their causal activity are here and now dependent on the causal activity of other causes. That is why I have spoken of a "hierarchy" rather than of a "series." What he is thinking of can be illustrated in this way. A son is dependent on his father, in the sense that he would not have existed except for the causal activity of his father. But when the son acts for himself, he is not dependent here and now on his father. But he is dependent here and now on other factors. Without the activity of the air, for instance, he could not himself act, and the life-preserving activity of the air is itself dependent here and now on other factors, and they in turn on other factors. I do not say that this illustration is in all respects adequate for the purpose; but it at least illustrates the fact that when Aquinas talks about an "order" of efficient causes he is not thinking of a series stretching back into the past, but of a hierarchy of causes, in which a subordinate member is here and now dependent on the causal activity of a higher member. If I wind up my watch at night, it then proceeds to work without further interference on my part. But the activity of the pen tracing these words on the page is here and now dependent on the activity of my hand, which in turn is here and now dependent on other factors.

The meaning of the rejection of an infinite regress should

now be clear. Aquinas is not rejecting the possibility of an infinite series as such. We have already seen that he did not think that anyone had ever succeeded in showing the impossibility of an infinite series of events stretching back into the past. Therefore he does not mean to rule out the possibility of an infinite series of causes and effects, in which a given member depended on the preceding member, say X on Y, but does not, once it exists, depend here and now on the present causal activity of the preceding member. We have to imagine, not a lineal or horizontal series, so to speak, but a vertical hierarchy, in which a lower member depends here and now on the present causal activity of the member above it. It is the latter type of series, if prolonged to infinity, which Aquinas rejects. And he rejects it on the ground that unless there is a "first" member, a mover which is not itself moved or a cause which does not itself depend on the causal activity of a higher cause, it is not possible to explain the "motion" or the causal activity of the lowest member. His point of view is this. Suppress the first unmoved mover and there is no motion or change here and now. Suppress the first efficient cause and there is no causal activity here and now. If therefore we find that some things in the world are changed, there must be a first unmoved mover. And if there are efficient causes in the world, there must be a first efficient, and completely non-dependent cause. The word "first" does not mean first in the temporal order, but supreme or first in the ontological order.

A remark on the word "cause" is here in place. What precisely Aquinas would have said to the David Humes either of the fourteenth century or of the modern era it is obviously impossible to say. But it is clear that he believed in real causal efficacy and real causal relations. He was aware, of course, that causal efficacy is not the object of vision in the sense in which patches of colors are objects of vision; but the human being, he considered, is aware of real causal relations and if we understand "perception" as involving the co-operation of sense and intellect, we can be said to "perceive" causality. And presumably he would have said that the sufficiency of a phenomenalistic interpretation of causality for purposes of physical science proves nothing against the validity of a metaphysical notion of causality. It is obviously possible to dispute whether his analyses of change or "motion" and of efficient causality are valid or invalid and whether there is such a thing as a hierarchy of causes. And our opinion about the validity or invalidity of his arguments for the existence of God will depend very largely on our answers to these questions. But mention of the mathematical infinite series is irrelevant to a discussion of his arguments. And it is this point which I have been trying to make clear.

In the third proof Aquinas starts from the fact that some things come into being and perish, and he concludes from this that it is possible for them to exist or not to exist: they do not exist "necessarily." He then argues that it is impossible for things which are of this kind to exist always; for "that which is capable of not existing, at some time does not exist." If all things were of this kind, at some time there would be nothing. Aquinas is clearly supposing for the sake of argument the hypothesis of infinite time, and his proof is designed to cover this hypothesis. He does not say that infinite time is impossible: what he says is that if time is infinite and if all things are capable of not existing, this potentiality would inevitably be fulfilled in infinite time. There would then be nothing. And if there had ever been nothing, nothing would now exist. For no thing can bring itself into existence. But it is clear as a matter of fact that there are things. Therefore it can never have been true to say that there was literally no thing. Therefore it is impossible that all things should be capable of existing or not existing. There must, then, be some necessary being. But perhaps it is necessary in the sense that it must exist if something else exists; that is to say, its necessity may be hypothetical. We cannot, however, proceed to infinity in the series or hierarchy of necessary beings. If we do so, we do not explain the presence here and now of beings capable of existing or not existing. Therefore we must affirm the existence of a being which is absolutely necessary (*per se necessarium*) and completely independent. "And all call this being *God*."

This argument may appear to be quite unnecessarily complicated and obscure. But it has to be seen in its historical context. As already mentioned, Aquinas designed his argument in such a way as to be independent of the question whether or not the world existed from eternity. He wanted to show that on either hypothesis there must be a necessary being. As for the introduction of hypothetical necessary beings, he wanted to show that even if there are such beings, perhaps within the universe, which are not corruptible in the sense in which a flower is corruptible, there must still be an absolutely independent being. Finally, in regard to terminology, Aquinas uses the common medieval expression "necessary being." He does not actually use the term "contingent being" in the argument and talks instead about "possible" beings; but it comes to the same thing. And though the words "contingent" and "necessary" are now applied to propositions rather than to beings, I have retained Aquinas' mode of speaking. Whether one accepts the argument or not, I do not think that there is any insuperable difficulty in understanding the line of thought.

The fourth argument is admittedly difficult to grasp. Aquinas argues that there are degrees of perfections in things. Different kinds of finite things possess different perfections in diverse limited degrees. He then argues not only that if there are different degrees of a perfection like goodness there is a supreme good to which other good things approximate but also that all limited degrees of goodness are caused by the supreme good. And since goodness is a convertible term with being, a thing being good in so far as it has being, the supreme good is the supreme being and the cause of being in all other things. "Therefore there is something which is the cause of the being and goodness and of every perfection in all other things; and this we call *God*."

Aquinas refers to some remarks of Aristotle in the *Metaphysics;* but this argument puts one in mind at once of Plato's *Symposium* and *Republic*. And the Platonic doctrine of participation seems to be involved. Aquinas was not immediately acquainted with either work, but the Platonic line of thought was familiar to him from other writers. And it has not disappeared from philosophy. Indeed, some of those theists who reject or doubt the validity of the "cosmological" arguments seem to feel a marked attraction for some variety of the fourth way, arguing that in the recognition of objective values we implicitly recognize God as the supreme value. But if the line of thought represented by the fourth way is to mean anything to the average modern reader, it has to be presented in a rather different manner from that in which it is expressed by Aquinas who was able to assume in his readers ideas and points of view which can no longer be presupposed.

Finally, the fifth proof, if we take its statement in the *Summa theologica* together with that in the *Summa contra Gentiles,* can be expressed more or less as follows. The activity and behaviour of each thing is determined by its form. But we observe material things of very different types co-operating in such a way as to produce and maintain a relatively stable world-order or system. They achieve an "end," the production and maintenance of a cosmic order. But non-intelligent material things certainly do not co-operate consciously in view of a purpose. If it is said that they co-operate in the realization of an end or purpose, this does not mean that they intend the realization of this order in a manner analogous to that in which a man can act consciously with a view to the achievement of a purpose. Nor, when Aquinas talks about operating "for an end" in this connection, is he thinking of the utility of certain things to the human race. He is not saying, for example, that grass grows to feed the sheep and that sheep exist in order that human beings should have food and clothing. It is of the unconscious co-operation of different kinds of material things in the production and maintenance of a relatively stable cosmic system that he is thinking, not of the benefits accruing to us from our use of certain objects. And his argument is that this co-operation on the part of heterogeneous material things clearly points to the existence of an extrinsic intelligent author of this co-operation, who operates with an end in view. If Aquinas had lived in the days of the evolutionary hypothesis, he would doubtless have argued that this hypothesis supports rather than invalidates the conclusion of the argument.

No one of these arguments was entirely new, as Aquinas himself was very well aware. But he developed them and arranged them to form a coherent whole. I do not mean that he regarded the validity of one particular argument as necessarily depending on the validity of the other four. He doubtless thought that each argument was valid in its own right. But, as I have already remarked, they conform to a certain pattern, and they are mutually complementary in the sense that in each argument things are considered from a different point of view or under a different aspect. They are so many different approaches to God.

Does any particular argument possess a special or preeminent importance? Modern Thomists often assert that the third proof, bearing explicitly on the existence of things, is fundamental. But if we look at the two *Summas,* we do not find Aquinas saying this. So far as he gives explicit preference to any particular proof it is to the first, which he declares, somewhat surprisingly, to be the clearest. Presumably he means that "motion" or change is so obvious and familiar that it forms a natural starting-point, though he may also have been influenced by the use which Aristotle made of the argument from motion. In any case it is this argument which he selects for a more elaborate discussion in the *Summa contra Gentiles,* while he does not treat at all of the third way in this work. So it cannot be said that Aquinas gives any special prominence to the third argument. At the same time I must confess that my sympathies are with those Thomists who regard this argument as fundamental and who restate it in other forms. And if it is true to say that Aquinas brought into prominence the existential aspect of metaphysics, it can hardly be said that this procedure is alien to his spirit. All the arguments, indeed, treat of dependence in some form or other. And I think that this idea will be found to be involved in all arguments for the existence of God which are in any real sense *a posteriori.* It seems to me to be involved even in those forms of the moral argument which some theists, who accept the Kantian criticism of the cosmological proofs, substitute for the traditional arguments. But it is the idea of existential dependence which most clearly introduces us to the metaphysical level. And it is the problem arising from the existence of finite and contingent things at all which most clearly points to the existence of a transfinite being. What I mean is this. Some people argue that mystical experience, for example, gives rise to a problem, in the sense that it calls for explanation, and that it is best explained on the hypothesis that this experience involves contact with an existent being, God. But there are others who admit the reality of the problem, namely that mystical experience calls for explanation, but who think that it can be satisfactorily explained without postulating God's existence. Thus whatever one may think of the right solution to the problem it is clear, as a matter of empirical fact, that it is possible to admit the reality of the problem and yet not admit that the solution involves affirming the existence of a transcendent being. But one can hardly admit that the existence of finite being at all constitutes a serious problem and at the same time maintain that the solution can be found anywhere else than in affirming the existence of the transfinite. If one does not wish to embark on the path which leads to the affirmation of transcendent being, however the latter may be described (if it is described at all), one has to deny the reality of the problem, assert that things "just are" and that the existential problem in question is a pseudo-problem. And if one refuses even to sit down at the chess-board and make a move, one cannot, of course, be checkmated. . . .

NOTES

[1] From *Aquinas,* by F. C. Copleston. Penguin Books, Baltimore, Md., 1961, pp. 117-127.

Criticism of the Argument

DAVID HUME

David Hume (1711-1776) described the cosmological argument as *a priori,* thereby illustrating the elasticity of these terms. He presumably meant that the cosmological argument is relatively *a priori* in comparison with the design argument with which he was mainly concerned in the *Dialogues Concerning Natural Religion.* For whilst the latter depends upon specific characteristics of the world, the cosmological proof rests upon the bare fact that anything exists which is not manifestly uncaused and self-explanatory.

In Part IX (which appears here in full) Hume formulates a basic and very important objection to the idea of a demonstrative proof of an existential proposition (i.e. any proposition of the form "x exists," including "God exists"). He has elsewhere distinguished "matters of fact and existence" from "the relations between ideas." Logical proof applies only in the latter sphere. We can demonstrate that "$2 + 2 = 4$," or that "if A is larger than B, and B than C, then A is larger than C"; but that New York is larger than Chicago, or that there are such things as chairs and tables, and other matters of fact and existence, are not knowable by logic alone but only through the various avenues of experience. As Hume puts this in our selection, "there is an evident absurdity in pretending to demonstrate a matter of fact, or to prove it by any arguments *a priori*. Nothing is demonstrable unless the contrary implies a contradiction. Nothing that is distinctly conceivable implies a contradiction. Whatever we conceive as existent, we can also conceive as nonexistent. There is no being, therefore, whose nonexistence implies a contradiction. Consequently there is no being whose existence is demonstrable" (p. 96).

Hume adds the point that even if we could validly infer that there is a necessarily existent reality it would not follow that this reality is anything other than the physical universe as a whole. For this might itself be eternal and uncaused.

❋

FROM *Dialogues Concerning Natural Religion*[1]

PART IX

But if so many difficulties attend the argument *a posteriori*, said Demea, had we not better adhere to that simple and sublime argument *a priori* which, by offering to us infallible demonstration, cuts off at once all doubt and difficulty? By this argument, too, we may prove the *infinity* of the Divine attributes, which, I am afraid, can never be ascertained with certainty from any other topic. For how can an effect which either is finite or, for aught we know, may be so—how can such an effect, I say, prove an infinite cause? The unity, too, of the Divine Nature it is very difficult, if not absolutely impossible, to deduce merely from contemplating the works of nature; nor will the uniformity alone of the plan, even were it allowed, give us any assurance of that attribute. Whereas the argument *a priori* . . .

You seem to reason, Demea, interposed Cleanthes, as if those advantages and conveniences in the abstract argument were full proofs of its solidity. But it is first proper, in my opinion, to determine what argument of this nature you choose to insist on; and we shall afterwards, from itself, better than from its *useful* consequences, endeavor to determine what value we ought to put upon it.

The argument, replied Demea, which I would insist on is the common one. Whatever exists must have a cause or reason of its existence, it being absolutely impossible for anything to produce itself or be the cause of its own existence. In mounting up, therefore, from effects to causes, we must either go on in tracing an infinite succession, without any ultimate cause at all, or must at last have recourse to some ultimate cause that is *necessarily* existent. Now that the first supposition is absurd may be thus proved. In the infinite chain or succession of causes and effects, each single effect is determined to exist by the power and efficacy of that cause which immediately preceded; but the whole eternal chain or succession, taken together, is not determined or caused by anything, and yet it is evident that it requires a cause or reason, as much as any particular object which begins to exist in time. The question is still reasonable why this particular succession of causes existed from eternity, and not any other succession or no succession at all. If there be no necessarily existent being, any supposition which can be formed is equally possible; nor is there any more absurdity in *nothing's* having existed from eternity than there is in that succession of causes which constitutes the universe. What was it, then, which determined *something* to exist rather than *nothing*, and bestowed being on a particular possibility, exclusive of the rest? *External causes*, there are supposed to be none. *Chance* is a word without a meaning. Was it *nothing*?

But that can never produce anything. We must, therefore, have recourse to a necessarily existent Being who carries the *reason* of his existence in himself, and who cannot be supposed not to exist, without an express contradiction. There is, consequently, such a Being—that is, there is a Deity.

I shall not leave it to Philo, said Cleanthes, though I know that the starting objections is his chief delight, to point out the weakness of this metaphysical reasoning. It seems to me so obviously ill-grounded, and at the same time of so little consequence to the cause of true piety and religion, that I shall myself venture to show the fallacy of it.

I shall begin with observing that there is an evident absurdity in pretending to demonstrate a matter of fact, or to prove it by any arguments *a priori*. Nothing is demonstrable unless the contrary implies a contradiction. Nothing that is distinctly conceivable implies a contradiction. Whatever we conceive as existent, we can also conceive as non-existent. There is no being, therefore, whose non-existence implies a contradiction. Consequently there is no being whose existence is demonstrable. I propose this argument as entirely decisive, and am willing to rest the whole controversy upon it.

It is pretended that the Deity is a necessarily existent being; and this necessity of his existence is attempted to be explained by asserting that, if we knew his whole essence or nature, we should perceive it to be as impossible for him not to exist, as for twice two not to be four. But it is evident that this can never happen, while our faculties remain the same as at present. It will still be possible for us, at any time, to conceive the non-existence of what we formerly conceived to exist; nor can the mind ever lie under a necessity of supposing any object to remain always in being; in the same manner as we lie under a necessity of always conceiving twice two to be four. The words, therefore, *necessary existence* have no meaning or, which is the same thing, none that is consistent.

But further, why may not the material universe be the necessarily existent Being, according to this pretended explication of necessity? We dare not affirm that we know all the qualities of matter; and, for aught we can determine, it may contain some qualities which, were they known, would make its non-existence appear as great a contradiction as that twice two is five. I find only one argument employed to prove that the material world is not the necessarily existent Being; and this argument is derived from the contingency both of the matter and the form of the world. "Any particle of matter," it is said, "may be *conceived* to be annihilated, and any form may be *conceived* to be altered. Such an annihilation or alteration, therefore, is not impossible."[2] But it seems a great partiality not to perceive that the same argument extends equally to the Deity, so far as we have any conception of him, and that the mind can at least imagine him to be non-existent or his attributes to be altered. It must be some unknown, inconceivable qualities which can make his non-existence appear impossible or his attributes unalterable; and no reason can be assigned why these qualities may not belong to matter. As they are altogether unknown and inconceivable, they can never be proved incompatible with it.

Add to this that in tracing an eternal succession of objects it seems absurd to inquire for a general cause or first author. How can anything that exists from eternity have a cause, since that relation implies a priority in time and a beginning of existence?

In such a chain, too, or succession of objects, each part is caused by that which preceded it, and causes that which succeeds it. Where then is the difficulty? But the *whole,* you say, wants a cause. I answer that the uniting of these parts into a whole, like the uniting of several distinct countries into one kingdom, or several distinct members into one body, is performed merely by an arbitrary act of the mind, and has no influence on the nature of things. Did I show you the particular causes of each individual in a collection of twenty particles of matter, I should think it very unreasonable should you afterwards ask me what was the cause of the whole twenty. This is sufficiently explained in explaining the cause of the parts.

Though the reasonings which you have urged, Cleanthes, may well excuse me, said Philo, from starting any further difficulties, yet I cannot forbear insisting still upon another topic. It is observed by arithmeticians that the products of 9 compose always either 9 or some lesser product of 9 if you add together all the characters of which any of the former products is composed. Thus, of 18, 27, 36, which are products of 9, you make 9 by adding 1 to 8, 2 to 7, 3 to 6. Thus 369 is a product also of 9; and if you add 3, 6, and 9, you make 18, a lesser product of 9.[3] To a superficial observer so wonderful a regularity may be admired as the effect either of chance or design; but a skilful algebraist immediately concludes it to be the work of necessity, and demonstrates that it must forever result from the nature of these numbers. Is it not probable, I ask, that the whole economy of the universe is conducted by a like necessity, though no human algebra can furnish a key which solves the difficulty? And instead of admiring the order of natural beings, may it not happen that, could we penetrate into the intimate nature of bodies, we should clearly see why it was absolutely impossible they could ever admit of any other disposition? So dangerous is it to introduce this idea of necessity into the present question! and so naturally does it afford an inference directly opposite to the religious hypothesis!

But dropping all these abstractions, continued Philo, and confining ourselves to more familiar topics, I shall venture to add an observation that the argument *a priori* has seldom been found very convincing, except to people of a metaphysical head who have accustomed themselves to abstract reasoning, and who, finding from mathematics that the understanding frequently leads to truth through obscurity, and contrary to first appearances, have transferred the same habit of thinking to subjects where it ought not to have place. Other people, even of good sense and the best inclined to religion, feel always some deficiency in such arguments, though they are not perhaps able to explain distinctly where it lies—a certain proof that men ever did and ever will derive their religion from other sources than from this species of reasoning.

NOTES

[1] Hafner Publishing Co., 1961, pp. 57-60.
[2] Dr. Clarke.
[3] *République des Lettres,* Aut 1685.

THE TELEOLOGICAL
ARGUMENT

The Watch and the Watchmaker

WILLIAM PALEY

William Paley (1743-1805), Archdeacon of Carlisle, wrote a number of apologetic works, of which the two most famous are his *Evidences of Christianity* (1794) and his *Natural Theology, or Evidences of the Existence and Attributes of the Deity collected from the Appearances of Nature* (1802), of which the opening chapter and a paragraph from chapter III are reprinted here.

❀

FROM *Natural Theology*

STATEMENT OF THE ARGUMENT

In crossing a heath, suppose I pitched my foot against a *stone,* and were asked how the stone came to be there, I might possibly answer, that, for anything I knew to the contrary, it had lain there for ever; nor would it, perhaps, be very easy to show the absurdity of this answer. But suppose I found a *watch* upon the ground, and it should be inquired how the watch happened to be in that place, I should hardly think of the answer which I had before given—that, for anything I knew, the watch might have always been there. Yet why should not this answer serve for the watch as well as for the stone? why is it not as admissible in the second case as in the first? For this reason, and for no other, viz., that, when we come to inspect the watch, we perceive (what we could not discover in the stone) that its several parts are framed and put together for a purpose, e.g. that they are so formed and adjusted as to produce motion, and that motion so regulated as to point out the hour of the day; that, if the different parts had been differently shaped from what they are, if a different size from what they are, or placed after any other manner, or in any other order than that in which they are placed, either no motion at all would have been carried on in the machine, or none which would have answered the use that is now served by it. To reckon up a few of the plainest of these parts, and of their offices, all tending to one result:—We see a cylindrical box containing a coiled elastic spring, which, by its endeavor to relax itself, turns round the box. We next observe a flexible chain (artificially wrought for the sake of flexure) communicating the action of the spring from the box to the fusee. We then find a series of wheels, the teeth of which catch in, and apply to, each other, conducting the motion from the fusee to the balance, and from the balance to the pointer, and, at the same time, by the size and shape of those wheels, so regulating that motion as to terminate in causing an index, by an equable and measured progression, to pass over a given space in a given time. We take notice that the wheels are made of brass, in order to keep them from rust; the springs of steel, no other metal being so elastic; that over the face of the watch there is placed a glass, a material employed in no other part of the work, but in the room of which, if there had been any other than a transparent substance, the hour could not be seen without opening the case. This mechanism being observed, (it requires indeed an examination of the instrument, and perhaps some previous knowledge of the subject, to perceive and understand it; but being once, as we have said, observed and understood,) the inference, we think, is inevitable, that the watch must have had a maker; that there must have existed, at some time, and at some place or other, an artificer or artificers who formed it for the purpose which we find it actually to answer; who comprehended its construction, and designed its use.

I. Nor would it, I apprehend, weaken the conclusion, that

we had never seen a watch made; that we had never known an artist capable of making one; that we were altogether incapable of executing such a piece of workmanship ourselves, or of understanding in what manner it was performed; all this being no more than what is true of some exquisite remains of ancient art, of some lost arts, and, to the generality of mankind, of the more curious productions of modern manufacture. Does one man in a million know how oval frames are turned? Ignorance of this kind exalts our opinion of the unseen and unknown artist's skill, if he be unseen and unknown, but raises no doubt in our minds of the existence and agency of such an artist, at some former time, and in some place or other. Nor can I perceive that it varies at all the inference, whether the question arise concerning a human agent, or concerning an agent of a different species, or an agent possessing, in some respect, a different nature.

II. Neither, secondly, would it invalidate our conclusion, that the watch sometimes went wrong, or that it seldom went exactly right. The purpose of the machinery, the design, and the designer, might be evident, and, in the case supposed, would be evident, in whatever way we accounted for the irregularity of the movement, or whether we could account for it or not. It is not necessary that a machine be perfect, in order to show with what design it was made; still less necessary, where the only question is, whether it were made with any design at all.

III. Nor, thirdly, would it bring any uncertainty into the argument, if there were a few parts of the watch, concerning which we could not discover, or had not yet discovered, in what manner they conduced to the general effect; or even some parts, concerning which we could not ascertain whether they conduced to that effect in any manner whatever. For, as to the first branch of the case, if by the loss, or disorder, or decay of the parts in question, the movement of the watch were found in fact to be stopped, or disturbed, or retarded, no doubt would remain in our minds as to the utility or intention of these parts, although we should be unable to investigate the manner according to which, or the connection by which, the ultimate effect depended upon their action or assistance; and the more complex is the machine, the more likely is this obscurity to arise. Then, as to the second thing supposed, namely, that there were parts which might be spared without prejudice to the movement of the watch, and that he had proved this by experiment, these superfluous parts, even if we were completely assured that they were such, would not vacate the reasoning which we had instituted concerning other parts. The indication of contrivance remained, with respect to them, nearly as it was before.

IV. Nor, fourthly, would any man in his senses think the existence of the watch, with its various machinery, accounted for, by being told that it was one out of possible combinations of material forms; that whatever he had found in the place where he found the watch, must have contained some internal configuration or other; and that this configuration might be the structure now exhibited, viz., of the works of a watch, as well as a different structure.

V. Nor, fifthly, would it yield his inquiry more satisfaction, to be answered, that there existed in things a principle of order, which had disposed the parts of the watch into their present form and situation. He never knew a watch made by the principle of order; nor can he even form to himself an idea of what is meant by a principle of order, distinct from the intelligence of the watchmaker.

VI. Sixthly, he would be surprised to hear that the mechanism of the watch was no proof of contrivance, only a motive to induce the mind to think so:

VII. And not less surprised to be informed, that the watch in his hand was nothing more than the result of the laws of *metallic* nature. It is a perversion of language to assign any law as the efficient, operative cause of anything. A law presupposes an agent; for it is only the mode according to which an agent proceeds; it implies a power; for it is the order according to which that power acts. Without this agent, without this power, which are both distinct from itself, the *law* does nothing, is nothing. The expression, "the law of metallic nature," may sound strange and harsh to a philosophic ear; but it seems quite as justifiable as some others which are more familiar to him such as "the law of vegetable nature," "the law of animal nature," or, indeed, as "the law of nature" in general, when assigned as the cause of phenomena in exclusion of agency and power, or when it is substituted into the place of these.

VIII. Neither, lastly, would our observer be driven out of his conclusion, or from his confidence in its truth, by being told that he knew nothing at all about the matter. He knows enough for his argument: he knows the utility of the end: he knows the subserviency and adaptation of the means to the end. These points being known, his ignorance of other points, his doubts concerning other points, affect not the certainty of his reasoning. The consciousness of knowing little need not beget a distrust of that which he does know. . . .

APPLICATION OF THE ARGUMENT

Every indication of contrivance, every manifestation of design, which existed in the watch, exists in the works of nature; with the difference, on the side of nature, of being greater and more, and that in a degree which exceeds all computation. I mean that the contrivances of nature surpass the contrivances of art, in the complexity, subtilty, and curiosity of the mechanism; and still more, if possible, do they go beyond them in number and variety; yet in a multitude of cases, are not less evidently mechanical, not less evidently contrivances, not less evidently accommodated to their end, or suited to their office, than are the most perfect productions of human ingenuity. . . .

Criticism of the Design Argument

DAVID HUME

Dialogues Concerning Natural Religion by David Hume[1] (published posthumously in 1779, three years after Hume's death) constitutes the classic critique of the design argument. It is a lamentable instance of the lack of com-

munication between the philosophical and theological
worlds that Paley was apparently unaware that his arguments had been devastatingly criticized by Hume twenty-
three years earlier.

❋

FROM *Dialogues Concerning Natural Religion*[2]

PART V

But to show you still more inconveniences, continued Philo,
in your anthropomorphism, please to take a new survey of
your principles. *Like effects prove like causes.* This is the
experimental argument; and this, you say too, is the sole theological argument. Now it is certain that the liker the effects
are which are seen and the liker the causes which are inferred, the stronger is the argument. Every departure on
either side diminishes the probability and renders the experiment less conclusive. You cannot doubt of the principle;
neither ought you to reject its consequences.

All the new discoveries in astronomy which prove the
immense grandeur and magnificence of the works of nature
are so many additional arguments for a Deity, according to
the true system of theism; but, according to your hypothesis
of experimental theism, they become so many objections, by
removing the effect still farther from all resemblance to the
effects of human art and contrivance. For if Lucretius, even
following the old system of the world, could exclaim:

> Quis regere immensi summam, quis habere profundi
> Indu manu validas potis est moderanter habenas?
> Quis pariter cœlos omnes convertere? et omnes
> Ignibus ætheriis terras suffire feraces?
> Omnibus inque locis esse omni tempore præsto?[3]

If Tully [Cicero] esteemed this reasoning so natural as to put
it into the mouth of his Epicurean:

> Quibus enim oculis animi intueri potuit vester Plato fabri-
> cam illam tanti operis, qua construi a Deo atque ædificari
> mundum facit? quæ molito? quæ ferramenta? qui vectes?

quæ machinæ? qui minstri tanti muneris fuerunt? quemad-
modum autem obedire et parere voluntati architecti aer,
ignis, aqua, terra potuerunt?[4]

If this argument, I say, had any force in former ages, how
much greater must it have at present when the bounds of
Nature are so infinitely enlarged and such a magnificent
scene is opened to us? It is still more unreasonable to form
our idea of so unlimited a cause from our experience of the
narrow productions of human design and invention.

The discoveries by microscopes, as they open a new universe in miniature, are still objections, according to you,
arguments, according to me. The further we push our re-
searches of this kind, we are still led to infer the universal
cause of all to be vastly different from mankind, or from any
object of human experience and observation.

And what say you to the discoveries in anatomy, chemistry, botany? . . . These surely are no objections, replied
Cleanthes; they only discover new instances of art and contrivance. It is still the image of mind reflected on us from
innumerable objects. Add a mind *like the human,* said Philo.
I know of no other, replied Cleanthes. And the liker, the
better, insisted Philo. To be sure, said Cleanthes.

Now, Cleanthes, said Philo, with an air of alacrity and
triumph, mark the consequences. *First,* by this method of
reasoning you renounce all claim to infinity in any of the
attributes of the Deity. For, as the cause ought to be proportioned to the effect, and the effect, so far as it falls under
our cognizance, is not infinite, what pretensions have we,
upon your suppositions, to ascribe that attribute to the Divine
Being? You will still insist that, by removing him so much
from all similarity to human creatures, we give in to the most
arbitrary hypothesis, and at the same time weaken all proofs
of his existence.

Secondly, you have no reason, on your theory, for ascrib-
ing perfection to the Deity, even in his finite capacity, or for
supposing him free from every error, mistake, or incoher-
ence, in his undertakings. There are many inexplicable difficulties in the works of nature which, if we allow a perfect

author to be proved *a priori,* are easily solved, and become only seeming difficulties from the narrow capacity of man, who cannot trace infinite relations. But according to your method of reasoning, these difficulties become all real, and, perhaps, will be insisted on as new instances of likeness to human art and contrivance. At least, you must acknowledge that it is impossible for us to tell, from our limited views, whether this system contains any great faults or deserves any considerable praise if compared to other possible and even real systems. Could a peasant, if the *Æneid* were read to him, pronounce that poem to be absolutely faultless, or even assign to it its proper rank among the productions of human wit, he who had never seen any other production?

But were this world ever so perfect a production, it must still remain uncertain whether all the excellences of the work can justly be ascribed to the workman. If we survey a ship, what an exalted idea must we form of the ingenuity of the carpenter who framed so complicated, useful, and beautiful a machine? And what surprise must we feel when we find him a stupid mechanic who imitated others, and copied an art which, through a long succession of ages, after multiplied trials, mistakes, corrections, deliberations, and controversies, had been gradually improving? Many worlds might have been botched and bungled, throughout an eternity, ere this system was struck out; much labor lost, many fruitless trials made, and a slow but continued improvement carried on during infinite ages in the art of world-making. In such subjects, who can determine where the truth, nay, who can conjecture where the probability lies, amidst a great number of hypotheses which may be proposed, and a still greater which may be imagined?

And what shadow of an argument, continued Philo, can you produce from your hypothesis to prove the unity of the Deity? A great number of men join in building a house or ship, in rearing a city, in framing a commonwealth; why may not several deities combine in contriving and framing a world? This is only so much greater similarity to human affairs. By sharing the work among several, we may so much further limit the attributes of each, and get rid of that extensive power and knowledge which must be supposed in one deity, and which, according to you, can only serve to weaken the proof of his existence. And if such foolish, such vicious creatures as man can yet often unite in framing and executing one plan, how much more those deities or demons, whom we may suppose several degrees more perfect!

To multiply causes without necessity is indeed contrary to true philosophy, but this principle applies not to the present case. Were one deity antecedently proved by your theory who were possessed of every attribute requisite to the production of the universe, it would be needless, I own, (though not absurd) to suppose any other deity existent. But while it is still a question whether all these attributes are united in one subject or dispersed among several independent beings, by what phenomena in nature can we pretend to decide the controversy? Where we see a body raised in a scale, we are sure that there is in the opposite scale, however concealed from sight, some counterpoising weight equal to it; but it is still allowed to doubt whether that weight be an aggregate of several distinct bodies or one uniform united mass. And if the weight requisite very much exceeds anything which we have ever seen conjoined in any single body, the former supposition becomes still more probable and natural. An intelligent being of such vast power and capacity as is necessary to produce the universe, or, to speak in the language of ancient philosophy, so prodigious an animal exceeds all analogy and even comprehension.

But further, Cleanthes: Men are mortal, and renew their species by generation; and this is common to all living creatures. The two great sexes of male and female, says Milton, animate the world. Why must this circumstance, so universal, so essential, be excluded from those numerous and limited deities? Behold, then, the theogeny of ancient times brought back upon us.

And why not become a perfect anthropomorphite? Why not assert the deity or deities to be corporeal, and to have eyes, a nose, mouth, ears, etc.? Epicurus maintained that no man had ever seen reason but in a human figure; therefore, the gods must have a human figure. And this argument, which is deservedly so much ridiculed by Cicero, becomes, according to you, solid and philosophical.

In a word, Cleanthes, a man who follows your hypothesis is able, perhaps, to assert or conjecture that the universe sometime arose from something like design; but beyond that position he cannot ascertain one single circumstance, and is left afterwards to fix every point of his theology by the utmost license of fancy and hypothesis. This world, for aught he knows, is very faulty and imperfect, compared to a superior standard, and was only the first rude essay of some infant deity who afterwards abandoned it, ashamed of his lame performance; it is the work only of some dependent, inferior deity, and is the object of derision to his superiors; it is the production of old age and dotage in some superannuated deity, and ever since his death has run on at adventures, from the first impulse and active force which it received from him. You justly give signs of horror, Demea, at these strange suppositions; but these, and a thousand more of the same kind, are Cleanthes' suppositions, not mine. From the moment the attributes of the Deity are supposed finite, all these have place. And I cannot, for my part, think that so wild and unsettled a system of theology is, in any respect, preferable to none at all.

These suppositions I absolutely disown, cried Cleanthes: they strike me, however, with no horror, especially when proposed in that rambling way in which they drop from you. On the contrary, they give me pleasure when I see that, by the utmost indulgence of your imagination, you never get rid of the hypothesis of design in the universe, but are obliged at every turn to have recourse to it. To this concession I adhere steadily; and this I regard as a sufficient foundation for religion. . . .

PART VIII

What you ascribe to the fertility of my invention, replied Philo, is entirely owing to the nature of the subject. In subjects adapted to the narrow compass of human reason there is commonly but one determination which carries probability or conviction with it; and to a man of sound judgment all other suppositions but that one appear entirely absurd and chimerical. But in such questions as the present, a hundred contradictory views may preserve a kind of imperfect analogy, and invention has here full scope to exert itself. Without any great effort of thought, I believe that I could, in an instant, propose other systems of cosmogony which would have some faint appearance of truth, though it is a thousand, a million to one if either yours or any one of mine be the true system.

For instance, what if I should revive the old Epicurean hypothesis? This is commonly, and I believe justly, esteemed the most absurd system that has yet been proposed; yet I know not whether, with a few alterations, it might not be brought to bear a faint appearance of probability. Instead of supposing matter infinite, as Epicurus did, let us suppose it finite. A finite number of particles is only susceptible of finite transpositions; and it must happen, in an eternal duration, that every possible order or position must be tried an infinite number of times. This world, therefore, with all its events, even the most minute, has before been produced and destroyed, and will again be produced and destroyed, without any bounds and limitations. No one who has a conception of the powers of infinite, in comparison of finite, will ever scruple this determination.

But this supposes, said Demea, that matter can acquire motion without any voluntary agent or first mover.

And where is the difficulty, replied Philo, of that supposition? Every event, before experience, is equally difficult and incomprehensible; and every event, after experience, is equally easy and intelligible. Motion, in many instances, from gravity, from elasticity, from electricity, begins in matter, without any known voluntary agent; and to suppose always, in these cases, an unknown voluntary agent is mere hypothesis and hypothesis attended with no advantages. The beginning of motion in matter itself is as conceivable *a priori* as its communication from mind and intelligence.

Besides, why may not motion have been propagated by impulse through all eternity, and the same stock of it, or nearly the same, be still upheld in the universe? As much is lost by the composition of motion, as much is gained by its resolution. And whatever the causes are, the fact is certain that matter is and always has been in continual agitation, as far as human experience or tradition reaches. There is not probably, at present, in the whole universe, one particle of matter at absolute rest.

And this very consideration, too, continued Philo, which we have stumbled on in the course of the argument suggests a new hypothesis of cosmogony that is not absolutely absurd and improbable. Is there a system, an order, an economy of things, by which matter can preserve that perpetual agitation which seems essential to it, and yet maintain a constancy in the forms which it produces? There certainly is such an economy, for this is actually the case with the present world. The continual motion of matter, therefore, in less than infinite transpositions, must produce this economy or order, and, by its very nature, that order, when once established, supports itself for many ages if not to eternity. But wherever matter is so poised, arranged, and adjusted, as to continue in perpetual motion, and yet preserve a constancy in the forms, its situation must, of necessity, have all the same appearance of art and contrivance which we observe at present. All the parts of each form must have a relation to each other and to the whole; and the whole itself must have a relation to the other parts of the universe, to the element in which the form subsists, to the materials with which it repairs its waste and decay, and to every other form which is hostile or friendly. A defect in any of these particulars destroys the form, and the matter of which it is composed is again set loose, and is thrown into irregular motions and fermentations till it unite itself to some other regular form. If no such form be prepared to receive it, and if there be a great quantity of this corrupted matter in the universe, the universe itself is entirely disordered, whether it be the feeble embryo of a world in its first beginnings that is thus destroyed or the rotten carcase of one languishing in old age and infirmity. In either case, a chaos ensues till finite though innumerable revolutions produce, at last, some forms whose parts and organs are so adjusted as to support the forms amidst a continued succession of matter.

Suppose (for we shall endeavor to vary the expression) that matter were thrown into any position by a blind, unguided force; it is evident that this first position must, in all probability, be the most confused and most disorderly imaginable, without any resemblance to those works of human contrivance which, along with a symmetry of parts, discover an adjustment of means to ends and a tendency to self-preservation. If the actuating force cease after this operation, matter must remain for ever in disorder and continue an immense chaos, without any proportion or activity. But suppose that the actuating force, whatever it be, still continues in matter, this first position will immediately give place to a second which will likewise, in all probability, be as disorderly as the first, and so on through many successions of changes and revolutions. No particular order or position ever continues a moment unaltered. The original force, still remaining in activity, gives a perpetual restlessness to matter. Every possible situation is produced, and instantly destroyed. If a glimpse or dawn of order appears for a moment, it is instantly hurried away and confounded by that never-ceasing force which actuates every part of matter.

Thus the universe goes on for many ages in a continued succession of chaos and disorder. But is it not possible that it may settle at last, so as not to lose its motion and active force (for that we have supposed inherent in it), yet so as to preserve an uniformity of appearance, amidst the continual motion and fluctuation of its parts? This we find to be the case with the universe at present. Every individual is perpetually changing, and every part of every individual; and yet the whole remains, in appearance, the same. May we not hope for such a position or rather be assured of it from the eternal revolutions of unguided matter; and may not this account for all the appearing wisdom and contrivance which is in the universe? Let us contemplate the subject a little, and we shall find that this adjustment if attained by matter of a seeming stability in the forms, with a real and perpetual revolution or motion of parts, affords a plausible, if not a true, solution of the difficulty.

It is in vain, therefore, to insist upon the uses of the parts in animals or vegetables, and their curious adjustment to each other. I would fain know how an animal could subsist unless its parts were so adjusted? Do we not find that it immediately perishes whenever this adjustment ceases, and that its matter, corrupting, tries some new form? It happens indeed that the parts of the world are so well adjusted that some regular form immediately lays claim to this corrupted matter; and if it were not so, could the world subsist? Must it not dissolve, as well as the animal, and pass through new positions and situations till in great but finite succession it fall, at last, into the present or some such order?

It is well, replied Cleanthes, you told us that this hypothesis was suggested on a sudden, in the course of the argument. Had you had leisure to examine it, you would soon have perceived the insuperable objections to which it is exposed. No form, you say, can subsist unless it possess those powers and organs requisite for its subsistence; some new order or economy must be tried, and so on, without intermission, till at last some order which can support and maintain itself is fallen upon. But according to this hypothesis, whence arise the many conveniences and advantages which men and all animals possess? Two eyes, two ears are not absolutely necessary for the subsistence of the species. Human race might have been propagated and preserved without horses, dogs, cows, sheep, and those innumerable fruits and products which serve to our satisfaction and enjoyment. If no camels had been created for the use of man in the sandy deserts of Africa and Arabia, would the world have been dissolved? If no loadstone had been framed to give that wonderful and useful direction to the needle, would human society and the human kind have been immediately extinguished? Though the maxims of nature be in general very frugal, yet instances of this kind are far from being rare; and any one of them is a sufficient proof of design—and of a benevolent design—which gave rise to the order and arrangement of the universe.

At least, you may safely infer, said Philo, that the foregoing hypothesis is so far incomplete and imperfect, which I shall not scruple to allow. But can we ever reasonably expect greater success in any attempts of this nature? Or can we ever hope to erect a system of cosmogony that will be liable to no exceptions, and will contain no circumstance repugnant to our limited and imperfect experience of the analogy of nature? Your theory itself cannot surely pretend to any such advantage, even though you have run into *anthropomorphism,* the better to preserve a conformity to common experience. Let us once more put it to trial. In all instances which we have ever seen, ideas are copied from real objects, and are ectypal, not archetypal, to express myself in learned terms. You reverse this order and give thought the precedence. In all instances which we have ever seen, thought has no influence upon matter except where that matter is so conjoined with it as to have an equal reciprocal influence upon it. No animal can move immediately anything but the members of its own body; and, indeed, the equality of action and reaction seems to be an universal law of nature; but your theory implies a contradiction to this experience. These instances, with many more which it were easy to collect (particularly the supposition of a mind or system of thought that is eternal or, in other words, an animal ingenerable and immortal)—these instances, I say, may teach all of us sobriety in condemning each other, and let us see that as no system of this kind ought ever to be received from a slight analogy, so neither ought any to be rejected on account of a small incongruity. For that is an inconvenience from which we can justly pronounce no one to be exempted.

All religious systems, it is confessed, are subject to great and insuperable difficulties. Each disputant triumphs in his turn, while he carries on an offensive war, and exposes the absurdities, barbarities, and pernicious tenets of his antagonist. But all of them, on the whole, prepare a complete triumph for the *sceptic,* who tells them that no system ought ever to be embraced with regard to such subjects: for this plain reason that no absurdity ought ever to be assented to with regard to any subject. A total suspense of judgment is here our only reasonable resource. And if every attack, as is commonly observed, and no defence among theologians is successful, how complete must be *his* victory who remains always, with all mankind, on the offensive, and has himself no fixed station or abiding city which he is ever, on any occasion, obliged to defend?

NOTES

[1] See pp. 93-94 for biographical note.

[2] Hafner Edition, *op. cit.*, pp. 37-41, 52-56.

[3] *De Rerum Natura*, Bk. XI, Chap. 2. "Who can rule the sum, who hold in his hand with controlling force the strong reins, of the immeasurable deep? Who can at once make all the different heavens to roll and warm with ethereal fires all the fruitful earths, or be present in all places at all times?" (Munro's trans.)

[4] *De Natura Deorum*, Bk. I, Chap. 8. "For with what eyes of the mind could your Plato see the construction of so vast a work which, according to him, God was putting together and building? What materials, what tools, what bars, what machines, what servants were employed in such gigantic work? How could the air, fire, water, and earth pay obedience and submit to the will of the architect?"

The Problem of Evil

JOHN STUART MILL

John Stuart Mill (1806-1873) forcibly presents, in its bearing upon the design argument, what is perhaps the most serious objection to theistic belief, namely, the problem of evil. This selection is from *Nature and Utility of Religion,* 1874.

❊

FROM *Nature and Utility of Religion*

For how stands the fact? That next to the greatness of these cosmic forces, the quality which most forcibly strikes everyone who does not avert his eyes from it is their perfect and absolute recklessness. They go straight to their end, without regarding what or whom they crush on the road. Optimists, in their attempts to prove that "whatever is, is right," are obliged to maintain, not that nature ever turns one step from her path to avoid trampling us into destruction, but that it would be very unreasonable in us to expect that she should. Pope's "Shall gravitation cease when you go by?" may be a just rebuke to anyone who should be so silly as to expect common human morality from nature. But if the question were between two men, instead of between a man and a natural phenomenon, that triumphant apostrophe would be thought a rare piece of impudence. A man who should persist in hurling stones or firing cannon when another man "goes by," and having killed him should urge a similar plea in exculpation, would very deservedly be found guilty of murder.

In sober truth, nearly all the things which men are hanged or imprisoned for doing to one another are nature's everyday performances. Killing, the most criminal act recognized by human laws, nature does once to every being that lives, and in a large proportion of cases after protracted tortures such as only the greatest monsters whom we read of ever purposely inflicted on their living fellow creatures. If by an arbitrary reservation we refuse to account anything murder but what abridges a certain term supposed to be allotted to human life, nature also does this to all but a small percentage of lives, and does it in all the modes, violent or insidious, in which the worst human beings take the lives of one another. Nature impales men, breaks them as if on the wheel, casts them to be devoured by wild beasts, burns them to death, crushes them with stones like the first Christian martyr, starves them with hunger, freezes them with cold, poisons them by the quick or slow venom of her exhalations, and has hundreds of other hideous deaths in reserve such as the ingenious cruelty of a Nabis or a Domitian never surpassed. All this nature does with the most supercilious disregard both of mercy and of justice, emptying her shafts upon the best and noblest indifferently with the meanest and worst; upon those who are engaged in the highest and worthiest enterprises, and often as the direct consequence of the noblest acts; and it might almost be imagined as a punishment for them. She mows down those on whose existence hangs the well-being of a whole people, perhaps the prospects of the human race for generations to come, with as little compunction as those whose death is a relief to themselves or a blessing to those under their noxious influence. Such are nature's dealings with life. Even when she does not intend to kill, she inflicts the same tortures in apparent wantonness. In the clumsy provision which she has made for that perpetual renewal of animal life, rendered necessary by the prompt termination she puts to it in every individual instance, no human being ever comes into the world but another human being is literally stretched on the rack for hours or days, not unfrequently issuing in death. Next to taking life (equal to it, according to a high authority) is taking the means by which we live; and nature does this, too, on the largest scale and with the most callous indifference. A single hurricane destroys the hopes of a season; a flight of locusts, or an inundation, desolates a district; a trifling chemical change in an edible root starves a million of people. The waves of the sea, like banditti, seize and appropriate the wealth of the rich and the little all of the poor with the same accompaniments of stripping, wounding, and killing as their human antitypes. Everything, in short, which the worst men commit either against life or property is perpetrated on a larger scale by natural agents. Nature has noyades more fatal than those of Carrier; her explosions of firedamp are as destructive as human artillery; her plague and cholera far surpass the poison cups of the Borgias. Even the love of "order" which is thought to be a following of the ways of nature is in fact a contradiction of them. All which people are accustomed to deprecate as "disorder" and its consequences is precisely a counterpart of nature's ways. Anarchy and the Reign of Terror are overmatched in injustice, ruin, and death by a hurricane and a pestilence. . . .

It is undoubtedly a very common fact that good comes out of evil, and, when it does occur, it is far too agreeable not to find people eager to dilate on it. But in the first place, it is quite as often true of human crimes as of natural calamities. The fire of London, which is believed to have had so salutary an effect on the healthiness of the city, would have produced that effect just as much if it had been really the work of the *furor papisticus* so long commemorated on the monument. The deaths of those whom tyrants or persecutors have made martyrs in any noble cause have done a service to mankind which would not have been obtained if they had died by accident or disease. Yet whatever incidental and unexpected benefits may result from crimes, they are crimes nevertheless. In the second place, if good frequently comes out of evil, the converse fact, evil coming out of good, is equally common. Every event, public or private, which, regretted on its occurrence, was declared providential at a later period on account of some unforeseen good consequence, might be matched by some other event, deemed fortunate at the time, but which proved calamitous or fatal to those whom it appeared to benefit. Such conflicts between the beginning and the end, or between the event and the expectation, are not only as frequent but as often held up to notice in the painful cases as in the agreeable, but there is not the same inclination to generalize on them or at all events they are not regarded by the moderns (though they were by the ancients) as similarly an indication of the divine purposes: men satisfy themselves with moralizing on the imperfect nature of our foresight, the uncertainty of events, and the vanity of human expectations. The simple fact is, human interests are so complicated, and the effects of any incident whatever so multitudinous, that if it touches mankind at all its influence on them is, in the great majority of cases, both good and bad. If the greater number of personal misfortunes have their good side, hardly any good fortune ever befell anyone which did not give either to the same or to some other person something to regret; and unhappily there are many misfortunes so overwhelming that their favorable side, if it exist, is entirely overshadowed and made insignificant, while the corresponding statement can seldom be made concerning blessings. The effects, too, of every cause depend so much on the circumstances which accidentally accompany it that many cases are sure to occur in which even the total result is markedly opposed to the predominant tendency; and thus not only evil has its good and good its evil side, but good often produces an overbalance of evil and evil an overbalance of good. This, however, is by no means the general tendency of either phenomenon. On the contrary, both good and evil naturally tend to fructify, each in its own kind, good producing good, and evil, evil. It is one of nature's general rules and part of her habitual injustice that "to him that hath shall be given, but from him that hath not shall be taken even that which he hath" [Matt. 25:29]. The ordinary and predominant tendency of good is toward more good. Health, strength, wealth, knowledge, virtue are not only good in themselves but facilitate and promote the acquisition of good, both of the same and of other kinds. The person who can learn easily is he who already knows much; it is the strong and not the sickly person who can do everything which most conduces to health; those who find it easy to gain money are not the poor but the rich; while health, strength, knowledge, talents are all means of acquiring riches, and riches are often an indispensable means of acquiring these. Again, *e converso,* whatever may be said of evil turning into good, the general tendency of evil is toward further evil. Bodily illness renders the body more susceptible of disease; it produces incapacity of exertion, sometimes debility of mind, and often the loss of means of subsistence. All severe pain, either bodily or mental, tends to increase the susceptibilities of pain forever after. Poverty is the parent of a thousand mental and moral evils. What is still worse, to be injured or oppressed, when habitual, lowers the whole tone of the character. One bad action leads to others, both in the agent himself, in the bystanders, and in the sufferers. All bad qualities are strengthened by habit, and all vices and follies tend to spread. Intellectual defects generate moral, and moral, intellectual; and every intellectual or moral defect generates others, and so on without end.

That much-applauded class of authors, the writers on natural theology, have, I venture to think, entirely lost their way and missed the sole line of argument which could have made

their speculations acceptable to anyone who can perceive
when two propositions contradict one another. They have ex-
hausted the resources of sophistry to make it appear that all
the suffering in the world exists to prevent greater—that misery exists for fear lest there should be misery: a thesis which,
if ever so well maintained, could only avail to explain and
justify the works of limited beings, compelled to labor under
conditions independent of their own will, but can have no
application to a Creator assumed to be omnipotent who, if he
bends to a supposed necessity, himself makes the necessity
which he bends to. If the maker of the world *can* all that he
will, he wills misery, and there is no escape from the conclusion. The more consistent of those who have deemed themselves qualified to "vindicate the ways of God to man" have
endeavored to avoid the alternative by hardening their hearts
and denying that misery is an evil. The goodness of God, they
say, does not consist in willing the happiness of his creatures
but their virtue; and the universe, if not a happy, is a just
universe. But waiving the objections to this scheme of ethics,
it does not at all get rid of the difficulty. If the Creator of
mankind willed that they should all be virtuous, his designs
are as completely baffled as if he had willed that they should
all be happy; and the order of nature is constructed with even
less regard to the requirements of justice than to those of
benevolence. If the law of all creation were justice and the
Creator omnipotent, then, in whatever amount suffering and
happiness might be dispensed to the world, each person's
share of them would be exactly proportioned to that person's
good or evil deeds; no human being would have a worse lot
than another without worse deserts; accident or favoritism
would have no part in such a world, but every human life
would be the playing out of a drama constructed like a perfect moral tale. No one is able to blind himself to the fact
that the world we live in is totally different from this, inso-
much that the necessity of redressing the balance has been
deemed one of the strongest arguments for another life
after death, which amounts to an admission that the order
of things in this life is often an example of injustice, not
justice. If it be said that God does not take sufficient account

of pleasure and pain to make them the reward or punishment of the good or the wicked, but that virtue is itself the greatest good and vice the greatest evil, then these at least ought to be dispensed to all according to what they have done to deserve them; instead of which every kind of moral depravity is entailed upon multitudes by the fatality of their birth, through the fault of their parents, of society, or of uncontrollable circumstances, certainly through no fault of their own. Not even on the most distorted and contracted theory of good which ever was framed by religious or philosophical fanaticism can the government of nature be made to resemble the work of a being at once good and omnipotent. . . .

Cosmic Teleology

F. R. TENNANT

F. R. Tennant (1866-1957) taught for many years at Cambridge University and is the author of *The Origin and Propagation of Sin,* 1902; *The Sources of the Doctrines of the Fall and Original Sin,* 1903; *The Concept of Sin,* 1912; *Miracle and Its Philosophical Presuppositions,* 1925; *Philosophical Theology,* Vol. I, 1928, Vol. II, 1930; *Philosophy of the Sciences,* 1932; *The Nature of Belief,* 1943. He is the most outstanding recent exponent of a religious belief which claims to arise solely out of philosophical reasoning. Theism is for him the most probable world-hypothesis. He does not profess to offer a strict logical demonstration of the existence of God, but a cumulative argument to the effect that theism is more probable than any other attempted explanation of the universe. His argument constitutes an expanded design argument, written in full awareness of Hume's criticisms.

❀

FROM *Philosophical Theology*[1]

The forcibleness of Nature's suggestion that she is the outcome of intelligent design lies not in particular cases of
adaptedness in the world, nor even in the multiplicity of
them. It is conceivable that every such instance may individually admit of explanation in terms of proximate causes
or, in the first instance, of explanation other than in terms
of cosmic or "external" teleology. And if it also admits of
teleological interpretation, that fact will not of itself constitute a rigorous certification of external design. The
forcibleness of the world's appeal consists rather in the
conspiration of innumerable causes to produce, by their
united and reciprocal action, and to maintain, a general order
of Nature. Narrower kinds of teleological argument, based
on surveys of restricted spheres of fact, are much more precarious then that for which the name of "the wider teleology"
may be appropriated in that the comprehensive design-
argument is the outcome of synopsis or conspection of the
knowable world.

The knowable world, however, is not identical with the
universe as to which, as a whole, we have no knowledge. It
may be objected, therefore, that to use the phrase "the
world" to denote both of these things seems to beg a vital
question. Of course, if trustworthy evidence of design in the
limited portion of the universe that we know were forthcoming, a world-designer would be "proved," and our ignorance
as to other parts would be irrelevant. But it is a graver objection—perhaps the gravest that the teleologist has to encounter
—that rich suggestions of design in the known world yield no
proof of design in the universe, since our ordered fragment
may be but a temporary and casual episode in the history
of the universe, an oasis in a desert of "chaos," a chance
product of mindless agency in a universe which has had
opportunity to produce all sorts of local and ephemeral
worlds within A World. To this objection it may be replied
that teleology does not profess to base itself on the principle
of "the inconceivability of the opposite," while interpretations
of the known cannot be refuted, even if they can be made

to appear more precarious, by considerations as to possibilities within the unknowable. Certainly a mechanical theory of the universe must not be tacitly assumed to which our known world gives the lie. More specifically it may be said that the ordered oasis is not an isolable fragment. It and the supposed desert or "chaos" are interdependent. It is because the desert is what it is that the oasis is what it is; and the one has orderedness only by permission, so to say, of the other. The force of the objection, indeed, seems to be derived from the assumption that our ordered world is due to some evolutionary process within the whole universe analogous to that secured within organic Nature by natural selection out of random variations. This is but conjecture or appeal to the unknown, and, confronted with the second law of thermodynamics, is overwhelmingly improbable. And if it includes the supposition that even unlimited re-shufflings of matter by mechanical forces can produce minds and personalities in a corner of the universe, it conflicts with knowledge. Further, if the nerve of the teleological argument be that design issues in the realization of ethical values, the spatio-temporal immensities of the universe become less significant than the petty oasis. Teleology, after all, is a value-concept; and magnitude and worth are incommensurable.

Nevertheless the inquiry that is here first to be undertaken, whether the knowable world, or Nature, has been devised by intelligence, is to be distinguished, though it cannot be separated, from the further inquiry, what the ultimate purpose or goal of the world-process is. The latter question may admit of no complete answer by man: reasonable belief as to the former involves but the application of mother-wit to forthcoming facts. A machine can evince intelligent contrivance or design to a man ignorant of engineering and unable to tell precisely what the machine is for. Once more, by way of making relevant distinctions, a teleological interpretation of Nature does not require that every detail in Nature was purposed or fore-ordained. Processes may inevitably produce by-products which, as such, were not purposed, but are the necessary outcome of processes by which a purpose is fulfilled.

The main fields of fact in which adaptation is conspicuous, and which have severally afforded data for particular arguments of the teleological kind and of restricted scope, are those of the knowability or intelligibility of the world (or the adaptation of thought to things), the internal adaptedness of organic beings, the fitness of the inorganic to minister to life, the aesthetic value of Nature, the world's instrumentality in the realization of moral ends, and the progressiveness in the evolutionary process culminating in the emergence of man with his rational and moral status. A brief examination of these fields in turn will not only enable us to estimate the respective strengths of the more or less independent arguments derived from them severally, but also to appreciate the interconnections within the world, and the comprehensive teleology which such interconnectedness suggests.

I. We may begin with the mutual adaptation of thought and things, Nature and Knowledge. The correspondence between human thought and the external world, rendering science possible, has evoked what may be called epistemological arguments for the being of God. Descartes accounted for the marvel, as it seemed to him, of this correspondence by invoking, as its necessary cause, the veracious Deity, whose existence he sought to prove—almost superfluously, on his own presuppositions—by other lines of reasoning. If a subject's "ideas" were as disparate from percepts and from external Objects as Descartes supposed, each class forming a closed system independent of the other, there might be something to be said for the invocation of divine agency to explain the elaborate correspondence between the two systems. But if our primary ideas of objects are but images of such objects defecated to pure transparency, or are but elements of the objective matter of perceptual experience isolated for thought by selective and restricted attention, then that they apply to the objects from which they have but been abstracted is no wonder to be supernaturally accounted for. And if, as in science, general ideas and the constituents of developed thought are determined and controlled by things external to thought, and so enjoy validity, there is no cause for amazement even at the preductiveness of theoretical physics. The mysterious element in knowledge does not lie where Descartes would place it: it lies deeper. Similarly, Shelley's apostrophe,

> O thou immortal Deity
> Whose throne is in the depths of human thought,

supposing it to have any relevance to the present context, errs as to the location of the "throne." It is in the world, as allowing itself to be thought about, rather than in our thinking, if anywhere, that considerations as to the penetrability of things by thought may lead teleology to enthrone its Deity. Reason might soliloquize: world or no world, I must think thus and thus, in order to think at all. Pure reason may have power to decree *how* thoughts must be linked in order to yield Thought, and certainly can without limit form ideas —as in the pure sciences—to which there is no knowable counterpart in Actuality; but it is powerless to prescribe to things *what* they shall be, and that they shall satisfy the demands of any pure science. The world might answer: you must think me thus and thus, as to my "what," and not otherwise, if you would know me. Nature will open to the right pass-word; but she has chosen it, not we. To revert to plain speech: the primary epistemological contribution to teleological reasoning consists in the fact that the world is more or less intelligible, in that it happens to be more or less a cosmos, when conceivably it might have been a self-subsistent and determinate "chaos" in which similar events never occurred, none recurred, universals had no place, relations no fixity, things no nexus of determination, and "real" categories no foothold. But whether such logico-mathematical order as has been found to obtain in our world bespeaks "chance"[2] in self-subsistent entities, or purposiveness in a designer or a creator, there is of course no logical method of deciding: the probability-calculus can gain no purchase. We know that similar ordering is sometimes due to human design; that it always is due to design we have no means of knowing. Again, the amenability of things to the more interpretative kind of knowledge, constituted by the "real" or the anthropic categories, shews that things, or their ontal counterparts, have so much of affinity with us as to be assimilable and to be understood, or alogically interpreted, as well as to be ordered by number, etc.: it does not of itself testify that the adaptedness is teleological. . . .

II. The adaptiveness that is so abundantly evinced in the organic world has already been discussed from the point of view of science and proximate causation. We have seen that if the behavior of matter be regarded as completely describable in terms of least action, shortest path, dissipation of kinetic energy, and so forth, matter must be regarded also as unable, of itself, to fall into such systems as organisms. There is indeed some tendency to-day in scientific circles to seek an organic conception of the physical atom, etc., rather than a mechanical conception of the organism. But as for the organic at the molar and phenomenal level of description, its formative principle, irreducible to rigid mechanism, is provided by mentality wherever we have reason to infer psychic behavior; there we can account for the facts of function and structure, heredity and progressive adaptation. Where, as in plants, there is no macroscopic evidence of psychic behavior, the formative principle, as yet mysterious to science, is further to seek. It may be that only in metaphysics such as spiritualistic monadism, or hylozoism of the microscopic order, is a natural explanation to be found. But in proportion as psychological or other explanation is forthcoming in the organic realm as a whole, resort to external or cosmic teleology in order to account for adaptations within the organism, becomes superfluous for the special sciences. So long as organisms were believed to have originated, in their present forms and with all their specialized organs "ready made," the argument that adaptation of part to whole, of whole to environment, and of organ to function implied design, was forcible. But its premiss became untenable when Darwin shewed that every organic structure had come to be what it now is through a long series of successive and gradual modifications. Gradualness of construction is in itself no proof of the absence of external design: it is not at this point that Darwinism delivered its alleged death-blow to teleology. The sting of Darwinism rather lay in the suggestion that proximate and "mechanical" causes were sufficient to produce the adaptations from which the teleology of the eighteenth century had argued to God. Assignable proximate causes, whether mechanical or not, are sufficient to dispose of the particular kind of teleological proof supplied by Paley. But the fact of organic evolution, even when the maximum of instrumentality is accredited to what is figuratively called natural selection, is not incompatible with teleology on a grander scale: as exponents of Darwinism were perhaps the first to recognize and to proclaim. Subversive of Paley's argument, it does not invalidate his theistic conclusion, nor even his view that every organism and organ is an end as well as a means. Indeed the science of evolution was the primary source of the wider teleology current for the last half century, as well as the main incentive to the recovery of the closely connected doctrine of divine immanence. This kind of teleology does not set out from the particular adaptations in individual organisms or species so much as from considerations as to the progressiveness of the evolutionary process and as to the organic realm as a whole; but its connection with the former class of facts belongs to the subject-matter of the present section.

The survival of the fittest presupposes the arrival of the fit, and throws no light thereupon. Darwin did not account for the origin of variations; their forthcomingness was simply a datum for him. It is of no great significance for the wider teleology that variations are not in all cases so indefinite or random, nor so infinitesimal and gradual, as was generally assumed in *The Origin of Species*. But it may be observed that, in the absence either of a mechanical or of an "internal" explanation of variation, room is left for the possibility that variation is externally predetermined or guided, so that not only the general trend of the organic process, but also its every detail, may be pre-ordained or divinely controlled. Even this observation is pointless save for those who regard a nexus of traceable proximate causes and a theistic interpretation as incompatibilities. Theism such as has over-emphasized the idea of God's immanence denies proximate causes as distinct from acts of God; and advocates of antitheistic mechanism sometimes appear to think that the traceability of proximate causes bespeaks the superfluity, to philosophy as well as to science, of the idea of God. Thus, in connection with the topic now before us, Weismann wrote: "It is certainly the absence of a theoretical definition of variability which leaves open the door for smuggling in a teleological power. A mechanical explanation of variability must form the basis of this side of natural selection." But theism, such as is sufficiently leavened with deism to distinguish itself from pantheism, and the world from a deified mechanism, is indifferent to the banishment of the Paleyan type of teleology which relied on particular organic adaptations, any one of which was deemed sufficient to prove a divine artificer; and at the same time it has no need of going to the extreme of asserting that God is "either everywhere or nowhere," or that He is nothing if not all. The discovery of organic evolution has caused the teleologist to shift his ground from special design in the products to directivity in the process, and plan in the primary collocations. It has also served to suggest that the organic realm supplies no better basis for teleological argument of the narrower type than does inorganic Nature. Indeed it suggests that, since the adaptiveness of an organism is non-teleological, the adaptiveness of the whole world may perhaps similarly be *Zweckmässigkeit ohne Zweck* [adaptation without a purpose]. But this suggestion calls for examination later.

III. Although teleologists in the past have generally set out from adaptations in organisms, it has occurred now and again to a theistic apologist, e.g. to Aquinas, that adaptation in inorganic Nature, where there cannot be a formative principle such as non-intelligent organisms evince, should more unequivocally bespeak external design. The teleologist of to-day, however, would rather call attention to the continuity of apparent purposiveness between the two realms, or to the dependence of adaptation in the one on adaptiveness in the other. Since Darwin, we have realized that organisms can only be understood in connection with their environment. And more recently it has been argued, as by Mr. Henderson, that the inorganic environment is as plainly adapted to life as living creatures are to their environment. The vast complexity of the physico-chemical conditions of life on the earth suggests to common sense that the inorganic world may retrospectively receive a biocentric explanation, which, if "unconscious purpose" do but restate the facts rather than account for them, and ungrounded coincidence be as humanly incredible as it is logically unassailable, becomes a teleological explanation. Waiving, as here irrelevant, the metaphysical possibility that what we call inorganic matter is an appearance of relatively unorganized spirit, we may say that if science is to be trusted when it regards the organic realm as later in time than the inorganic world, and when it asserts that the processes, which made the emergence and persistence of life possible, would have been precisely the same had life not emerged at all, then there would seem to be a development of this fitness for life, involving convergence of innumerable events towards a result, as if that result were an end to which the inorganic processes were means. The fitness of our world to be the home of living beings depends upon certain primary conditions, astronomical, thermal, chemical, etc., and on the coincidence of qualities apparently not causally connected with one another, the number of which would doubtless surprise anyone wholly unlearned in the sciences; and these primary conditions, in their turn, involve many of secondary order. Unique assemblages of unique properties on so vast a scale being thus essential to the maintenance of life, their forthcomingness makes the inorganic world seem in some respects comparable with an organism. It is suggestive of a formative principle. But, if there be such a principle, it is not conceivable after analogy with the life and mind of organisms, and cannot be said to be intrinsic or internal; because the inorganic—at the molar and phenomenal level of explanation—is devoid of life, and—at any level of explanation—is devoid of intelligence and foresight. Unless cosmic teleology is invoked, the intricate adaptations that have been mentioned must be referred by the dualist to a mechanically controlled concourse of atoms, and by the pluralistic spiritualist to conative monads that are no more capable of conspiration than are inert particles.

Such is the teleological appeal of this field of facts to commonsense reasonableness, or mother-wit, which regards the "probability," that the apparent preparedness of the world to be a theatre of life is due to "chance," as infinitesimally small. It remains to ask whether either science or logic is able to abate the forcibleness of this appeal.

Science does not seem to lessen the convincingness of the argument now before us when it suggests that (as if organic chemistry were irrelevant), had the conditions upon which life, as we know it, depends been wholly or partly different, other forms of organism might equally well have emerged, adapted to the altered environment: silicon perhaps replacing carbon in another kind of protoplasm, and iron replacing calcium phosphate in skeletons. For the point is that, for the existence of any forms of life that we may conceive, the necessary environment, whatever its nature, must be complex and dependent on a multiplicity of coincident conditions, such as are not reasonably attributable to blind forces or to pure mechanism. Nor, again, can science explain the adaptation of the inorganic environment to life after the manner in which Darwinism, its sufficiency being assumed, explains progressive adaptations in organisms without resort to design. Of a struggle for existence between rival worlds, out of which ours has survived as the fittest, we have no knowledge upon which to draw. Natural selection cannot here be invoked; and if the term "evolution" be applicable at all to the whole world-process, it must have a different meaning from that which it bears in Darwinian biology. Presumably the world is comparable with a single throw of dice. And common sense is not foolish in suspecting the dice to have been loaded.

But here the logician intervenes. He will first point out that the remarkableness, or surprisingness, of manifold coincidences, evoking our teleological explanation of them, is but a fact pertaining to human psychology, unless "remarkable" means what he calls antecedently improbable. He will then remind us that a remarkable world might result from "one throw" in spite of there being indefinitely large chances against it, just as double sixes may be cast in one's first toss of two unloaded dice, although the adverse odds are 35 to 1. But his most harmful observation will be that, if the world be the sole instance of its kind, or be analogous to a single throw, there can be no talk of chances or of antecedent probability in connection with our question. Sound as this caution is, it does not affect the teleologist; for, when he calls coincidence on the vast scale improbable, he has in mind not mathematical probability, or a logical relation, but the alogical probability which is the guide of life and which has been found to be the ultimate basis of all scientific induction. If teleology here strays from the path of logical rectitude into one marked by logicians with a warning-post, it does so in the light-hearted company of common sense and inductive science. Science has been so continuously successful in its venturesomeness that the wise-head, logic, now lets it pass without remonstrance; but theology, though arm in arm with science, receives a reprimand. The teleologist is told that there is no antecedent probability, as to the existence of the intelligent Being invoked to explain adaptation suggestive of intelligent activity, after observation of the facts in question, unless there was an appreciable probability, before observation of them, that such a Being exists. Robinson Crusoe can be said to have inferred Friday from footprints legitimately, because he already knew that men existed and that they could reach his island; but the teleologist does not know beforehand that any superhuman being exists, and therefore cannot legitimately reason from what apparently are Mind-prints to their divine causation. But some favoritism would seem to be shewn to science in this illustration; for when we inquire how Crusoe originally got his knowledge as to the existence of fellow-men who can not only make footprints but also supply service and friendship, we find that it seems to have been mediated in much the same way as is the teleologist's belief in God. It is true that in the former case there is a psychologically stronger compulsion, a nearer analogy, and a more immediate and constantly reiterated verification-process than in the latter; but the origination of our belief in fellow-subjects, like remarkableness of coincidences, is ultimately an affair of human psychology and life, of teleology and not of logic or of direct apprehension of soul-substance. Moreover, though we have no "knowledge" of a spirit above man in the hierarchy of spirits that we "know," neither have we knowledge that there is no such being. Knowledge leaves room for the faith which teleology involves; and the faith-venture is similar *in kind* to that on which all scientific knowledge relies. Previously to verification of his faith the teleologist need ask of science no further recognition than this. He would but insist that, in so far as relations with logic are concerned, it is not true that science rests on reason while, in a corresponding sense, teleology rests on unreason.

IV. Besides possessing a structure that happens to render it habitable by living creatures and intelligible to some of them, the world is a bearer of values, thus evincing affinity with beings such as can appreciate as well as understand. The beauty and sublimity of Nature have been made the basis of a special teleological argument; and if, as standing by itself, this argument falls short of cogency, the facts from which it sets out may be said to form a link in the chain of evidence which comprehensive teleology presents. The few considerations that lend themselves to either of these uses do not call for lengthy or subtle disputation; and fortunately it is not necessary to enter the scientifically trackless domain of aesthetics in order to ascertain their bearing on theism. Whether the adaptation to our faculties, involved in aesthetic estimation, be, as Kant thought, formal and the same for all, though subjective; whether it be subjectively constituted and not the same for all; whether beauty be wholly Objective and literally intrinsic to Nature: these controversial questions are here immaterial. For the doctrine that aesthetic value is constituted by feeling does not imply that the feeling is not objectively evoked, as if we could see beauty when and where we chose. It has a parallel in the phenomenalist theory of knowledge: that is to say, beauty is not created by minds out of nothing, but is subjectively made out of *rapport* with the ontal. Thus diverse theories as to the constitution of beauty may be said to have in common the implication that the ontal world is ultimately responsible for the evocation of aesthetic thrills and sentiments, though the value-judgments evoked by the same "perceptual" Objects are different in different percipients. Theories differ but as to what exactly is intrinsic, whether that is intrinsic to Nature as ontal or as phenomenal, and how much is subjectively contributed. And whatever be our proportioning of the shares of the human mind and external Reality in constituting aesthetic value, the dependence or non-dependence of beauty on design will not be affected by it. There is a point in Toby Veck's remark as to the chimes: "If I hear 'em, what does it matter whether they speak it or not?" Yet "We receive but what we give,"[8] in this connection, is a partial truth because it suppresses the fact that our giving is solicited by a prior and different gift to us. If we minimise phenomenal Nature's gift by denying that her beauty is intrinsic, as is form or color, we must allow to ontal Nature an intrinsic constitution such that minds can make beauty as well as nomic order out of it. And the more we magnify man's part in this making, phenomenalizing, and appreciating, the more motivation have we to believe that Nature is meaningless and valueless without God behind it and man in front; and that is what teleology in its comprehensiveness, and the aesthetic argument in its particularity, endeavor to establish.

The latter argument, at least in its more popular forms, treats the beauty of Nature as Paley treated organic adaptations. That it discusses the beauty of the world, as we now contemplate it, as if it were a "special creation" with no past history or development, may not signify. The weak spot in what purports to be a special proof of theism lies rather in the assumption that, since in human art a beautiful or sublime production is the outcome of human design, similar effects must everywhere be due to design. This generalization is all too precarious; it can hardly be maintained that arrangements of matter, accounted beautiful, humanly caused but not contrived or selectively constructed with a view to exciting aesthetic admiration, *never* occur. Prescience or purpose is involved in art; but art is not necessarily the sole source of beauty. We may deem some of Kant's criticisms of the teleological explanation of the beautiful and the sublime to be captious, and such explanation to be natural and reasonable; but it is hardly necessitated by the considerations on which this would-be coercive argument relies.

The aesthetic argument for theism becomes more persuasive when it renounces all claim to proof and appeals to alogical probability. And it becomes stronger when it takes as the most significant fact not the forthcomingness of beautiful phenomena but what may be called, with almost negligible need of qualification, the saturation of Nature with beauty. On the telescopic and on the microscopic scale, from the starry heaven to the siliceous skeleton of the diatom, in her inward parts (if scientific imagination be veridical) as well as on the surface, in flowers that "blush unseen" and gems that the "unfathomed caves of ocean bear," Nature is sublime or beautiful, and the exceptions do but prove the rule. However various be the taste for beauty, and however diverse the levels of its education or the degrees of its refinement, Nature elicits aesthetic sentiment from men severally and collectively; and the more fastidious becomes this taste, the more poignantly and the more lavishly does she gratify it. Indeed, from contemplation of Nature, whose "every prospect pleases," the atheist might be led to conclude that processes only need *not* to be fraught with aesthetic design in order to excite, almost without fail, aesthetic admiration. But his generalization would become untenable as soon as he bethought himself of similar causal *nexa* into which human agency, seeking any end save beauty, enters. In general, man's productions (other than professed works of art), and almost only they, are aesthetically vile. An automobile, with its noises, stench, etc., can disgust all our senses simultaneously, and is not wholly untypical; while human output of larger scale is often not only unsightly and otherwise offensive in itself, but mars the fair face of Nature. Here, then, are two kinds of agency, *ex hypothesi* proceeding with indifference to the realization of aesthetic values: we might almost say the one never achieves, while the other never misses, the beautiful. And the same contrast subsists between their processes as between their products. Compare, e.g., "the rattling looms and the hammering noise of human workshops" with Nature's silent or musical constructiveness; or the devastating stinks of chemical works with Nature's fragrant distillations. "In the very act of laboring as a machine [Nature] also sleeps as a picture."[4]

If "God made the country" whereas man made the town—and the black country—we have a possible explanation of these things; but if the theism contained in this saying be rejected, explanation does not seem to be forthcoming. The universality of Nature's beauty,—to speak as if beauty were the same for all and were intrinsic—is a generalization roughly comparable with the uniformity of natural law. That natural Objects evoke aesthetic sentiment is as much a fact about them as that they obey the laws of motion or that they have such and such chemical composition. And this potency is not coextensive with "mechanicalness," or absence of aesthetic design, as man's utilitarian productions shew. Nor can Nature's mechanism be regarded as a sufficient cause of the adaptiveness to our subjectivity in which beauty consists; for we may still ask why *Nature's* mechanism affects us in such wise that we deem her sublime and beautiful, since mere mechanism, as such, is under no universal necessity to do so, and what we may call human mechanisms usually fail to do so. Yet this potency, describable as the Objective factor in beauty, belongs to Nature's very texture. And our scientific knowledge that the world-elements are ordered by number brings us no nearer to understanding why Nature is comparable with elaborately polyphonic music, or a harmony of many combined melodies.

It may further be observed that, in so far as the mechanical stability and the analytic intelligibility of the inorganic world are concerned, beauty is a superfluity. Also that in the organic world aesthetic pleasingness of color, etc., seems to possess survival-value on but a limited scale, and then is not to be identified with the complex and intellectualized aesthetic sentiments of humanity, which apparently have no survival-value. From the point of view of science, beauty proper is, in both its subjective and its objective factors, but a by-product, an epiphenomenon, a biologically superfluous accompaniment of the cosmic process. Once more then lucky accidents and coincidences bewilderingly accumulate until the idea of purposiveness, already lying to hand as indispensable within the sphere of human conduct, is applied to effect the substitution of reasonable, if alogical, probability for groundless contingency. If we do apply this category of design to the whole time-process, the beauty of Nature may not only be assigned a cause but also a meaning, or a revelational function. It may then be regarded as no mere by-product, like physical evil, in a teleologically ordered world whose *raison d' être* is the realization of other values—the moral and the religious. Indeed Nature's potency to evoke aesthetic sentiment, however otiose in the cosmic process studied by science, is efficient in the world's *rapport* with man. From its very origination religious experience seems to have been conditioned by the impressiveness or the awesomeness of natural phenomena, suggestive of an invisible and mysterious presence. Aesthetic values are closely associated, and often are inextricably interwoven, with ethico-religious values. God reveals Himself, to such as have differentiated these valuations, in many ways; and some men enter His Temple by the Gate Beautiful. Values alone can provide guidance as to the world's meaning, structure being unable to suggest more than intelligent power. And beauty may well be *a* meaning. That is the element of sense contained in the romanticist's paradox, beauty is truth, or truth is beauty.

It may be remarked by the way that if sensuous beauty be accounted a world-meaning, so far will the anthropocentric factor in interpretation of the world become accentuated. For as to the ontal counterpart to sensory beauty, or what Nature's beauty is for the Creator Himself, we cannot speculate. If Nature's beauty embody a purpose *of* God, it would seem to be a purpose *for* man, and to bespeak that God is "mindful of him." Theistically regarded, Nature's beauty is of a piece with the world's intelligibility and with its being a theatre for moral life; and thus far the case for theism is strengthened by aesthetic considerations.

NOTES

[1] Vol. II, chapter IV, "Cosmic Teleology," pp. 79-93 (Cambridge: The University Press, and New York: The Cambridge University Press, 1930).

[2] By "chance" is here meant absence of a sufficient ground. The word, as commonly used, carries several meanings; and which of them is to the fore in any context where the term subsequently appears will perhaps not need to be stated. Among its senses the following may be mentioned. It may signify an event not as yet included by known law, or one which, in that it is unique, is absolutely non-subsumable under a general law; or one that is determined by causes as to which we have but imperfect, or perhaps no relevant, knowledge. It may simply exclude final causation, and then denote the non-purposed. It may even suggest the supposed indeterminateness, which can never actually subsist, e.g. of a configuration.

[3] . . . We receive but what we give,
   And in our life alone does Nature live:
   Ours is her wedding-garment, ours her shroud!
                    —S. T. Coleridge, "Dejection: An Ode."

[4] J. B. Mozley, *University Sermons,* 6th ed., p. 123.

THE MORAL ARGUMENT

God as a Postulate of Practical Reason

IMMANUEL KANT

Immanuel Kant, whose criticism of the ontological argument appears earlier (pp. 39f.), also rejected the cosmological and teleological arguments. In addition to his piecemeal critique of each of these traditional arguments, it follows from his critical philosophy that pure or theoretical reason cannot make pronouncements referring beyond the boundaries of human experience and cannot therefore establish the reality of transcendent entities. He did not however conclude from this limitation of theoretical reason that there is no transcendent God. Having removed religious belief from the sphere of theoretical reason Kant sought to re-establish it on a different ground altogether, as something that is necessarily presupposed in the operations of practical or moral reason. The reality of God is a *postulate* of practical reason. This is the argument of the following section from Kant's *Critique of Practical Reason*. (Book II, Chapter II, section V, translated by Thomas Kingsmill Abbott, *Kant's Theory of Ethics*, 4th edition, 1889, pp. 220-229.)

❊

The Existence of God as a Postulate of Practical Reason

In the foregoing analysis the moral law led to a practical problem which is prescribed by pure reason alone, without the aid of any sensible motives, namely, that of the necessary completeness of the first and principal element of the *sum-*

mum bonum, viz. Morality; and as this can be perfectly solved only in eternity, to the postulate of *immortality.* The same law must also lead us to affirm the possibility of the second element of the *summum bonum,* viz. Happiness proportioned to that morality, and this on grounds as disinterested as before, and solely from impartial reason; that is, it must lead to the supposition of the existence of a cause adequate to this effect; in other words, it must postulate the *existence of God,* as the necessary condition of the possibility of the *summum bonum* (an object of the will which is necessarily connected with the moral legislation of pure reason). We proceed to exhibit this connection in a convincing manner.

Happiness is the condition of a rational being in the world with whom *everything goes according to his wish and will;* it rests, therefore, on the harmony of physical nature with his whole end, and likewise with the essential determining principle of his will. Now the moral law as a law of freedom commands by determining principles, which ought to be quite independent on nature and on its harmony with our faculty of desire (as springs). But the acting rational being in the world is not the cause of the world and of nature itself. There is not the least ground, therefore, in the moral law for a necessary connection between morality and proportionate happiness in a being that belongs to the world as part of it, and therefore dependent on it, and which for that reason cannot by his will be a cause of this nature, nor by his own power make it thoroughly harmonize, as far as his happiness is concerned, with his practical principles. Nevertheless, in the practical problem of pure reason, i.e. the necessary pursuit of the *summum bonum,* such a connection is postulated as necessary: we ought to endeavor to promote the *summum bonum,* which, therefore, must be possible. Accordingly, the existence of a cause of all nature, distinct from nature itself and containing the principle of this connection, namely, of the exact harmony of happiness with morality, is also *postulated.* Now, this supreme cause must contain the principle of the harmony of nature, not merely with a law of the will of rational beings, but with the conception of this *law,* in so far as they make it the *supreme determining principle of the will*, and consequently not merely with the form of morals, but with their morality as their motive, that is, with their moral character. Therefore, the *summum bonum* is possible in the world only on the supposition of a supreme Being having a causality corresponding to moral character. Now a being that is capable of acting on the conception of laws is an *intelligence* (a rational being), and the causality of such a being according to this conception of laws is his *will*; therefore the supreme cause of nature, which must be presupposed as a condition of the *summum bonum*, is a being which is the cause of nature by *intelligence* and *will*, consequently its author, that is God. It follows that the postulate of the possibility of the *highest derived good* (the best world) is likewise the postulate of the reality of a *highest original good*, that is to say, of the existence of God. Now it was seen to be a duty for us to promote the *summum bonum*; consequently it is not merely allowable, but it is a necessity connected with duty as a requisite, that we should presuppose the possibility of this *summum bonum*; and as this is possible only on condition of the existence of God, it inseparably connects the supposition of this with duty; that is, it is morally necessary to assume the existence of God.

It must be remarked here that this moral necessity is *subjective*, that is, it is a want, and not *objective*, that is, itself a duty, for there cannot be a duty to suppose the existence of anything (since this concerns only the theoretical employment of reason). Moreover it is not meant by this that it is necessary to suppose the existence of God *as a basis of all obligation in general* (for this rests, as has been sufficiently proved, simply on the autonomy of reason itself). What belongs to duty here is only the endeavor to realize and promote the *summum bonum* in the world, the possibility of which can therefore be postulated; and as our reason finds it not conceivable except on the supposition of a supreme intelligence, the admission of this existence is therefore connected with the consciousness of our duty, although the admission itself belongs to the domain of speculative reason. Considered in respect of this alone, as a principle of explanation, it may be called a *hypothesis*, but in reference to the intelligibility of an object given us by the moral law (the *summum bonum*), and consequently of a requirement for practical purposes, it may be called *faith,* that is to say a pure *rational faith,* since pure reason (both in its theoretical and its practical use) is the sole source from which it springs. . . .

The doctrine of Christianity, even if we do not yet consider it as a religious doctrine, gives, touching this point, a conception of the *summum bonum* (the kingdom of God), which alone satisfies the strictest demand of practical reason. The moral law is holy (unyielding) and demands holiness of morals, although all the moral perfection to which man can attain is still only virtue, that is, a rightful disposition arising from *respect* for the law, implying consciousness of a constant propensity to transgression, or at least a want of purity, that is, a mixture of many spurious (not moral) motives of obedience to the law, consequently a self-esteem combined with humility. In respect then of the holiness which the Christian law requires, this leaves the creature nothing but a progress *in infinitum,* but for that very reason it justifies him in hoping for an endless duration of his existence. The *worth* of a character *perfectly* accordant with the moral law is infinite, since the only restriction on all possible happiness in the judgment of a wise and all-powerful distributor of it is the absence of conformity of rational beings to their duty. But the moral law of itself does not *promise* any happiness, for according to our conceptions of an order of nature in general, this is not necessarily connected with obedience to the law. Now Christian morality supplies this defect (of the second indispensable element of the *summum bonum*) by representing the world, in which rational beings devote themselves with all their soul to the moral law, as a *kingdom of God,* in which nature and morality are brought into a harmony foreign to each of itself, by a holy Author who makes the derived *summum bonum* possible. *Holiness* of life is prescribed to them as a rule even in this life, while the welfare proportioned to it, namely, *bliss,* is represented as attainable only in an eternity; because the *former* must always be the pattern of their conduct in every state, and progress towards it is already possible and necessary in this life; while the *latter,* under the name of happiness, cannot be attained at all in this world (so far as our own power is concerned), and therefore is made simply an object of hope. Nevertheless, the Christian principle of *morality* itself is not theological (so as to be heteronomy) but is autonomy of pure practical reason, since it does not make the knowledge of God and his will the foundation of these laws, but only of the attainment of the *summum bonum,* on condition of following these laws, and it does not even place the proper *spring* of this obedience in the desired results, but solely in the conception of duty, as that of which the faithful observance alone constitutes the worthiness to obtain those happy consequences.

In this manner the moral laws lead through the conception of the *summum bonum* as the object and final end of pure practical reason to *religion,* that is, to the *recognition of all duties as divine commands, not as sanctions, that is to say, arbitrary ordinances of a foreign will and contingent in themselves, but* as essential *laws* of every free will in itself, which, nevertheless, must be regarded as commands of the Supreme Being, because it is only from a morally perfect (holy and good) and at the same time all-powerful will, and consequently only through harmony with this will that we can hope to attain the *summum bonum* which the moral law makes it our duty to take as the object of our endeavors. Here again, then, all remains disinterested and founded merely on duty; neither fear nor hope being made the fundamental springs, which if taken as principles would destroy the whole moral worth of actions. The moral law commands me to make the highest possible good in a world the ultimate object of all my conduct. But I cannot hope to effect this otherwise than by the harmony of my will with that of a holy and good Author of the world; and although the conception of the *summum bonum* as a whole, in which the greatest happiness is conceived as combined in the most exact proportion with the highest degree of moral perfection (possible in creatures), includes *my own happiness,* yet it is not this that is the determining principle of the will which is enjoined to promote the *summum bonum,* but the moral law, which on the contrary limits by strict conditions my unbounded desire of happiness.

Hence also morality is not properly the doctrine how we should *make* ourselves happy, but how we should become *worthy* of happiness. It is only when religion is added that there also comes in the hope of participating some day in happiness in proportion as we have endeavored to be not unworthy of it.

A man is *worthy* to possess a thing or a state when his possession of it is in harmony with the *summum bonum*. We can now easily see that all worthiness depends on moral conduct, since in the conception of the *summum bonum* this constitutes the condition of the rest (which belongs to one's state), namely, the participation of happiness. Now it follows from this that *morality* should never be treated as a *doctrine of happiness,* that is, an instruction how to become happy; for it has to do simply with the rational condition (*conditio sine qua non*) of happiness, not with the means of attaining it. But when morality has been completely expounded (which merely imposes duties instead of providing rules for selfish desires), then, first, after the moral desire to promote the *summum bonum* (to bring the kingdom of God to us) has been awakened, a desire founded on a law, and which could not previously arise in any selfish mind, and when for the behoof of this desire the step to religion has been taken, then this ethical doctrine may be also called a doctrine of happiness, because the *hope* of happiness first begins with religion only.

We can also see from this that, when we ask what is *God's ultimate end* in creating the world, we must not name the *happiness* of the rational beings in it, but the *summum bonum,* which adds a further condition to that wish of such beings, namely, the condition of being worthy of happiness, that is, the *morality* of these same rational beings, a condition which alone contains the rule by which only they can hope to share in the former at the hand of a *wise* Author. For as *wisdom* theoretically considered signifies *the knowledge of the summum bonum,* and practically *the accordance of the will with the summum bonum,* we cannot attribute to a supreme independent wisdom an end based merely on *goodness.* For we cannot conceive the action of this goodness (in respect of the happiness of rational beings) as suitable to the highest original good, except under the restrictive conditions of harmony with the holiness of his will. Therefore those who placed the end of creation in the glory of God (provided that this is not conceived anthropomorphically as a desire to be praised) have perhaps hit upon the best expression. For nothing glorifies God more than that which is the most estimable thing in the world, respect for His command, the observance of the holy duty that His law imposes on us, when there is added thereto His glorious plan of crowning such a beautiful order of things with corresponding happiness. If the latter (to speak humanly) makes Him worthy of love, by the *former* He is an object of adoration. Even men can never acquire respect by benevolence alone, though they may gain love, so that the greatest beneficence only procures them honor when it is regulated by worthiness.

That in the order of ends, man (and with him every rational being) *is an end in himself,* that is, that he can never be used merely as a means by any (not even by God) without being at the same time an end also himself, that therefore *humanity* in our person must be *holy* to ourselves, this follows now of itself because he is the *subject of the moral law,* in other words, of that which is holy in itself, and on account of which and in agreement with which alone can anything be termed holy. For this moral law is founded on the autonomy of his will, as a free will which by its universal laws must necessarily be able to agree with that to which it is to submit itself.

The Moral Argument

HASTINGS RASHDALL

The "moral argument" for the existence of God, first established in the modern world by Kant, has been developed and varied by a number of subsequent thinkers, and was especially popular in the Anglo-Saxon world in the first decades of the present century. Hastings Rashdall (1858-1924) formulated the argument in a way which has been followed by many other writers.

❋

FROM *The Theory of Good and Evil*[1]

THE MORAL ARGUMENT

We have seen that certain metaphysical presuppositions as to the nature of knowledge and the nature of the self are necessary to the very existence of an ethical system which can be regarded as representing and justifying the deliverances of the moral consciousness. When we have admitted that knowledge is not mere subjective feeling or passive experience, that the self is as real as or more real than any "thing" of which Physical Science can tell us, and that the self causes certain events which are commonly spoken of as its actions, then we are able to recognize the reality of duty, of ideals, of a good which includes right conduct. And *prima facie* it might appear that the truth and validity of these ideals are independent of any particular conclusions as to the ultimate nature of things which go beyond these simple presuppositions. The man who wishes to see any meaning in the deliverances of his own moral consciousness and to represent to himself the attempt to live up to the ideal which they set before him as an intelligible and rational aim, must assume this much about knowledge and about the self; but it may possibly be contended that he need assume nothing further about the ultimate nature of things, except that it is a Universe, part of whose nature is to produce this moral consciousness of his. And it is no doubt true that the Agnostic (in Metaphysic or Theology) cannot be convicted of any positive inconsistency, if he simply accepts the dictates of his moral consciousness as final, and says: "I know nothing as to the ultimate source of these moral ideas, except that they come to me in the same way as the rest of my knowledge, or anything as to the ultimate outcome of this moral life which I feel to be incumbent upon me. I simply know the meaning of the good, and that it is right for me to aim at it, and that I can, to

some extent, bring it into existence by my voluntary action."
Psychologically this attitude is a possible one. The term
"good" or "right" does not contain any *explicit* reference to
any theological or metaphysical theory of the Universe. The
proposition that some things are right, others wrong, is not
in any sense an inference or deduction from any such theory;
it is an immediate datum or deliverance of consciousness. The
truth is assented to, and acted upon, by men of all religions
or of none, by persons who hold most dissimilar views as to
the ultimate nature of the Universe, and by men who profess
to have no theory of the Universe at all. And it is impossible to say that the words "good" and "right" have no
meaning for such persons or an entirely different meaning
from what they have for the Metaphysician who refuses to
acquiesce in Agnosticism. In this sense it is of the highest
possible importance to recognize what is sometimes spoken
of as the "independence of Morality." But it remains a
further question whether the true meaning of Morality is
capable of being made explicit, and of being reconciled or
harmonized with other facts of our knowledge or experience
without necessitating the adoption of certain views concerning the ultimate nature of things and the rejection of certain
other views. If this should turn out to be the case, Morality
will be in exactly the same position as any other part of our
knowledge. So long as we refuse to bring any piece of our
knowledge or experience into connection with any other part
of it, the particular piece of knowledge cannot be shown to
be either consistent or inconsistent with such other parts of
our knowledge. So long as that is the case, it may no doubt
from a high metaphysical attitude be maintained that this
knowledge may not be altogether true, since it may require
to be corrected and limited in order to bring it into harmony
with other parts of our knowledge: for the only test that
we have of the validity of any part of our knowledge is its
capacity for being harmonized or co-ordinated with the rest
of it. But, from a rough practical point of view, it is
possible to be certain of the truth of Science without holding
any metaphysical position at all: and in that sense it is
equally possible to combine a strong conviction of the reality

or objective validity of moral distinctions with complete Agnosticism as to the general nature of the Universe, though in practice Agnosticism is very apt to involve negative assumptions the irreconcilability of which with what is implied in the idea of moral obligation, can with difficulty remain unrecognized. But after all the question remains whether this refusal to bring one part of our knowledge into connection with the rest is a reasonable attitude of mind. It is always easy to escape inconsistency by resolutely shutting our eyes to a portion of the facts, by refusing to think of or arbitrarily stopping the process of thought at some particular point. When we ask whether a certain intellectual attitude is ultimately reasonable, we presuppose that we are making up our minds to look at the whole of the facts. Agnosticism is not a reasonable attitude of mind when it is possible to know. And the question arises whether, when the attempt to harmonize and so to justify our beliefs is honestly made, the man who wishes to defend and rationalize his practical recognition of moral obligation may not be forced into the alternative of giving up his ethical creed or of giving up certain views of the Universe which reflection has shown to be inconsistent with that creed.

Are there then any metaphysical positions about the ultimate nature of things which logically exclude the idea of an objective Moral Law? Let us suppose, for instance, that, without giving up that bare minimum of metaphysical belief about the self which we have found to be absolutely presupposed in the very idea of Morality, a man has nevertheless adopted a materialistic or naturalistic view of the world to this extent—that he believes that the origin of the self, and of the knowledge which resides in the self, may actually be traced to certain material processes of a Reality in which previously no mind resided except as a "promise and potency" of the future. Such a man is not, indeed, technically in the most thorough-going sense of the word a Materialist if he admits that after all a true view of the Universe must include a recognition of the spiritual nature which the Universe has ultimately, by whatever process, evolved. And it is quite right to emphasize the difference between a position of this kind and the old confused puzzle-headed Materialism which was inclined to look on matter and motion as real things and on thought, feeling (with perhaps some not very logical exception in favor of pleasure and pain), emotion, aspiration, ideals as mere arbitrary inventions or hallucinations. But, putting aside for the present the purely metaphysical difficulties of such a position, we have to ask how it must affect our attitude towards Morality.

So long as the ultimate reality of things is regarded as purely material, so long as material process is regarded as the sole cause or source or ground of mind and all its contents, there is always the possibility of scepticism as to the knowledge of which this material world has somehow delivered itself. Our knowledge may be conceived of as representing, not the real truth of things, but the way in which it is most conducive to the survival of the race that we should think of them. Error and delusion may be valuable elements in Evolution; to a certain extent it is undeniable, from any metaphysical standpoint, that they have actually been so. But on the naturalistic view of things the doubt arises not merely whether this or that particular belief of ours is a delusion, but whether human thought in general may not wholly fail to correspond with Reality, whether thought *qua* thought may not be a delusion, whether (to put it still more paradoxically) the more rational a man's thought becomes, the more faithfully the individual adheres to the canons of human Reason, the wider may be the gulf between his thinking and the facts. Arguments might no doubt be found for putting away such an "unmotived" doubt as to the truthworthiness of our knowledge about ordinary matters of fact—its self-consistency, the constant correspondence of the predictions which it makes with subsequent experience, the practical serviceableness for the purposes of life of its assumed validity, and the uselessness of entertaining doubts as to the trustworthiness of our faculties which from the nature of the case can be neither confirmed nor refuted; though after all such arguments at bottom assume the validity of thought. But these considerations do not apply in the same degree to moral knowledge. It is often possible to explain in a sense this or that particular ethical belief by the history of the race, the environment of the individual, and the like. Such considerations do not shake belief in the ultimate validity of moral distinctions for an Idealist who believes that the Universe owes its very existence to the Mind which assures him of these distinctions (though he is aware that the evolution of his individual mind has been conditioned by physical processes and social environment); but they wear a totally different aspect for one who has no general *a priori* reason for assuming a correspondence of thought with things. The Idealist has every reason for believing the ultimate moral ideas to be true that he has for believing any other ideas to be true, though he realizes that he does not know the whole truth, and that his knowledge of this or ignorance of that element in the moral ideal (like his knowledge or ignorance of ordinary scientific truth) is in part explicable by the accident of antecedents or environment. But to the man who regards all spiritual life as a mere inexplicable incident in the career of a world which is essentially material (were it not for the human and animal minds which it is known to have produced) and as a whole essentially purposeless, there is no conclusive reason why all moral ideas—the very conception of "value," the very notion that one thing is intrinsically better than another, the very conviction that there is something which a man ought to do—may not be merely some strange illusion due to the unaccountable freaks of a mindless process or to the exigencies of natural selection. It cannot be said that a man who allowed such doubts to shake or modify his allegiance to the dictates of Morality, where they do not happen to coincide with his actual desires or inclinations, would be doing anything essentially unreasonable. Reasonable conduct would for him mean merely "conduct conformable to his own private reason": intrinsically or absolutely reasonable or unreasonable conduct could not exist in a world which was not itself the product of Reason or governed by its dictates.

Another way of putting much the same difficulty is this. We say that the Moral Law has a real existence, that there is such a thing as an absolute Morality, that there is something absolutely true or false in ethical judgments, whether we or any number of human beings at any given time actually think so or not. Such a belief is distinctly implied in what we mean by Morality. The idea of such an unconditional, objectively valid, Moral Law or ideal undoubtedly exists as a psychological fact. The question before us is whether it is capable of theoretical justification. We must then face the question *where* such an ideal exists, and what manner of existence we are to attribute to it. Certainly it is to be found, wholly and completely, in no individual human consciousness. Men actually think differently about moral questions, and there is no empirical reason for supposing that they will ever do otherwise. Where then and how does the moral ideal really exist? As regards matters of fact or physical law, we have no difficulty in satisfying ourselves that there is an objective reality which is what it is irrespectively of our beliefs or disbeliefs about it. For the man who supposes that objective reality resides in the things themselves, our ideas about them are objectively true or false so far as they correspond or fail to correspond with this real and independent archetype, though he might be puzzled to give a metaphysical account of the nature of this "correspondence" between experience and a Reality whose *esse* is something other than to be experienced. In the physical region the existence of divergent ideas does not throw doubt upon the existence of a reality independent of our ideas. But in the case of moral ideals it is otherwise. On materialistic or naturalistic assumptions the moral ideal can hardly be regarded as a real thing. Nor could it well be regarded as a property of any real thing: it can be no more than an aspiration, a product of the imagination, which may be useful to stimulate effort in directions in which we happen to want to move, but which cannot compel respect when we feel no desire to act in conformity with it. An absolute Moral Law or moral ideal cannot exist *in* material things. And it does not (we have seen) exist in the mind of this or that individual. Only if we believe in the existence of a Mind for which the true moral ideal is already in some sense real, a Mind which is the source of whatever is true in our own moral judgments, can we rationally think of the moral ideal as no less real than the world itself. Only so can we believe in an absolute standard of right and wrong, which is as independent of this or that man's actual ideas and actual desires as the facts of material nature. The belief in God, though not (like the belief in a real and an active self) a postulate of there being any such thing as Morality at all, is the logical presupposition of an "objective" or absolute Morality. A moral ideal can exist nowhere and nohow but in a mind; an absolute moral ideal can exist only in a Mind from which all Reality is derived.[2] Our moral ideal can only claim objective validity in so far as it can rationally be regarded as the revelation of a moral ideal eternally existing in the mind of God.

We may be able, perhaps, to give some meaning to Morality without the postulate of God, but not its true or full meaning. If the existence of God is not a postulate of all Morality, it is a postulate of a sound Morality; for it is essential to that belief which vaguely and implicitly underlies all moral beliefs, and which forms the very heart of Morality in its highest, more developed, more explicit forms. The truth that the moral ideal is what it is whether we like it or not is the most essential element in what the popular consciousness understands by "moral obligation." Moral obligation means moral objectivity. That *at least* seems to be implied in any legitimate use of the term: at least it implies the existence of an absolute, objective moral idea. And such a belief we have seen imperatively to demand an explanation of the Universe which shall be idealistic or at least spiritualistic, which shall recognize the existence of a Mind whose thoughts are the standard of truth and falsehood alike in Morality and in respect of all other existence. In other words, objective Morality implies the belief in God. The belief in God, if not so obviously and primarily a postulate of Morality as the belief in a permanent spiritual and active self, is still a postulate of a Morality which shall be able fully to satisfy the demands of the moral consciousness. It may conveniently be called the secondary postulate of Morality. . . .

The course of events must itself be governed by the same Mind which is the source of our moral ideas, and be ultimately directed towards the ends which the moral ideal, disclosed, however imperfectly, in the moral consciousness of man, sets up as the goal and canon of human conduct. The Universe itself must have a purpose or rational end, a purpose which a perfect Reason would pronounce to be good. The end which our Reason sets before us as the true end of conduct must be the end likewise of the Mind from which that Reason is derived. This seems speculatively necessary if Morality is to be regarded as ultimately and in the fullest sense rational—rational not merely from the point of view of this or that actual intelligence, or even from the point of view of all human intelligences, but from the point of view of all Reason whatever, universally, absolutely. And, as it is speculatively necessary, so it is, if not practically necessary in every individual case, at least highly conducive to Morality in practice that it should be believed that the ends which Morality sets before itself are destined to be realized. Unless the Universe be rational, no course of conduct can be said to be wholly and absolutely rational; we could only say "I am so constituted" or at the very most "*we* are so constituted that this or that seems rational to me or to us." And the Universe is not rational because there is a rational intelligence *for* whom it exists; if it is to be in the true sense rational, it must be directed towards ends which a rational intelligence would pronounce good.[3] I do not say that without this belief Morality would become irrational; moral conduct would still be as rational as anything could be in an irrational Universe, i.e. it would seem rational to some persons who think that they see clearly. And a man to whom it appeared good to diminish human suffering, and who desired that which he saw to be good, would still allow himself to be influenced by the desire, even though he thought or suspected that the Universe was very bad—though of course if his view of the ultimate badness of things reached a certain intensity, the encouragement of universal suicide might present itself to him as the only way to attain his end. But a belief of this kind is obviously one not calculated to encourage or stimulate what is ordinarily called Morality. To some minds no doubt the impulse to fight against the evil in a world in which evil was the stronger power would always seem good and noble. But Pessimism is not the belief about the Universe which is best calculated to call forth the highest energies even of the noblest souls. Still less is it calculated to foster the ethical education of those (and they are the vast majority, especially as regards the earlier stages of the individual's moral life) who recognize the intrinsic goodness of the Moral Law, but whose desire to fulfil it is faintly and fitfully struggling against a host of conflicting impulses. The belief that the Universe has a rational end is speculatively a postulate of an absolute or unconditional Morality: and the speculative necessity is one which is evident enough to minds of by no means a highly speculative cast. A Morality which is not absolute or unconditional is not Morality as it presents itself to the developed moral consciousness.

NOTES

[1] Vol. II (Oxford: The Clarendon Press and New York: The Oxford University Press, 1907), Book III, Chapter I, sections IV and V, pp. 206-213, 219-220.

[2] Or at least a mind by which all Reality is controlled.—Rashdall.

[3] Much confusion has been caused by the ambiguity of the word "rational." It may mean "intelligible" or "reducible to a coherent system such that one part of it could (with adequate insight) be inferred from another." In this sense the Universe might be rational if it were a sort of infernal machine. Or it may mean (and that is the only sense in which we ought to talk about a reality which includes events as "rational") realizing an end which is absolutely good.—Rashdall.

THE ARGUMENT FROM
RELIGIOUS EXPERIENCE

Statement of the Argument

A. E. TAYLOR

A. E. Taylor (1869-1945) was both a leading authority on
Plato and a leading Anglo-Catholic apologist for Christianity. The argument from religious experience was not
the only or the main strand in his own apologetic (see *The
Faith of a Moralist,* 1930, and *Does God Exist?,* 1945),
but nevertheless he has provided what is probably the best
available exposition of it in his essay "The Vindication of
Religion" from which the following excerpt is taken.

✱

FROM *The Vindication of Religion*[1]

III. FROM GOD TO GOD

To use phraseology which is more familiar to us of to-day,
we have to consider the worth of the so-called "religious
experience" as testimony to the reality of its own object,
and there is no line of argument which lends itself more
readily to abuse. Every kind of faddist and fanatic will appeal as readily to "experience" for testimony to his own pet
fancies as the credulous appeal to the "evidence of their
senses" for proof of the existence of ghosts or the reality of
sorcery. We seriously need to remember, as the Bishop of
Manchester has recently reminded us, that just as the "artist's
experience" means the way in which the *whole* natural realm
is experienced by the man who is an artist, **so** "religious

experience" means not some isolated group of bizarre experiences but the special way in which the whole of life is experienced by the "religious" man. And yet, true as this is, the very statement implies that there are some experiences which stand out in the life of the religious man as characteristically predominant and determining the coloring of his whole experience of the world. This is equally true of the artist. A man with the artist's eye, we very rightly say, "sees beauty" everywhere, while a man without it goes through life not seeing beauty anywhere, or at best seeing it only occasionally, where it is too prominent to be missed. Still no one doubts that even a man highly endowed with the gifts of the artist has to develop his sense for the beautiful. If he comes to find it present where the rest of us would never suspect it at all but for the teaching we may get from his work, this must be because he began by being specially alive to and interested in its presence where it is more visibly displayed. This again means that, however truly beauty may pervade the whole of things, there are special regions where its presence is most manifest and obvious. What is characteristic of the artist is that he makes just these elements of experience a key to unlock the meaning of the rest. So the religious man, no doubt, means the man who sees the whole of reality under the light of a specific illumination, but he has come to see all things in that light by taking certain arresting pieces or phases of his experience as the key to the meaning of the rest. In this sense we may properly speak of specifically religious experiences, as we may speak of a man's experience in the presence of a wonderful picture or musical composition, or at a moment when a weighty decision which will color the whole tenour of his future conduct has to be made, as specifically aesthetic or moral experiences. The question is whether there really are such specific experiences or whether what have been supposed to be so are only illusions, misinterpretations of experiences which contain nothing unique.

This question is not settled by the admission that some experiences which have been reckoned by those who have had them as religious are illusory. All experience is liable to misinterpretation. We must not argue that sense-perception does not reveal a world of really existing bodies, which are no illusions of our imagination, on the ground that there are such things as dreams and hallucinations, any more than we may argue from the general reality of the things perceived by sense to the reality of dream-figures or ghosts. So again we may neither argue that there is no real beauty in the visible world because the best of us are capable of sometimes finding it where it is not, nor that because there is real beauty, every supposed beauty detected by any man must be real. In a sense, "everything is given." If there were no arresting perception of beauty in the region of color or tone, we should never come to be on the look out for it where it is less manifest. On the other hand, every man's immediate verdict on beauty is not to be trusted. We have to learn how to interpret our experience in the light of the judgment of the artist who is specially endowed with a fine discrimination of beauty and has cultivated his eye or ear by long and careful attention to the aesthetic aspects of the sensible world before we can trust our own immediate "taste" for color or line or tone. So, too, in matters of morality, if a man has no direct perception of what "ought" means, it is impossible to convey that meaning to him; but a man would be led sadly astray in his morality if he assumed that his own first judgments of right and wrong are infallible. He needs to learn "sound judgment in all things" by a training which puts him in possession of the moral tradition of a high-minded society, and by comparing his own judgment in cases of perplexity with that of men of high character, ripe reflection, and rich knowledge of life. (This is why, though without conscientiousness there can be no true moral goodness, the faddist, who insists on treating his own "private" conscience as infallible, is a mere moral nuisance.)

We may readily admit, then, that much which the experiencer is inclined to take for "religious" experience is illusion. He may mistake the vague stirrings and impulses of sex, or aesthetic sensibility, or even pure illusions of sense or perception, for the self-revelation of the divine, just as any of us may, in favorable conditions, mistake what he has merely dreamed of for an event of waking life. And such confusions may very well lie at the bottom of widespread aberrations; they may account very largely for the puerility of many of the "religious" beliefs of mankind, and the lewd or bloody practices which defile so many of our ritual cults. And we must insist that if there are specific and unique religious experiences, they must not all be taken "at their face-value"; like all other alleged experiences they stand in need of "interpretation" in the light of the judgment of the "expert" who is at once keenly sensible of the actual "experience," and has brought a tried and sane judgment to bear upon it.[2] We thus find ourselves face to face with a second question, and we have to ask (a) are there specific *data* which furnish the basis for a "religious" interpretation of life, and (b) if there are, who are the "experts" whose interpretation of the *data* should guide the interpretation?

(a) As to the first question. It has, as we all know, been denied that there are any specific data to furnish such an interpretation with its starting-point. The supposed *data* have been explained away, now as ordinary physical facts misunderstood by the curious but ignorant savage, now as emotional reactions to dreams, fear of the dark or of lonely places, now as vague emotional reactions attendant on the different sexual modifications characteristic of adolescence, and in other ways. The question is whether *all* the known facts can be disposed of without remainder in this fashion. *A priori* we have no right to assume that this can be done. It may be true, for example, that "conversions" are more common at or shortly after the reaching of puberty than at any other time of life. It is equally true that the same period is often marked by the sudden appearance of other new interests or the sudden intensification of old ones. Thus a boy often suddenly develops a vivid interest in literature, or a new sensitiveness to art, in the years of dawning manhood. Clearly this does not prove that the qualities we admire in literary style or in painting or music are not really there, but only supposed to be there in virtue of an illusion of sexuality. *A priori* it is just as likely that the effect of a crisis which affects our whole bodily and mental life should be to awaken a heightened perception of a reality previously veiled from our eyes, as to create the "illusion" of a reality which is not there. The experiences of adolescence may be, as a matter of my private history, the occasion of my first discovery of beauties in Keats or Chopin which I do not find in the ordinary rhymester or manufacturer of "music" for the piano. But how does this prove that in reality the poetry of Keats does not differ from that of writers for the provincial newspaper, or the music of Chopin from the average waltz or polka? The problem is not how I came to make a certain "find," but what the worth of the "find" may be.

So with the part played by fear of the dark or of desert solitudes in creating beliefs in gods. The real question is not whether emotions of this kind may not have influenced men's religious emotions and beliefs, but whether the emotions and beliefs, however they may have been developed, *contain* nothing more than such fears or contain something else which is quite specific, just as musical perception may be prompted or quickened by adolescence but certainly, *when once it is there,* contains a quite specific core or kernel of its own. However our sensibility to music began, it is quite certain that what we perceive when we appreciate it is nothing sexual. There are, I honestly believe, men who only respond to the appeal of music so far as it, crudely or subtly, is made to sexual feeling, but such men are the typically "unmusical." What they value is not musical beauty itself, but a mass of suggestions which have to be got rid of before one can begin to appreciate "pure" music at all, exactly as one has to get rid of the tendency to demand that a picture shall "tell a story" before one can begin to understand the values of color, line, disposal of light and shade. We have also to be on our guard against the standing "psychologist's fallacy" which no one has done more to expose than Dr. Otto in the work to which reference has already been made.[3] It is too often assumed that because there is an *analogy* between our mental attitude towards an object of our adoration and our attitude towards something we fear, or something which attracts us sexually, the two attitudes must be the same. Thus our reverence for the God we worship is in some ways like our dread of a strange and powerful natural object; our love for God is in some ways like the feelings of a devoted human lover, as the language of religious devotion is enough to prove. But it does not in the least follow that the likeness is more than a likeness; it is still perfectly possible that even the rudest savage's attitude in the presence of that which he "worships" has a character of its own quite distinct, e.g., from his mere fear of a formidable beast or of the dangers of the dark. Since language has been primarily adapted to express our attitude towards "things of this world," when we want to speak of our attitude in the presence of our *numina* we have to make shift, as best we can, with words which properly designate an analogous but different attitude. The psychologist and anthropologist are only too apt to take these makeshift expressions *au pied de la lettre*; because we have to say that we "fear" or "love" God, they assume that we mean no more than when we say that we are afraid of an angry bull or that we love a young lady. Thus the specifically "religious" character of certain experiences, if it is really there, eludes them because they have not taken Bacon's warning against the *idola fori* [idols of the market place] which arises from excessive belief in the adequacy of language. They have not understood that the name of GOD is necessarily the "ineffable" name.

That civilized men, in the presence of anything they take as divine, have this sense of being face to face with the "ineffable" is quite certain, and we can see by reading the cruder utterances of the uncivilized in the light of what has grown out of them that they too must have it. It is the great service of Dr. Otto to the philosophy of religion that he has worked out this line of thought in full detail in his careful analysis of the meanings of "holy" and corresponding words, as revealed by the historical study of language and literature. The main point to be made is that, as far back as we can trace the beginnings of religion, the "holy," even if it is no more than an oddly shaped stone, does not simply mean the strange or the formidable; it means, at the lowest, the "uncanny," and the "uncanny" is precisely that which does not simply belong to "this" everyday world, but directly impresses us as manifesting in some special way the presence of "the other" world. As such, it repels and attracts at once, is at once the awful and the worshipful, but above all in both aspects the absolutely transcendent and "*other*-worldly." At different levels of spiritual development the object which awakens this special sense of being in the presence of the "absolutely transcendent" may be very different. A low savage may feel it in the presence of what to us is simply a quaintly shaped stone or a queer-looking hill; the prophet feels it, and is crushed by the sense of its transcendent "otherness," in his vision of the Lord of hosts; the disciples of Christ feel it in the presence of a living man, who is also their friend and teacher, when we read of Him that "he was going before them on the road and they were *astounded* (ἐθαμβοῦντο), and as they followed they were *terrified* (ἐφοβοῦντο)" (Mark 10:32). It is precisely the same feeling which has prompted, e.g., the utterance of the words of institution in the Eucharist *sotto voce*, and inspired the old Eucharistic hymn σιδησάτω πᾶσα σὰρξ βροτεια ["let all mortal flesh be silent"],[4] as well as the modern saying that if Shakespeare came into the room we should all stand up, but if Jesus Christ came into the room we should all kneel down. It is equally the same sense of being in the presence of the wholly "other-worldly" which finds expression in such an exclamation as the prophet's "Woe is me for I am unclean, for mine eyes have seen the Lord of hosts," or St. Peter's "Depart from me, for I am a sinful man." We should quite misunderstand such language if we read it as a confession of any special wrongdoing on the part of prophet or apostle. It is the universal voice of the mutable and temporal brought face to face with the absolutely eternal; hence in Scripture even the sinless seraphim are said to "veil their faces" as they stand before their Lord. This, again, is why it has been the belief of all peoples that he who sees a god dies.

As nearly as we can express our attitude towards that which awakens this sense of being immediately in the presence of the "other-worldly" by any one word, we may say that it is the attitude of "worship." But even here we need to remember the inadequacy of language. In our own Marriage Office the bridegroom speaks of "worshipping" the bride; a mayor or a police magistrate is to this day officially "his worship." The word *worship,* like all other words, is really hopelessly inadequate to express the attitude a man experiences in the presence of what he feels to be the "absolutely other" made directly manifest. (We do not say anything, we are simply silent when we kneel at the *Incarnatus Est.*) Yet it is hard to believe that the most sceptical among us does not know the experience. There are those to whom it is present as a constant experience during their lives, and those to whom it comes but seldom; there are those who bestow their "worship" on inadequate objects, like the man who "worships" his money or his mistress. But it is as doubtful whether there is really any man who has never worshipped anything as it is doubtful whether there is any man who has never feared or never loved. The experience moreover seems to be specially characteristic of man; as the Greeks said, "Man is the only animal who has gods." (Possibly indeed, the attitude of some dogs to their masters may offer a remote analogy, but we must remember that these are dogs who have been brought up by man and become at any rate distantly humanized by the process. There is no reason to think that "Yellow Dog Dingo" could ever have developed in this way.)

And again, there can be little doubt that the men in whom the spirit of true worship has been most constantly present are they who show us human nature at its best. It is the "brutalized" man who is marked by the temper of habitual irreverence. Even if we judge of men solely by what they have effected in the way of "social reform," history seems to show that the men who have achieved most for the service of man in this world are men whose hearts have been set on something which is not of this world; "the advance of civilization is in truth a sort of by-product of Christianity, not its chief aim."[5] We may reasonably draw the conclusion that religion is just as much a unique characteristic and interest of humanity as love of truth, love of beauty, love of country, and that the saint's "experience" is no more to be dismissed as an illusion than the thinker's, the artist's, or the patriot's.

(b) Of course, like all other immediate experiences, the peculiar experience of the immediate presence of the divine requires interpretation and criticism. A man may be moved to adoration by an unworthy and inadequate object, like the heathen who "in his blindness, bows down to wood and stone," or the lover who lavishes his spiritual treasure on a light woman. Religion is not proved to be an illusion by its aberrations, any more than science by the labor wasted on squaring the circle or seeking the elixir and the philosopher's stone, or love by the havoc it makes of life when it is foolishly bestowed. The sane judgment of reflection is required to direct and correct all our human activities. We are neither to suppose that there is no way to God because some ways which have been found promising at first have led astray, nor yet that because there is a way, any way that mankind have tried must be as good a road to the goal as any other. We may freely assert that even the most puerile and odious "religions" have had their value; they have this much at least of worth about them that those who have practiced them have been right in their conviction that the "other-world" is really there to be sought for. But to draw the conclusion that "all religions are equally good," or even, like the "Theosophists," that at any rate every religion is the best for those who practice it, and that we are not to carry the Gospel to the heathen because they are not at a level to appreciate it, is like arguing that all supposed "science" is equally good, or that we ought to abstain from teaching the elements of natural science to a Hindu because his own traditional notions about astronomy and geography are "the best he is capable of." Views of this kind rest in the end on an absurd personal self-conceit, and a denial of our common humanity. A true religion, like a true science, is not the monopoly of a little aristocracy of superior persons; it is for everyone. We may not be able to teach the mass, even of our own fellow-countrymen, more than the first elements of any science, but we must see to it that what we do teach them is as true as we can make it. And so even more with religion, because of its direct relation with the whole conduct of life. A savage may be capable only of very elementary notions about God and the unseen world, but at least we can see to it that the ideas he has are not defiled by cruelty or lewdness. Not to say that you never know how far the capacity of *any* mind for receiving true ideas extends, until you have tried it. The "Theosophist" usually claims to show a broad-minded humanity, which he contrasts complacently with the "narrowness" of the Christian who wishes all mankind to share his faith. But he belies his own profession the moment he begins his habitual disparagement of the missionary. To say that in religion, or in any other department of life, the vile or foolish is good enough for your neighbor is the arrogance of the half-educated. The neighbor whom we are to love as ourselves deserves at our hands the best we can possibly bring him.

The point I chiefly want to make, however, is that the specific experience of contact with the divine not only needs interpretation, like all other experience, but that, though it is the directest way of access to the "wholly other," it is not the only way. If we are to reach God in this life, so far as it is permitted, we need to integrate the "religious experience" with the suggestions conveyed to us by the knowledge of Nature and of our own being. It seems clear that in its crudest manifestations the experience of this direct contact is not specifically connected with superiority in knowledge or in moral character. At a sufficiently low level of intelligence we find the idiot regarded as God-possessed in virtue of his very idiocy. (He is supposed to be in touch with the transcendent "other" because he is so manifestly out of touch with our "this-world" daily life.)[6] And the "holy men" of barbaric peoples are very seldom men who show anything we should call moral superiority over their neighbors. Even among ourselves it is often the simple and ignorant who make on us the impression of spending their lives most in the sense of God's presence, and again the men who show themselves most keenly sensitive to "religious impressions" are by no means always among the most faultless. Indeed, "moral excellence" itself, without humility, seems only too often to close the soul's eye to the eternal. A self-absorbed prig is in deeper spiritual blindness than many an open sinner. But if we would look at the Lord "all at once," we must of course integrate the glimpses we get in our moments of direct adoring contact with all that Nature and Morality suggest of the abiding source of them both. In particular, we need to have the conception of the "holy," as the object of adoration, transformed in such a way that it is fragrant with moral import before "Be ye holy because I am holy" can become the supreme directing note for the conduct of life. In principle this work of integrating our experience has been already accomplished for us by Christianity, with its double inheritance from the Jewish prophets and the Greek philosophers who freed their "reasonable worship" from entanglement in the follies and foulnesses of the old "nature-religions." But the root of the old errors is in every one of us; we cannot enter into the highest religious experience available to us except by a perpetual fresh interpretation of the given for ourselves. We may have Moses and the prophets and Paul and the evangelists, and yet, without personal watching unto prayer, all this will not avail to ensure that we shall think Christianly of the unseen, or that our sense of its reality will of itself lead us to a noble life rich in good works. And this answers for us the question "Who are the experts?" The true "expert critic" of the constructions and hypotheses of science is the man who has already learned what the men of science have to teach him. The true expert critic of the painter or the musician must first have learned to see with the painter's eye and hear with the musician's ear. Without this qualification, mere acuteness and ingenuity are wasted. In the end, all effectual criticism must be of what a man has first seen and felt for himself. So the verdict on the religious life if it is to count must come from the men who have first made it their own by living it. Only they can tell "how much there is in it."

NOTES

[1] From *Essays Catholic and Critical,* edited by Edward Gordon Selwyn (London: The Society for Promoting Christian Knowledge; New York: The Macmillan Company, 1926), pp. 70-80.

[2] This sort of interpretation is needed even for sense-perception. Any one who has, e.g., ever used a microscope must remember how he had at first to learn to "see" with it. At first the beginner does not "see" what his teacher says is there to be seen, or (*experto crede*) he "sees" a great deal that is not there. I can vividly recollect the trouble I had in this matter when first shown sections of the spinal medulla under the microscope. Cp. again the sharp disputes of astronomers about many of the markings which some of them claim to have "seen" on the disc of Mars.
—Taylor.

[3] Rudolf Otto. *The Idea of the Holy*, trans. by J. W. Harvey (London: Oxford University Press, 1923).

[4] *See* the working out of this thought in Otto, *op. cit.*, chap. xiv., pp. 159ff.—Taylor.

[5] W. R. Inge, *Personal Religion and the Life of Devotion*, p. 84; *cf. ibid.* pp. 59-60. A careful study of the debt of "civilisation" to St. Francis would afford an admirable illustration. No one in the course of many centuries has done more for "civilisation"; no one, probably, ever thought less about it.—Taylor.

[6] *Cf.* Wordsworth's application to idiots of the words "Their life is hid with Christ in God."—Taylor.

2

Discussions
and
Questionings

A Debate on the Existence of God

BERTRAND RUSSELL and F. C. COPLESTON

Bertrand Russell, O.M., F.R.S. (1872-), third Earl Russell, probably the greatest living British philosopher, and author of works too numerous to list here, has long been an outspoken critic both of Christian belief and of Christian practice. Some of his writings on these topics are collected in *Why I Am Not a Christian* (London, George Allen & Unwin Ltd., 1957), from which the following debate is reprinted. The debate was originally broadcast by the British Broadcasting Corporation in 1948. For biographical note on Father Copleston, see p. 86 of this volume.

❋

The Existence of God

COPLESTON: As we are going to discuss the existence of God, it might perhaps be as well to come to some provisional agreement as to what we understand by the term "God." I presume that we mean a supreme personal being—distinct from the world and creator of the world. Would you agree—provisionally at least—to accept this statement as the meaning of the term "God"?

RUSSELL: Yes, I accept this definition.

COPLESTON: Well, my position is the affirmative position that such a being actually exists, and that His existence can be proved philosophically. Perhaps you would tell me if your position is that of agnosticism or of atheism. I mean, would you say that the non-existence of God can be proved?

RUSSELL: No, I should not say that: my position is agnostic.

COPLESTON: Would you agree with me that the problem of God is a problem of great importance? For example, would you agree that if God does not exist, human beings and human history can have no other purpose than the purpose they choose to give themselves, which—in practice—is likely to mean the purpose which those impose who have the power to impose it?

RUSSELL: Roughly speaking, yes, though I should have to place some limitation on your last clause.

COPLESTON: Would you agree that if there is no God—no absolute Being—there can be no absolute values? I mean, would you agree that if there is no absolute good that the relativity of values results?

RUSSELL: No, I think these questions are logically distinct. Take, for instance, G. E. Moore's *Principia Ethica,* where he maintains that there is a distinction of good and evil, that both of these are definite concepts. But he does not bring in the idea of God to support that contention.

COPLESTON: Well, suppose we leave the question of good till later, till we come to the moral argument, and I give first a metaphysical argument. I'd like to put the main weight on the metaphysical argument based on Leibniz's argument from "Contingency" and then later we might discuss the moral argument. Suppose I give a brief statement on the metaphysical argument and that then we go on to discuss it?

RUSSELL: That seems to me to be a very good plan.

THE ARGUMENT FROM CONTINGENCY

COPLESTON: Well, for clarity's sake, I'll divide the argument into distinct stages. First of all, I should say, we know that there are at least some beings in the world which do not contain in themselves the reason for their existence. For example, I depend on my parents, and now on the air, and on food, and so on. Now, secondly, the world is simply the real or imagined totality or aggregate of individual objects, none of which contain in themselves alone the reason for their existence. There isn't any world distinct from the objects which form it, any more than the human race is something apart from the members. Therefore, I should say, since objects or events exist, and since no object of experience contains within itself the reason of its existence, this reason, the totality of objects, must have a reason external to itself.

That reason must be an existent being. Well, this being is either itself the reason for its own existence, or it is not. If it is, well and good. If it is not, then we must proceed farther. But if we proceed to infinity in that sense, then there's no explanation of existence at all. So, I should say, in order to explain existence, we must come to a being which contains within itself the reason for its own existence, that is to say, which cannot not-exist.

RUSSELL: This raises a great many points and it is not altogether easy to know where to begin, but I think that, perhaps, in answering your argument, the best point at which to begin is the question of necessary being. The word "necessary" I should maintain, can only be applied significantly to propositions. And, in fact, only to such as are analytic—that is to say—such as it is self-contradictory to deny. I could only admit a necessary being if there were a being whose existence it is self-contradictory to deny. I should like to know whether you would accept Leibniz's division of propositions into truths of reason and truths of fact. The former— the truths of reason—being necessary.

COPLESTON: Well, I certainly should not subscribe to what seems to be Leibniz's idea of truths of reason and truths of fact, since it would appear that, for him, there are in the long run only analytic propositions. It would seem that for Leibniz truths of fact are ultimately reducible to truths of reason. That is to say, to analytic propositions, at least for an omniscient mind. Well, I couldn't agree with that. For one thing, it would fail to meet the requirements of the experience of freedom. I don't want to uphold the whole philosophy of Leibniz. I have made use of his argument from contingent to necessary being, basing the argument on the principle of sufficient reason, simply because it seems to me a brief and clear formulation of what is, in my opinion, the fundamental metaphysical argument for God's existence.

RUSSELL: But, to my mind, "a necessary proposition" has got to be analytic. I don't see what else it can mean. And analytic propositions are always complex and logically somewhat late. "Irrational animals are animals" is an analytic proposition; but a proposition such as "This is an animal" can never be analytic. In fact, all the propositions that can be analytic are somewhat late in the build-up of propositions.

COPLESTON: Take the proposition "If there is a contingent being then there is a necessary being." I consider that that proposition hypothetically expressed is a necessary proposition. If you are going to call every necessary proposition an analytic proposition, then—in order to avoid a dispute in terminology—I would agree to call it analytic, though I don't consider it a tautological proposition. But the proposition is a necessary proposition only on the supposition that there is a contingent being. That there is a contingent being actually existing has to be discovered by experience, and the proposition that there is a contingent being is certainly not an analytic proposition, though once you know, I should maintain, that there is a contingent being, it follows of necessity that there is a necessary being.

RUSSELL: The difficulty of this argument is that I don't admit the idea of a necessary being and I don't admit that there is any particular meaning in calling other beings "contingent." These phrases don't for me have a significance except within a logic that I reject.

COPLESTON: Do you mean that you reject these terms because they won't fit in with what is called "modern logic"?

RUSSELL: Well, I can't find anything that they could mean. The word "necessary," it seems to me, is a useless word, except as applied to analytic propositions, not to things.

COPLESTON: In the first place, what do you mean by "modern logic"? As far as I know, there are somewhat differing systems. In the second place, not all modern logicians surely would admit the meaninglessness of metaphysics. We both know, at any rate, one very eminent modern thinker whose knowledge of modern logic was profound, but who certainly did not think that metaphysics are meaningless or, in particular, that the problem of God is meaningless. Again, even if all modern logicians held that metaphysical terms are meaningless, it would not follow that they were right. The proposition that metaphysical terms are meaningless seems to me to be a proposition based on an assumed philosophy. The dogmatic position behind it seems to be this: What will not go into my machine is non-existent, or it is meaningless; it is the expression of emotion. I am simply trying to point out that anybody who says that a particular system of modern logic is the sole criterion of meaning is saying something that is over dogmatic; he is dogmatically insisting that a part of philosophy is the whole of philosophy. After all, a "contingent" being is a being which has not in itself the complete reason for its existence, that's what I mean by a contingent being. You know, as well as I do, that the existence of neither of us can be explained without reference to something or somebody outside us, our parents, for example. A "necessary" being, on the other hand, means a being that must and cannot not-exist. You may say that there is no such being, but you will find it hard to convince me that you do not understand the terms I am using. If you do not understand them, then how can you be entitled to say that such a being does not exist, if that is what you do say?

RUSSELL: Well, there are points here that I don't propose to go into at length. I don't maintain the meaninglessness of metaphysics in general at all. I maintain the meaninglessness of certain particular terms—not on any general ground, but simply because I've not been able to see an interpretation of those particular terms. It's not a general dogma—it's a particular thing. But those points I will leave out for the moment. And I will say that what you have been saying brings us back, it seems to me, to the ontological argument that there is a being whose essence involves existence, so that his existence is analytic. That seems to me to be impossible, and it raises, of course, the question what one means by existence, and as to this, I think a subject named can never be significantly said to exist but only a subject described. And that existence, in fact, quite definitely is not a predicate.

COPLESTON: Well, you say, I believe, that is bad grammar, or rather bad syntax to say, for example, "T. S. Eliot exists"; one ought to say, for example, "He, the author of *Murder in the Cathedral*, exists." Are you going to say that the proposition, "The cause of the world exists," is without meaning? You may say that the world has no cause; but I fail to see how you can say that the proposition that "the cause of the world exists" is meaningless. Put it in the form of a question: "Has the world a cause?" or "Does a cause of the world exist?" Most people surely would understand the question, even if they don't agree about the answer.

RUSSELL: Well, certainly the question "Does the cause of the world exist?" is a question that has meaning. But if you say "Yes, God is the cause of the world" you're using God as a proper name; then "God exists" will not be a statement that has meaning; that is the position that I'm maintaining. Because, therefore, it will follow that it cannot be an analytic proposition ever to say that this or that exists. For example, suppose you take as your subject "the existent round-square," it would look like an analytic proposition that "the existent round-square exists," but it doesn't exist.

COPLESTON: No, it doesn't, then surely you can't say it doesn't exist unless you have a conception of what existence is. As to the phrase "existent round-square," I should say that it has no meaning at all.

RUSSELL: I quite agree. Then I should say the same thing in another context in reference to a "necessary being."

COPLESTON: Well, we seem to have arrived at an impasse. To say that a necessary being is a being that must exist and cannot not-exist has for me a definite meaning. For you it has no meaning.

RUSSELL: Well, we can press the point a little, I think. A being that must exist and cannot not-exist, would surely, according to you, be a being whose essence involves existence.

COPLESTON: Yes, a being the essence of which is to exist. But I should not be willing to argue the existence of God simply from the idea of His essence because I don't think we have any clear intuition of God's essence as yet. I think we have to argue from the world of experience to God.

RUSSELL: Yes, I quite see the distinction. But, at the same time, for a being with sufficient knowledge it would be true to say "Here is this being whose essence involves existence!"

COPLESTON: Yes, certainly if anybody saw God, he would see that God must exist.

RUSSELL: So that I mean there is a being whose essence

involves existence although we don't know that essence. We only know there is such a being.

COPLESTON: Yes, I should add we don't know the essence *a priori*. It is only *a posteriori* through our experience of the world that we come to a knowledge of the existence of that being. And then one argues, the essence and existence must be identical. Because if God's essence and God's existence were not identical, then some sufficient reason for this existence would have to be found beyond God.

RUSSELL: So it all turns on this question of sufficient reason, and I must say you haven't defined "sufficient reason" in a way that I can understand—what do you mean by sufficient reason? You don't mean cause?

COPLESTON: Not necessarily. Cause is a kind of sufficient reason. Only contingent being can have a cause. God is His own sufficient reason; and He is not cause of Himself. By sufficient reason in the full sense I mean an explanation adequate for the existence of some particular being.

RUSSELL: But when is an explanation adequate? Suppose I am about to make a flame with a match. You may say that the adequate explanation of that is that I rub it on the box.

COPLESTON: Well, for practical purposes—but theoretically, that is only a partial explanation. An adequate explanation must ultimately be a total explanation, to which nothing further can be added.

RUSSELL: Then I can only say that you're looking for something which can't be got, and which one ought not to expect to get.

COPLESTON: To say that one has not found it is one thing; to say that one should not look for it seems to me rather dogmatic.

RUSSELL: Well, I don't know. I mean, the explanation of one thing is another thing which makes the other thing dependent on yet another, and you have to grasp this sorry scheme of things entire to do what you want, and that we can't do.

COPLESTON: But are you going to say that we can't, or we shouldn't even raise the question of the existence of the whole of this sorry scheme of things—of the whole universe?

RUSSELL: Yes. I don't think there's any meaning in it at all. I think the word "universe" is a handy word in some connections, but I don't think it stands for anything that has a meaning.

COPLESTON: If the word is meaningless, it can't be so very handy. In any case, I don't say that the universe is something different from the objects which compose it (I indicated that in my brief summary of the proof), what I'm doing is to look for the reason, in this case the cause of the objects—the real or imagined totality of which constitute what we call the universe. You say, I think, that the universe—or my existence if you prefer, or any other existence—is unintelligible?

RUSSELL: First may I take up the point that if a word is meaningless it can't be handy. That sounds well but isn't in fact correct. Take, say, such a word as "the" or "than." You can't point to any object that those words mean, but they are very useful words; I should say the same of "universe." But leaving that point, you ask whether I consider that the universe is unintelligible. I shouldn't say unintelligible—I think it is without explanation. Intelligible, to my mind, is a different thing. Intelligible has to do with the thing itself intrinsically and not with its relations.

COPLESTON: Well, my point is that what we call the world is intrinsically unintelligible, apart from the existence of God. You see, I don't believe that the infinity of the series of events—I mean a horizontal series, so to speak—if such an infinity could be proved, would be in the slightest degree relevant to the situation. If you add up chocolates you get chocolates after all and not a sheep. If you add up chocolates to infinity, you presumably get an infinite number of chocolates. So if you add up contingent beings to infinity, you still get contingent beings, not a necessary being. An infinite series of contingent beings will be, to my way of thinking, as unable to cause itself as one contingent being. However, you say, I think, that it is illegitimate to raise the question of what will explain the existence of any particular object?

RUSSELL: It's quite all right if you mean by explaining it, simply finding a cause for it.

COPLESTON: Well, why stop at one particular object? Why

shouldn't one raise the question of the cause of the existence of all particular objects?

RUSSELL: Because I see no reason to think there is any. The whole concept of cause is one we derive from our observation of particular things; I see no reason whatsoever to suppose that the total has any cause whatsoever.

COPLESTON: Well, to say that there isn't any cause is not the same thing as saying that we shouldn't look for a cause. The statement that there isn't any cause should come, if it comes at all, at the end of the enquiry, not the beginning. In any case, if the total has no cause, then to my way of thinking it must be its own cause, which seems to me impossible. Moreover, the statement that the world is simply there if in answer to a question, presupposes that the question has meaning.

RUSSELL: No, it doesn't need to be its own cause, what I'm saying is that the concept of cause is not applicable to the total.

COPLESTON: Then you would agree with Sartre that the universe is what he calls "gratuitous"?

RUSSELL: Well, the word "gratuitous" suggests that it might be something else; I should say that the universe is just there, and that's all.

COPLESTON: Well, I can't see how you can rule out the legitimacy of asking the question how the total, or anything at all comes to be there. Why something rather than nothing, that is the question? The fact that we gain our knowledge of causality empirically, from particular causes, does not rule out the possibility of asking what the cause of the series is. If the word "cause" were meaningless or if it could be shown that Kant's view of the matter were correct, the question would be illegitimate I agree; but you don't seem to hold that the word "cause" is meaningless, and I do not suppose you are a Kantian.

RUSSELL: I can illustrate what seems to me your fallacy. Every man who exists has a mother, and it seems to me your argument is that therefore the human race must have a mother, but obviously the human race hasn't a mother— that's a different logical sphere.

COPLESTON: Well, I can't really see any parity. If I were

saying "every object has a phenomenal cause, therefore, the whole series has a phenomenal cause," there would be a parity; but I'm not saying that; I'm saying, every object has a phenomenal cause if you insist on the infinity of the series —but the series of phenomenal causes is an insufficient explanation of the series. Therefore, the series has not a phenomenal cause but a transcendent cause.

RUSSELL: That's always assuming that not only every particular thing in the world, but the world as a whole must have a cause. For that assumption I see no ground whatever. If you'll give me a ground I'll listen to it.

COPLESTON: Well, the series of events is either caused or it's not caused. If it is caused, there must obviously be a cause outside the series. If it's not caused then it's sufficient to itself, and if it's sufficient to itself it is what I call necessary. But it can't be necessary since each member is contingent, and we've agreed that the total is no reality apart from its members, therefore, it can't be necessary. Therefore, it can't be (caused)—uncaused—therefore it must have a cause. And I should like to observe in passing that the statement "the world is simply there and is inexplicable" can't be got out of logical analysis.

RUSSELL: I don't want to seem arrogant, but it does seem to me that I can conceive things that you say the human mind can't conceive. As for things not having a cause, the physicists assure us that individual quantum transition in atoms have no cause.

COPLESTON: Well, I wonder now whether that isn't simply a temporary inference.

RUSSELL: It may be, but it does show that physicists' minds can conceive it.

COPLESTON: Yes, I agree, some scientists—physicists—are willing to allow for indetermination within a restricted field. But very many scientists are not so willing. I think that Professor Dingle, of London University, maintains that the Heisenberg uncertainty principle tells us something about the success (or the lack of it) of the present atomic theory in correlating observations, but not about nature in itself, and many physicists would accept this view. In any case, I don't see how physicists can fail to accept the theory in practice, even if they don't do so in theory. I cannot see how science could be conducted on any other assumption than that of order and intelligibility in nature. The physicist presupposes, at least tacitly, that there is some sense in investigating nature and looking for the causes of events, just as the detective presupposes that there is some sense in looking for the cause of a murder. The metaphysician assumes that there is sense in looking for the reason or cause of phenomena, and, not being a Kantian, I consider that the metaphysician is as justified in his assumption as the physicist. When Sartre, for example, says that the world is gratuitous, I think that he has not sufficiently considered what is implied by "gratuitous."

RUSSELL: I think—there seems to me a certain unwarrantable extension here; a physicist looks for causes; that does not necessarily imply that there are causes everywhere. A man may look for gold without assuming that there is gold everywhere; if he finds gold, well and good, if he doesn't he's had bad luck. The same is true when the physicists look for causes. As for Sartre, I don't profess to know what he means, and I shouldn't like to be thought to interpret him, but for my part, I do think the notion of the world having an explanation is a mistake. I don't see why one should expect it to have, and I think what you say about what the scientist assumes is an over-statement.

COPLESTON: Well, it seems to me that the scientist does make some such assumption. When he experiments to find out some particular truth, behind that experiment lies the assumption that the universe is not simply discontinuous. There is the possibility of finding out a truth by experiment. The experiment may be a bad one, it may lead to no result, or not to the result that he wants, but that at any rate there is the possibility, through experiment, of finding out the truth that he assumes. And that seems to me to assume an ordered and intelligible universe.

RUSSELL: I think you're generalizing more than is necessary. Undoubtedly the scientist assumes that this sort of thing is likely to be found and will often be found. He does not assume that it will be found, and that's a very important matter in modern physics.

COPLESTON: Well, I think he does assume or is bound to

assume it tacitly in practice. It may be that, to quote Professor Haldane, "when I light the gas under the kettle, some of the water molecules will fly off as vapor, and there is no way of finding out which will do so," but it doesn't follow necessarily that the idea of chance must be introduced except in relation to our knowledge.

RUSSELL: No it doesn't—at least if I may believe what he says. He's finding out quite a lot of things—the scientist is finding out quite a lot of things that are happening in the world, which are, at first, beginnings of causal chains—first causes which haven't in themselves got causes. He does not assume that everything has a cause.

COPLESTON: Surely that's a first cause within a certain selected field. It's a relatively first cause.

RUSSELL: I don't think he'd say so. If there's a world in which most events, but not all, have causes, he will then be able to depict the probabilities and uncertainties by assuming that this particular event you're interested in probably has a cause. And since in any case you won't get more than probability that's good enough.

COPLESTON: It may be that the scientist doesn't hope to obtain more than probability, but in raising the question he assumes that the question of explanation has a meaning. But your general point then, Lord Russell, is that it's illegitimate even to ask the question of the cause of the world?

RUSSELL: Yes, that's my position.

COPLESTON: If it's a question that for you has no meaning, it's of course very difficult to discuss it, isn't it?

RUSSELL: Yes, it is very difficult. What do you say—shall we pass on to some other issue?

RELIGIOUS EXPERIENCE

COPLESTON: Let's. Well, perhaps I might say a word about religious experience, and then we can go on to moral experience. I don't regard religious experience as a strict proof of the existence of God, so the character of the discussion changes somewhat, but I think it's true to say that the best explanation of it is the existence of God. By religious experience I don't mean simply feeling good. I mean a loving, but unclear, awareness of some object which irresistibly seems to the experiencer as something transcending the self, something transcending all the normal objects of experience, something which cannot be pictured or conceptualized, but of the reality of which doubt is impossible—at least during the experience. I should claim that cannot be explained adequately and without residue, simply subjectively. The actual basic experience at any rate is most easily explained on the hypotheses that there is actually some objective cause of that experience.

RUSSELL: I should reply to that line of argument that the whole argument from our own mental states to something outside us, is a very tricky affair. Even where we all admit its validity, we only feel justified in doing so, I think, because of the consensus of mankind. If there's a crowd in a room and there's a clock in a room, they can all see the clock. The fact that they can all see it tends to make them think that it's not an hallucination: whereas these religious experiences do tend to be very private.

COPLESTON: Yes, they do. I'm speaking strictly of mystical experience proper, and I certainly don't include, by the way, what are called visions. I mean simply the experience, and I quite admit it's indefinable, of the transcendent object or of what seems to be a transcendent object. I remember Julian Huxley in some lecture saying that religious experience, or mystical experience, is as much a real experience as falling in love or appreciating poetry and art. Well, I believe that when we appreciate poetry and art we appreciate definite poems or a definite work of art. If we fall in love, well, we fall in love with somebody and not with nobody.

RUSSELL: May I interrupt for a moment here. That is by no means always the case. Japanese novelists never consider that they have achieved a success unless large numbers of real people commit suicide for love of the imaginary heroine.

COPLESTON: Well, I must take your word for these goings on in Japan. I haven't committed suicide, I'm glad to say, but I have been strongly influenced in the taking of two important steps in my life by two biographies. However, I must say I see little resemblance between the real influence of those books on me and the mystic experience proper, so far, that is, as an outsider can obtain an idea of that experience.

RUSSELL: Well, I mean we wouldn't regard God as being on the same level as the characters in a work of fiction. You'll admit there's a distinction here?

COPLESTON: I certainly should. But what I'd say is that the best explanation seems to be the not purely subjectivist explanation. Of course, a subjectivist explanation is possible in the case of certain people in whom there is little relation between the experience and life, in the case of deluded people and hallucinated people, and so on. But when you get what one might call the pure type, say St. Francis of Assisi, when you get an experience that results in an overflow of dynamic and creative love, the best explanation of that it seems to me is the actual existence of an objective cause of the experience.

RUSSELL: Well, I'm not contending in a dogmatic way that there is not a God. What I'm contending is that we don't know that there is. I can only take what is recorded as I should take other records and I do find that a very great many things are reported, and I am sure you would not accept things about demons and devils and what not—and they're reported in exactly the same tone of voice and with exactly the same conviction. And the mystic, if his vision is veridical, may be said to know that there are devils. But I don't know that there are.

COPLESTON: But surely in the case of the devils there have been people speaking mainly of visions, appearances, angels or demons and so on. I should rule out the visual appearances, because I think they can be explained apart from the existence of the object which is supposed to be seen.

RUSSELL: But don't you think there are abundant recorded cases of people who believe that they've heard Satan speaking to them in their hearts, in just the same way as the mystics assert God—and I'm not talking now of an external vision, I'm talking of a purely mental experience. That seems to be an experience of the same sort as mystics' experience of God, and I don't see that from what mystics tell us you can get any argument for God which is not equally an argument for Satan.

COPLESTON: I quite agree, of course, that people have imagined or thought they have heard or seen Satan. And I have no wish in passing to deny the existence of Satan. But I do not think that people have claimed to have experienced Satan in the precise way in which mystics claim to have experienced God. Take the case of a non-Christian, Plotinus. He admits the experience is something inexpressible, the object is an object of love, and therefore, not an object that causes horror and disgust. And the effect of that experience is, I should say, borne out, or I mean the validity of the experience is borne out in the records of the life of Plotinus. At any rate it is more reasonable to suppose that he had that experience if we're willing to accept Porphyry's account of Plotinus's general kindness and benevolence.

RUSSELL: The fact that a belief has a good moral effect upon a man is no evidence whatsoever in favor of its truth.

COPLESTON: No, but if it could actually be proved that the belief was actually responsible for a good effect on a man's life, I should consider it a presumption in favor of some truth, at any rate of the positive part of the belief not of its entire validity. But in any case I am using the character of the life as evidence in favor of the mystic's veracity and sanity rather than as a proof of the truth of his beliefs.

RUSSELL: But even that I don't think is any evidence. I've had experiences myself that have altered my character profoundly. And I thought at the time at any rate that it was altered for the good. Those experiences were important, but they did not involve the existence of something outside me, and I don't think that if I'd thought they did, the fact that they had a wholesome effect would have been any evidence that I was right.

COPLESTON: No, but I think that the good effect would attest your veracity in describing your experience. Please remember that I'm not saying that a mystic's mediation or interpretation of his experience should be immune from discussion or criticism.

RUSSELL: Obviously the character of a young man may be— and often is—immensely affected for good by reading about some great man in history, and it may happen that the great man is a myth and doesn't exist, but the boy is just as much affected for good as if he did. There have been such people. Plutarch's *Lives* take Lycurgus as an example, who certainly did not exist, but you might be very much influenced by reading Lycurgus under the impression that he had previously existed. You would then be influenced by an object that you'd loved, but it wouldn't be an existing object.

COPLESTON: I agree with you on that, of course, that a man may be influenced by a character in fiction. Without going into the question of what it is precisely that influences him (I should say a real value) I think that the situation of that man and of the mystic are different. After all the man who is influenced by Lycurgus hasn't got the irresistible impression that he's experienced in some way the ultimate reality.

RUSSELL: I don't think you've quite got my point about these historical characters—these unhistorical characters in history. I'm not assuming what you call an effect on the reason. I'm assuming that the young man reading about this person and believing him to be real loves him—which is quite easy to happen, and yet he's loving a phantom.

COPLESTON: In one sense he's loving a phantom that's perfectly true, in the sense, I mean, that he's loving X or Y who doesn't exist. But at the same time, it is not, I think, the phantom as such that the young man loves; he perceives a real value, an idea which he recognizes as objectively valid, and that's what excites his love.

RUSSELL: Well, in the same sense we had before about the characters in fiction.

COPLESTON: Yes, in one sense the man's loving a phantom—perfectly true. But in another sense he's loving what he perceives to be a value.

THE MORAL ARGUMENT

RUSSELL: But aren't you now saying in effect, I mean by God whatever is good or the sum total of what is good—the system of what is good, and, therefore, when a young man loves anything that is good he is loving God. Is that what you're saying, because if so, it wants a bit of arguing.

COPLESTON: I don't say, of course, that God is the sum-total or system of what is good in the pantheistic sense; I'm not a pantheist, but I do think that all goodness reflects God in some way and proceeds from Him, so that in a sense the man who loves what is truly good, loves God even if he doesn't advert to God. But still I agree that the validity of such an interpretation of a man's conduct depends on the recognition of God's existence, obviously.

RUSSELL: Yes, but that's a point to be proved.

COPLESTON: Quite so, but I regard the metaphysical argument as probative, but there we differ.

RUSSELL: You see, I feel that some things are good and that other things are bad. I love the things that are good, that I think are good, and I hate the things that I think are bad. I don't say that these things are good because they participate in the Divine goodness.

COPLESTON: Yes, but what's your justification for distinguishing between good and bad or how do you view the distinction between them?

RUSSELL: I don't have any justification any more than I have when I distinguish between blue and yellow. What is my justification for distinguishing between blue and yellow? I can see they are different.

COPLESTON: Well, that is an excellent justification, I agree. You distinguish blue and yellow by seeing them, so you distinguish good and bad by what faculty?

RUSSELL: By my feelings.

COPLESTON: By your feelings. Well, that's what I was asking. You think that good and evil have reference simply to feeling?

RUSSELL: Well, why does one type of object look yellow and another look blue? I can more or less give an answer to that thanks to the physicists, and as to why I think one sort of thing good and another evil, probably there is an answer of the same sort, but it hasn't been gone into in the same way and I couldn't give it you.

COPLESTON: Well, let's take the behavior of the Commandant of Belsen. That appears to you as undesirable and evil and to me too. To Adolf Hitler we suppose it appeared as something good and desirable. I suppose you'd have to admit that for Hitler it was good and for you it is evil.

RUSSELL: No, I shouldn't quite go so far as that. I mean, I

think people can make mistakes in that as they can in other things. If you have jaundice you see things yellow that are not yellow. You're making a mistake.

COPLESTON: Yes, one can make mistakes, but can you make a mistake if it's simply a question of reference to a feeling or emotion? Surely Hitler would be the only possible judge of what appealed to his emotions.

RUSSELL: It would be quite right to say that it appealed to his emotions, but you can say various things about that among others, that if that sort of thing makes that sort of appeal to Hitler's emotions, then Hitler makes quite a different appeal to my emotions.

COPLESTON: Granted. But there's no objective criterion outside feeling then for condemning the conduct of the Commandant of Belsen, in your view?

RUSSELL: No more than there is for the color-blind person who's in exactly the same state. Why do we intellectually condemn the color-blind man? Isn't it because he's in the minority?

COPLESTON: I would say because he is lacking in a thing which normally belongs to human nature.

RUSSELL: Yes, but if he were in the majority, we shouldn't say that.

COPLESTON: Then you'd say that there's no criterion outside feeling that will enable one to distinguish between the behavior of the Commandant of Belsen and the behavior, say, of Sir Stafford Cripps or the Archbishop of Canterbury.

RUSSELL: The feeling is a little too simplified. You've got to take account of the effects of actions and your feelings towards those effects. You see, you can have an argument about it if you say that certain sorts of occurrences are the sort you like and certain others the sort you don't like. Then you have to take account of the effects of actions. You can very well say that the effects of the actions of the Commandant of Belsen were painful and unpleasant.

COPLESTON: They certainly were, I agree, very painful and unpleasant to all the people in the camp.

RUSSELL: Yes, but not only to the people in the camp, but to outsiders contemplating them also.

COPLESTON: Yes, quite true in imagination. But that's my point. I don't approve of them, and I know you don't approve of them, but I don't see what ground you have for not approving of them, because after all, to the Commandant of Belsen himself, they're pleasant, those actions.

RUSSELL: Yes, but you see I don't need any more ground in that case than I do in the case of color perception. There are some people who think everything is yellow, there are people suffering from jaundice, and I don't agree with these people. I can't prove that the things are not yellow, there isn't any proof, but most people agree with me that they're not yellow, and most people agree with me that the Commandant of Belsen was making mistakes.

COPLESTON: Well, do you accept any moral obligation?

RUSSELL: Well, I should have to answer at considerable length to answer that. Practically speaking—yes. Theoretically speaking I should have to define moral obligation rather carefully.

COPLESTON: Well, do you think that the word "ought" simply has an emotional connotation?

RUSSELL: No, I don't think that, because you see, as I was saying a moment ago, one has to take account of the effects, and I think right conduct is that which would probably produce the greatest possible balance in intrinsic value of all the acts possible in the circumstances, and you've got to take account of the probable effects of your action in considering what is right.

COPLESTON: Well, I brought in moral obligation because I think that one can approach the question of God's existence in that way. The vast majority of the human race will make, and always have made, some distinction between right and wrong. The vast majority I think has some consciousness of an obligation in the moral sphere. It's my opinion that the perception of values and the consciousness of moral law and obligation are best explained through the hypothesis of a transcendent ground of value and of an author of the moral law. I do mean by "author of the moral law" an arbitrary author of the moral law. I think, in fact, that those modern atheists who have argued in the converse way "there is no

God; therefore, there are no absolute values and no absolute law," are quite logical.

RUSSELL: I don't like the word "absolute." I don't think there is anything absolute whatever. The moral law, for example, is always changing. At one period in the development of the human race, almost everybody thought cannibalism was a duty.

COPLESTON: Well, I don't see that differences in particular moral judgments are any conclusive argument against the universality of the moral law. Let's assume for the moment that there are absolute moral values, even on that hypothesis it's only to be expected that different individuals and different groups should enjoy varying degrees of insight into those values.

RUSSELL: I'm inclined to think that "ought," the feeling that one has about "ought" is an echo of what has been told one by one's parents or one's nurses.

COPLESTON: Well, I wonder if you can explain away the idea of the "ought" merely in terms of nurses and parents. I really don't see how it can be conveyed to anybody in other terms than itself. It seems to me that if there is a moral order bearing upon the human conscience, that that moral order is unintelligible apart from the existence of God.

RUSSELL: Then you have to say one or other of two things. Either God only speaks to a very small percentage of mankind—which happens to include yourself—or He deliberately says things that are not true in talking to the consciences of savages.

COPLESTON: Well, you see, I'm not suggesting that God actually dictates moral precepts to the conscience. The human being's ideas of the content of the moral law depends certainly to a large extent on education and environment, and a man has to use his reason in assessing the validity of the actual moral ideas of his social group. But the possibility of criticising the accepted moral code presupposes that there is an objective standard, that there is an ideal moral order, which imposes itself (I mean the obligatory character of which can be recognized). I think that the recognition of this ideal moral order is part of the recognition of contingency. It implies the existence of a real foundation of God.

RUSSELL: But the law-giver has always been, it seems to me, one's parents or someone like. There are plenty of terrestrial law-givers to account for it, and that would explain why people's consciences are so amazingly different in different times and places.

COPLESTON: It helps to explain differences in the perception of particular moral values, which otherwise are inexplicable. It will help to explain changes in the matter of the moral law in the content of the precepts as accepted by this or that nation, or this or that individual. But the form of it, what Kant calls the categorical imperative, the "ought," I really don't see how that can possibly be conveyed to anybody by nurse or parent because there aren't any possible terms, so far as I can see, with which it can be explained. It can't be defined in other terms than itself, because once you've defined it in other terms than itself you've explained it away. It's no longer a moral "ought." It's something else.

RUSSELL: Well, I think the sense of "ought" is the effect of somebody's imagined disapproval, it may be God's imagined disapproval, but it's somebody's imagined disapproval. And I think that is what is meant by "ought."

COPLESTON: It seems to me to be external customs and taboos and things of that sort which can most easily be explained simply through environment and education, but all that seems to me to belong to what I call the matter of the law, the content. The idea of the "ought" as such can never be conveyed to a man by the tribal chief or by anybody else, because there are no other terms in which it could be conveyed. It seems to me entirely—[Russell breaks in].

RUSSELL: But I don't see any reason to say that—I mean we all know about conditioned reflexes. We know that an animal, if punished habitually for a certain sort of act, after a time will refrain. I don't think the animal refrains from arguing within himself, "Master will be angry if I do this." He has a feeling that that's not the thing to do. That's what we can do with ourselves and nothing more.

COPLESTON: I see no reason to suppose that an animal has

a consciousness of moral obligation; and we certainly don't regard an animal as morally responsible for his acts of disobedience. But a man has a consciousness of obligation and of moral values. I see no reason to suppose that one could condition all men as one can "condition" an animal, and I don't suppose you'd really want to do so even if one could. If "behaviorism" were true, there would be no objective moral distinction between the emperor Nero and St. Francis of Assisi. I can't help feeling, Lord Russell, you know, that you regard the conduct of the Commandant at Belsen as morally reprehensible, and that you yourself would never under any circumstances act in that way, even if you thought, or had reason to think, that possibly the balance of the happiness of the human race might be increased through some people being treated in that abominable manner.

RUSSELL: No. I wouldn't imitate the conduct of a mad dog. The fact that I wouldn't do it doesn't really bear on this question we're discussing.

COPLESTON: No, but if you were making a utilitarian explanation of right and wrong in terms of consequences, it might be held, and I suppose some of the Nazis of the better type would have held that although it's lamentable to have to act in this way, yet the balance in the long run leads to greater happiness. I don't think you'd say that, would you? I think you'd say that that sort of action is wrong—and in itself, quite apart from whether the general balance of happiness is increased or not. Then, if you're prepared to say that, then I think you must have some criterion of right and wrong, that is outside the criterion of feeling, at any rate. To me, that admission would ultimately result in the admission of an ultimate ground of value in God.

RUSSELL: I think we are perhaps getting into confusion. It is not direct feeling about the act by which I should judge, but rather a feeling as to the effects. And I can't admit any circumstances in which certain kinds of behavior, such as you have been discussing, would do good. I can't imagine circumstances in which they would have a beneficial effect. I think the persons who think they do are deceiving themselves. But if there were circumstances in which they would have a beneficial effect, then I might be obliged, however reluctantly, to say—"Well, I don't like these things, but I will acquiesce in them," just as I acquiesce in the Criminal Law, although I profoundly dislike punishment.

COPLESTON: Well, perhaps it's time I summed up my position. I've argued two things. First, that the existence of God can be philosophically proved by a metaphysical argument; secondly, that it is only the existence of God that will make sense of man's moral experience and of religious experience. Personally, I think that your way of accounting for man's moral judgments leads inevitably to a contradiction between what your theory demands and your own spontaneous judgments. Moreover, your theory explains moral obligation away, and explaining away is not explanation. As regards the metaphysical argument, we are apparently in agreement that what we call the world consists simply of contingent beings. That is, of beings no one of which can account for its own existence. You say that the series of events needs no explanation: I say that if there were no necessary being, no being which must exist and cannot not-exist, nothing would exist. The infinity of the series of contingent beings, even if proved, would be irrelevant. Something does exist; therefore, there must be something which accounts for this fact, a being which is outside the series of contingent beings. If you had admitted this, we could then have discussed whether that being is personal, good, and so on. On the actual point discussed, whether there is or is not a necessary being, I find myself, I think, in agreement with the great majority of classical philosophers.

You maintain, I think, that existing beings are simply there, and that I have no justification for raising the question of the explanation of their existence. But I would like to point out that this position cannot be substantiated by logical analysis; it expresses a philosophy which itself stands in need of proof. I think we have reached an impasse because our ideas of philosophy are radically different; it seems to me that what I call a part of philosophy, that you call the whole, insofar at least as philosophy is rational. It seems to me, if you will pardon my saying so, that besides your own logical system—which you call "modern" in opposition to antiquated logic (a tendentious adjective)—you maintain a philosophy which cannot be substantiated by logical analysis. After all, the problem of God's existence is an existential problem whereas logical analysis does not deal directly with problems of existence. So it seems to me, to declare that the terms involved in one set of problems are meaningless because they are not required in dealing with another set of problems, is to settle from the beginning the nature and extent of philosophy, and that is itself a philosophical act which stands in need of justification.

RUSSELL: Well, I should like to say just a few words by way of summary on my side. First, as to the metaphysical argument: I don't admit the connotations of such a term as "contingent" or the possibility of explanation in Father Copleston's sense. I think the word "contingent" inevitably suggests the possibility of something that wouldn't have this what you might call accidental character of just being there, and I don't think is true except in the purely causal sense. You can sometimes give a causal explanation of one thing as being the effect of something else, but that is merely referring one thing to another thing and there's no—to my mind—explanation in Father Copleston's sense of anything at all, nor is there any meaning in calling things "contingent" because there isn't anything else they could be. That's what I should say about that, but I should like to say a few words about Father Copleston's accusation that I regard logic as all philosophy—that is by no means the case. I don't by any means regard logic as all philosophy. I think logic is an essential part of philosophy and logic has to be used in philosophy, and in that I think he and I are at one. When the logic that he uses was new—namely, in the time of Aristotle, there had to be a great deal of fuss made about it; Aristotle made a lot of fuss about that logic. Nowadays it's become old and respectable, and you don't have to make so much fuss about it. The logic that I believe in is comparatively new, and therefore I have to imitate Aristotle in making a fuss about it; but it's not that I think it's all philosophy by any means—I don't think so. I think it's an important part of philosophy, and when I say that, I don't find a meaning for this or that word, that is a position of detail based upon what I've found out about that particular word, from thinking about it. It's not a general position that all words that are used in metaphysics are nonsense, or anything like that which I don't really hold.

As regards the moral argument, I do find that when one studies anthropology or history, there are people who think it their duty to perform acts which I think abominable, and I certainly can't, therefore, attribute Divine origin to the matter of moral obligation, which Father Copleston doesn't ask me to; but I think even the form of moral obligation, when it takes the form of enjoining you to eat your father or what not, doesn't seem to me to be such a very beautiful and noble thing; and, therefore, I cannot attribute a Divine origin to this sense of moral obligation, which I think is quite easily accounted for in quite other ways.

God as a Projection of the Human Mind

LUDWIG FEUERBACH

Ludwig Feuerbach (1804-1872) was perhaps the most profound of the nineteenth century Atheists. His influential book, *Das Wesen des Christentums,* published in 1841, appeared in an English translation by the novelist George Eliot in 1853. Feuerbach's basic contention is that in his religions man projects a magnified image of himself upon the universe.

❋

FROM *The Essence of Christianity*[1]

In the perceptions of the senses consciousness of the object is distinguishable from consciousness of self; but in religion, consciousness of the object and self-consciousness coincide. The object of the senses is out of man, the religious object is within him, and therefore as little forsakes him as his self-consciousness or his conscience; it is the intimate, the closest object. "God," says Augustine, for example, "is nearer, more related to us, and therefore more easily known by us, than sensible, corporeal things."[2] The object of the senses is in itself indifferent—independent of the disposition or of the judgment; but the object of religion is a selected object; the most excellent, the first, the supreme being; it essentially presupposes a critical judgment, a discrimination between the divine and the non-divine, between that which is worthy of adoration and that which is not worthy.[3] And here may be applied, without any limitation, the proposition: the object of any subject is nothing else than the subject's own nature taken objectively. Such as are a man's thoughts and dispositions, such is his God; so much worth as a man has, so much and no more has his God. Consciousness of God is self-consciousness, knowledge of God is self-knowledge. By his God thou knowest the man, and by the man his God; the two are identical. Whatever is God to a man, that is his heart and soul; and conversely, God is the manifested inward nature, the expressed self of a man,—religion the solemn unveiling of a man's hidden treasures, the revelation of his intimate thoughts, the open confession of his love-secrets.

But when religion—consciousness of God—is designated as the self-consciousness of man, this is not to be understood as affirming that the religious man is directly aware of this identity; for, on the contrary, ignorance of it is fundamental to the peculiar nature of religion. To preclude this misconception, it is better to say, religion is man's earliest and also indirect form of self-knowledge. Hence, religion everywhere precedes philosophy, as in the history of the race, so also in that of the individual. Man first of all sees his nature as if *out of* himself, before he finds it in himself. His own nature is in the first instance contemplated by him as that of another being. Religion is the childlike condition of humanity; but the child sees his nature—man—out of himself; in childhood a man is an object to himself, under the form of another man. Hence the historical progress of religion consists in this: that what by an earlier religion was regarded as objective, is now recognized as subjective; that is, what was formerly contemplated and worshipped as

God is now perceived to be something *human*. What was at first religion becomes at a later period idolatry; man is seen to have adored his own nature. Man has given objectivity to himself, but has not recognized the object as his own nature: a later religion takes this forward step; every advance in religion is therefore a deeper self-knowledge. But every particular religion, while it pronounces its predecessors idolatrous, excepts itself—and necessarily so, otherwise it would no longer be religion—from the fate, the common nature of all religions: it imputes only to other religions what is the fault, if fault it be, of religion in general. Because it has a different object, a different tenor, because it has transcended the ideas of preceding religions, it erroneously supposes itself exalted above the necessary eternal laws which constitute the essence of religion—it fancies its object, its ideas, to be superhuman. But the essence of religion, thus hidden from the religious, is evident to the thinker, by whom religion is viewed objectively, which it cannot be by its votaries. And it is our task to show that the antithesis of divine and human is altogether illusory, that it is nothing else than the antithesis between the human nature in general and the human individual; that, consequently, the object and contents of the Christian religion are altogether human.

Religion, at least the Christian, is the relation of man to himself, or more correctly to his own nature (*i.e.*, his subjective nature);[4] but a relation to it, viewed as a nature apart from his own. The divine being is nothing else than the human being, or, rather, the human nature purified, freed from the limits of the individual man, made objective —*i.e.*, contemplated and revered as another, a distinct being. All the attributes of the divine nature are, therefore, attributes of the human nature.[5]

In relation to the attributes, the predicates, of the Divine Being, this is admitted without hesitation, but by no means in relation to the subject of these predicates. The negation of the subject is held to be irreligion, nay, atheism; though not so the negation of the predicates. But that which has no predicates or qualities, has no effect upon me; that which has no effect upon me has no existence for me. To deny all the qualities of a being is equivalent to denying the being himself.

A being without qualities is one which cannot become an object to the mind, and such a being is virtually non-existent. Where man deprives God of all qualities, God is no longer anything more to him than a negative being. To the truly religious man, God is not a being without qualities, because to him he is a positive, real being. The theory that God cannot be defined, and consequently cannot be known by man, is therefore the offspring of recent times, a product of modern unbelief.

As reason is and can be pronounced finite only where man regards sensual enjoyment, or religious emotion, or æsthetic contemplation, or moral sentiment, as the absolute, the true; so the proposition that God is unknowable or undefinable, can only be enunciated and become fixed as a dogma, where this object has no longer any interest for the intellect; where the real, the positive, alone has any hold on man, where the real alone has for him the significance of the essential, of the absolute, divine object, but where at the same time, in contradiction with this purely worldly tendency, there yet exist some old remains of religiousness. On the ground that God is unknowable, man excuses himself to what is yet remaining of his religious conscience for his forgetfulness of God, his absorption in the world: he denies God practically by his conduct,—the world has possession of all his thoughts and inclinations,—but he does not deny him theoretically, he does not attack his existence; he lets that rest. But this existence does not affect or incommode him; it is a merely negative existence, an existence without existence, a self-contradictory existence,—a state of being which, as to its effects, is not distinguishable from non-being. The denial of determinate, positive predicates concerning the divine nature is nothing else than a denial of religion, with, however, an appearance of religion in its favor, so that it is not recognized as a denial; it is simply a subtle, disguised atheism. The alleged religious horror of limiting God by positive predicates is only the irreligious wish to know nothing more of God, to banish God from the mind. Dread of limitation is dread of existence. All real existence, *i.e.*, all existence which is truly such, is qualitative, determinative existence. He who earnestly believes in the

Divine existence is not shocked at the attributing even of gross sensuous qualities to God. He who dreads an existence that may give offense, who shrinks from the grossness of a positive predicate, may as well renounce existence altogether. A God who is injured by determinate qualities has not the courage and the strength to exist. Qualities are the fire, the vital breath, the oxygen, the salt of existence. An existence in general, an existence without qualities, is an insipidity, an absurdity. But there can be no more in God than is supplied by religion. Only where man loses his taste for religion, and thus religion itself becomes insipid, does the existence of God become an insipid existence—an existence without qualities.

There is, however, a still milder way of denying the divine predicates than the direct one just described. It is admitted that the predicates of the divine nature are finite, and, more particularly, human qualities, but their rejection is rejected; they are even taken under protection, because it is necessary to man to have a definite conception of God, and since he is man he can form no other than a human conception of him. In relation to God, it is said, these predicates are certainly without any objective validity; but to me, if he is to exist for me, he cannot appear otherwise than as he does appear to me, namely, as a being with attributes analogous to the human. But this distinction between what God is in himself, and what he is for me destroys the peace of religion, and is besides in itself an unfounded and untenable distinction. I cannot know whether God is something else in himself or for himself than he is for me; what he is to me is to me all that he is. For me, there lies in these predicates under which he exists for me, what he is in himself, his very nature; he is for me what he can alone ever be for me. The religious man finds perfect satisfaction in that which God is in relation to himself; of any other relation he knows nothing, for God is to him what he can alone be to man. In the distinction above stated, man takes a point of view above himself, *i.e.*, above his nature, the absolute measure of his being; but this transcendentalism is only an illusion; for I can make the distinction between the object as it is in itself, and the object as it is for me, only where an object can really appear otherwise to me, not where it appears to me such as the absolute measure of my nature determines it to appear—such as it must appear to me. It is true that I may have a merely subjective conception, *i.e.*, one which does not arise out of the general constitution of my species; but if my conception is determined by the constitution of my species, the distinction between what an object is in itself, and what it is for me ceases; for this conception is itself an absolute one. The measure of the species is the absolute measure, law, and criterion of man. And, indeed, religion has the conviction that its conceptions, its predicates of God, are such as every man ought to have, and must have, if he would have the true ones—that they are the conceptions necessary to human nature; nay, further, that they are objectively true, representing God as he is. To every religion the gods of *other* religions are only notions concerning God, but its own conception of God is to it God himself, the true God—God such as he is in himself. Religion is satisfied only with a complete Deity, a God without reservation; it will not have a mere phantasm of God; it demands God himself. Religion gives up its own existence when it gives up the nature of God; it is no longer a truth when it renounces the possession of the true God. Scepticism is the arch-enemy of religion; but the distinction between object and conception—between God as he is in himself, and God as he is for me—is a sceptical distinction, and therefore an irreligious one.

That which is to man the self-existent, the highest being, to which he can conceive nothing higher—that is to him the Divine Being. How then should he inquire concerning this being, what he is in himself? If God were an object to the bird, he would be a winged being: the bird knows nothing higher, nothing more blissful, than the winged condition. How ludicrous would it be if this bird pronounced: To me God appears as a bird, but what he is in himself I know not. To the bird the highest nature is the bird-nature; take from him the conception of this, and you take from him the conception of the highest being. How, then, could he ask whether God in himself were winged? To ask whether God is in himself what he is for me, is to ask whether God is God, is to lift oneself above one's God, to rise up against him.

Wherever, therefore, this idea, that the religious predicates are only anthropomorphisms, has taken possession of a man, there has doubt, has unbelief, obtained the mastery of faith. And it is only the inconsequence of faint-heartedness and intellectual imbecility which does not proceed from this idea to the formal negation of the predicates, and from thence to the negation of the subject to which they relate. If thou doubtest the objective truth of the predicates, thou must also doubt the objective truth of the subject whose predicates they are. If thy predicates are anthropomorphisms, the subject of them is an anthropomorphism too. If love, goodness, personality, &c., are human attributes, so also is the subject which thou presupposest, the existence of God, the belief that there is a God, an anthropomorphism—a presupposition purely human. Whence knowest thou that the belief in a God at all is not a limitation of man's mode of conception? Higher beings—and thou supposest such—are perhaps so blest in themselves, so at unity with themselves, that they are not hung in suspense between themselves and a yet higher being. To know God and not oneself to be God, to know blessedness and not oneself to enjoy it, is a state of disunity, of unhappiness. Higher beings know nothing of this unhappiness; they have no conception of that which they are not.

Thou believest in love as a divine attribute because thou thyself lovest; thou believest that God is a wise, benevolent being because thou knowest nothing better in thyself than benevolence and wisdom; and thou believest that God exists, that therefore he is a subject—whatever exists is a subject, whether it be defined as substance, person, essence, or otherwise—because thou thyself existest, art thyself a subject. Thou knowest no higher human good than to love, than to be good and wise; and even so thou knowest no higher happiness than to exist, to be a subject; for the consciousness of all reality, of all bliss, is for thee bound up in the consciousness of being a subject, of existing. God is an existence, a subject to thee, for the same reason that he is to thee a wise, a blessed, a personal being. The distinction

between the divine predicates and the divine subject is only
this, that to thee the subject, the existence, does not appear
an anthropomorphism, because the conception of it is necessarily involved in thy own existence as a subject, whereas
the predicates do appear anthropomorphisms, because their
necessity—the necessity that God should be conscious, wise,
good, &c.,—is not an immediate necessity, identical with
the being of man, but is evolved by his self-consciousness,
by the activity of his thought. I am a subject, I exist, whether
I be wise or unwise, good or bad. To exist is to man the
first datum; it constitutes the very idea of the subject; it is
presupposed by the predicates. Hence man relinquishes the
predicates, but the existence of God is to him a settled,
irrefragable, absolutely certain, objective truth. But, nevertheless, this distinction is merely an apparent one. The
necessity of the subject lies only in the necessity of the
predicate. Thou art a subject only in so far as thou art a
human subject; the certainty and reality of thy existence lie
only in the certainty and reality of thy human attributes.
What the subject is lies only in the predicate; the predicate is
the *truth* of the subject—the subject only the personified,
existing predicate, the predicate conceived as existing. Subject and predicate are distinguished only as existence and
essence. The negation of the predicates is therefore the
negation of the subject. What remains of the human subject
when abstracted from the human attributes? Even in the
language of common life the divine predicates—Providence,
Omniscience, Omnipotence—are put for the divine subject.

The certainty of the existence of God, of which it has
been said that it is as certain, nay, more certain to man than
his own existence, depends only on the certainty of the
qualities of God—it is in itself no immediate certainty. To
the Christian the existence of the Christian God only is a
certainty; to the heathen that of the heathen God only. The
heathen did not doubt the existence of Jupiter, because he
took no offence at the nature of Jupiter, because he could
conceive of God under no other qualities, because to him
these qualities were a certainty, a divine reality. The reality
of the predicate is the sole guarantee of existence.

Whatever man conceives to be true, he immediately con-

ceives to be real (that is, to have an objective existence),
because, originally, only the real is true to him—true in
opposition to what is merely conceived, dreamed, imagined.
The idea of being, of existence, is the original idea of truth;
or, originally, man makes truth dependent on existence,
subsequently, existence dependent on truth. Now God is the
nature of man regarded as absolute truth,—the truth of man;
but God, or, what is the same thing, religion, is as various
as are the conditions under which man conceives this his
nature, regards it as the highest being. These conditions, then,
under which man conceives God, are to him the truth, and
for that reason they are also the highest existence, or rather
they are existence itself; for only the emphatic, the highest
existence, is existence, and deserves this name. Therefore,
God is an existent, real being, on the very same ground that
he is a particular, definite being; for the qualities of God
are nothing else than the essential qualities of man himself,
and a particular man is what he is, has his existence, his
reality, only in his particular conditions. Take away from the
Greek the quality of being Greek, and you take away his
existence. On this ground it is true that for a definite positive
religion—that is, relatively—the certainty of the existence
of God is *immediate*; for just as involuntarily, as necessarily,
as the Greek was a Greek, so necessarily were his gods
Greek beings, so necessarily were they real, existent beings.
Religion is that conception of the nature of the world and of
man which is essential to, *i.e.*, identical with, a man's nature.
But man does not stand above this his necessary conception;
on the contrary, it stands above him; it animates, determines,
governs him. The necessity of a proof, of a middle term to
unite qualities with existence, the possibility of a doubt, is
abolished. Only that which is apart from my own being is
capable of being doubted by me. How then can I doubt of
God, who is my being? To doubt of God is to doubt of myself. Only when God is thought of abstractly, when his
predicates are the result of philosophic abstraction, arises the
distinction or separation between subject and predicate, existence and nature—arises the fiction that the existence or the
subject is something else than the predicate, something immediate, indubitable, in distinction from the predicate, which

is held to be doubtful. But this is only a fiction. A God who
has abstract predicates has also an abstract existence. Existence, being, varies with varying qualities.

The identity of the subject and predicate is clearly evi-
denced by the progressive development of religion, which is
identical with the progressive development of human culture.
So long as man is in a mere state of nature, so long is his
god a mere nature-god—a personification of some natural
force. Where man inhabits houses, he also encloses his gods
in temples. The temple is only a manifestation of the value
which man attaches to beautiful buildings. Temples in
honor of religion are in truth temples in honor of architecture.
With the emerging of man from a state of savagery and wild-
ness to one of culture, with the distinction between what is
fitting for man and what is not fitting, arises simultaneously
the distinction between that which is fitting and that which
is not fitting for God. God is the idea of majesty, of the
highest dignity: the religious sentiment is the sentiment of
supreme fitness. The later more cultured artists of Greece
were the first to embody in the statues of the gods the ideas
of dignity, of spiritual grandeur, of imperturbable repose and
serenity. But why were these qualities in their view attributes,
predicates of God? Because they were in themselves regarded
by the Greeks as divinities. Why did those artists exclude all
disgusting and low passions? Because they perceived them to
be unbecoming, unworthy, unhuman, and consequently un-
godlike. The Homeric gods eat and drink;—that implies
eating and drinking is a divine pleasure. Physical strength
is an attribute of the Homeric gods: Zeus is the strongest
of the gods. Why? Because physical strength, in and by
itself, was regarded as something glorious, divine. To the
ancient Germans the highest virtues were those of the war-
rior; therefore their supreme god was the god of war, Odin,
—war, "the original or oldest law." Not the attribute of the
divinity, but the divineness or deity of the attribute, is the
first true Divine Being. Thus what theology and philosophy
have held to be God, the Absolute, the Infinite, is not God;
but that which they have held not to be God is God:
namely, the attribute, the quality, whatever has reality. Hence
he alone is the true atheist to whom the predicates of the

Divine Being,—for example, love, wisdom, justice,—are nothing; not he to whom merely the subject of these predicates is nothing. And in no wise is the negation of the subject necessarily also a negation of the predicates considered in themselves. These have an intrinsic, independent reality; they force their recognition upon man by their very nature; they are self-evident truths to him; they prove, they attest themselves. It does not follow that goodness, justice, wisdom, are chimæras because the existence of God is a chimæra, nor truths because this is a truth. The idea of God is dependent on the idea of justice, of benevolence; a God who is not benevolent, not just, not wise, is no God; but the converse does not hold. The fact is not that a quality is divine because God has it, but that God has it because it is in itself divine: because without it God would be a defective being. Justice, wisdom, in general every quality which constitutes the divinity of God, is determined and known by itself independently, but the idea of God is determined by the qualities which have thus been previously judged to be worthy of the divine nature; only in the case in which I identify God and justice, in which I think of God immediately as the reality of the idea of justice, is the idea of God self-determined. But if God as a subject is the determined, while the quality, the predicate, is the determining, then in truth the rank of the godhead is due not to the subject, but to the predicate.

Not until several, and those contradictory, attributes are united in one being, and this being is conceived as personal— the personality being thus brought into especial prominence —not until then is the origin of religion lost sight of, is it forgotten that what the activity of the reflective power has converted into a predicate distinguishable or separable from the subject, was originally the true subject. Thus the Greeks and Romans deified accidents as substances; virtues, states of mind, passions, as independent beings. Man, especially the religious man, is to himself the measure of all things, of all reality. Whatever strongly impresses a man, whatever produces an unusual effect on his mind, if it be only a peculiar, inexplicable sound or note, he personifies as a divine being. Religion embraces all the objects of the world: everything existing has been an object of religious reverence; in the

nature and consciousness of religion there is nothing else
than what lies in the nature of man and in his consciousness
of himself and of the world. Religion has no material exclusively its own. In Rome even the passions of fear and
terror had their temples. The Christians also made mental
phenomena into independent beings, their own feelings into
qualities of things, the passions which governed them into
powers which governed the world, in short, predicates of
their own nature, whether recognized as such or not, into
independent subjective existences. Devils, cobolds, witches,
ghosts, angels, were sacred truths as long as the religious
spirit held undivided sway over mankind. . . .

Now, when it is shown that what the subject is lies entirely
in the attributes of the subject; that is, that the predicate is
the true subject; it is also proved that if the divine predicates
are attributes of the human nature, the subject of those
predicates is also of the human nature. But the divine
predicates are partly general, partly personal. The general
predicates are the metaphysical, but these serve only as external points of support to religion; they are not the characteristic definitions of religion. It is the personal predicates
alone which constitute the essence of religion—in which the
Divine Being is the object of religion. Such are, for example,
that God is a Person, that he is the moral Lawgiver, the
Father of mankind, the Holy One, the Just, the Good, the
Merciful. It is, however, at once clear, or it will at least be
clear in the sequel, with regard to these and other definitions,
that, especially as applied to a personality, they are purely
human definitions, and that consequently man in religion—
in his relation to God—is in relation to his own nature; for
to the religious sentiment these predicates are not mere conceptions, mere images, which man forms of God, to be distinguished from that which God is in himself, but truths,
facts, realities. Religion knows nothing of anthropomorphisms; to it they are not anthropomorphisms. It is the very
essence of religion, that to it these definitions express the
nature of God. They are pronounced to be images only by
the understanding, which reflects on religion, and which
while defending them yet before its own tribunal denies them.
But to the religious sentiment God is a real Father, real

Love and Mercy; for to it he is a real, living, personal being, and therefore his attributes are also living and personal. Nay, the definitions which are the most sufficing to the religious sentiment are precisely those which give the most offence to the understanding, and which in the process of reflection on religion it denies. Religion is essentially emotion; hence, objectively also, emotion is to it necessarily of a divine nature. Even anger appears to it an emotion not unworthy of God, provided only there be a religious motive at the foundation of this anger.

But here it is also essential to observe, and this phenomenon is an extremely remarkable one, characterizing the very core of religion, that in proportion as the divine subject is in reality human, the greater is the apparent difference between God and man; that is, the more, by reflection on religion, by theology, is the identity of the divine and human denied, and the human, considered as such, is depreciated.[6] The reason of this is, that as what is positive in the conception of the divine being can only be human, the conception of man, as an object of consciousness, can only be negative. To enrich God, man must become poor; that God may be all, man must be nothing. But he desires to be nothing in himself, because what he takes from himself is not lost to him, since it is preserved in God. Man has his being in God; why then should he have it in himself? Where is the necessity of positing the same thing twice, of having it twice? What man withdraws from himself, what he renounces in himself, he only enjoys in an incomparably higher and fuller measure in God.

NOTES

[1] Harper Torchbooks Edition, 1957, pp. 12-22, 25-26 (George Eliot's translation).

[2] De Genesi ad litteram, l. v. c. 16.

[3] "Unusquisque vestrum non cogitat, *prius* se debere Deum *nosse,* quam *colere.*"—M. Minucii Felicis Octavianus, c. 24.

[4] The meaning of this parenthetic limitation will be clear in the sequel.

[5] "Les perfections de Dieu sont celles de nos âmes, mais il les possede sans bornes—il y a en nous quelque puissance, quelque connaissance, quelque bonté, mais elles sont toutes entières en

Dieu."—Leibniz (Théod. Preface). "Nihil in anima esse putemus eximium, quod non etiam divinæ naturæ proprium sit—Quidquid a Deo alienum extra definitionem animæ."—St. Gregorius Nyss. "Est ergo, ut videtur, disciplinarum omnium pulcherrima et maxima se ipsum nosse; si quis enim se ipsum norit, Deum cognoscet." —Clemens Alex. (Pæd. l. iii. c. 1).

6 Inter creatorem et creaturam non potest tanta similitudo notari, quin inter eos major sit dissimilitudo notanda.—Later. Conc. can. 2. (Summa Omn. Conc. Carranza. Antw. 1559. p. 326.) The last distinction between man and God, between the finite and infinite nature, to which the religious speculative imagination soars, is the distinction between Something and Nothing, Ens and Non-Ens; for only in Nothing is all community with other beings abolished.

The Irrelevance of Proofs from the Biblical Point of View

JOHN BAILLIE

In this passage John Baillie (1886-1960), late Professor of Divinity at Edinburgh University, summarizes an important aspect of the data concerning the problem of divine existence, namely the point of view of the Biblical writers. Baillie's own constructive contribution is contained in other parts of his book *Our Knowledge of God*, from which this section is taken, and in *The Sense of the Presence of God* (London: Oxford University Press, 1963).

❊

FROM *Our Knowledge of God*[1]

I have said that Plato's Greece was the source of the tradition according to which the existence of God requires and admits of proof by argument. Was, then, such a tradition wholly absent from the Palestinian and Scriptural background of Christianity? Let us see.

First, as to the Old Testament. Dr. Henry Sloane Coffin once preached a sermon in New York on the commandment "Thou shalt have no other gods," which began with the words, "Had this commandment been written for our day and place, it would rather have read, 'Thou shalt have at least one God.'" That puts very well the difference between Bible times and our own. The danger then was not that men should believe in no gods but that they should believe in too many. None of the Old Testament writers treats of the existence of deity as if it were an open question or in any sense problematic. They betray no consciousness that there were any in Israel who denied it. There are, indeed, three or four passages in the literature which look at first sight like exceptions to this statement, but a close examination of them shows that they are not so in reality. In the tenth psalm we read of murderous criminals who despise Jehovah and whose thoughts amount to the declaration that "There is no God." It is perhaps not entirely clear whether the poet has in mind inimical surrounding nations or certain Israelite free-booters who have been causing trouble, but in either case most of the commentators are concerned to make the point that this is "not a denial of the divine existence, but of His presence and interposition."[2] This is made clear enough by the rest of the psalm, where the thoughts in the criminals' minds are said rather to be "God does not punish," "God has forgotten, He has hidden His face, He never sees." Again in the fourteenth psalm, which is the same as the fifty-third, we read of fools or impious men who say in their heart "There is no God," but again the commentators make the point that it is God's effective presence rather than His existence that is being denied, so that we should perhaps translate "No God is here." Much the same may be said of the attitude of mind ascribed by Jeremiah to many of the inhabitants of Jerusalem, both the poor and ignorant folk and also those of high degree. Some translators render, "They have denied Jehovah and said, He is not"; but others prefer to render, "They have belied Jehovah and said, He will do nothing."[3] It seems clear that in all these passages we have to do not with intellectual perplexity but with sinful evasion—with the wicked man's attempt to persuade himself that he can go through with his wickedness and yet escape divine judgment. As for the nations surrounding Israel, they had, of course, their own gods and did not worship Jehovah or trust either in His power or in His goodwill, but that such a deity as Jehovah existed it probably never occurred to them to question; just as the Israelites themselves never perhaps came to think the gods of the surrounding nations out of all existence, though they did come to regard them as mere demonic "powers of darkness" inhabiting the underworld. The question in those days was not "What gods exist?" but "What gods must I worship?"

It is therefore natural enough that no attempt should be made in the Old Testament to establish the divine existence by means of argument. In that same chapter of Jeremiah we do indeed find such a passage as the following: "Hear now this, O foolish people, and without understanding; which have eyes, and see not; which have ears, and hear not; Fear ye not me? saith the Lord: will ye not tremble at my presence, which have placed the sand for the bound of the sea by a perpetual decree, that it cannot pass it; and though the waves thereof toss themselves, yet can they not prevail; though they roar, yet can they not pass over it? But this people hath a revolting and a rebellious heart; they are revolted and gone."[4] This, however, is not an argument for God's existence but a reminder of the inexorable character of His commandments. And so it is generally. "When psalmist or prophet," writes Sir George Adam Smith, "calls Israel to lift their eyes to the hills, or to behold how the heavens declare the glory of God, or to listen to that unbroken tradition which day passes to day and night to night, of the knowledge of the Creator, it is not proofs to doubting minds which he offers: it is spiritual nourishment to hungry souls. These are not arguments—they are sacraments."[5] It is not until we reach Philo that we first find a Jew who acknowledges the existence of atheism and seeks to rebut it with argument; but it is Greek atheism that the Alexandrian has in mind and it is with the cosmology of Plato's *Timaeus* that he rebuts it! All through the Old Testament it is assumed that the knowledge of God rests, not on cosmological speculation, but on the revelation of Himself which He has vouchsafed—on the theophanies of Mount Sinai, on the laws He gave to Moses, on the words He spoke to the prophets.

In this respect, then, the Old Testament literature occupies the same position as that of Greek literature before the rise of the philosophic movement. Yet it is remarkable how often this fact was obscured from the minds of Christian scholars during the long reign of rationalism. It was hardly a welcome discovery to the early seventeenth century when Pascal wrote, *"C'est une chose admirable que jamais auteur canonique ne s'est servi de la nature pour prouver Dieu."* [It is remarkable that never does a biblical writer use Nature to prove God.][6] Nor was it even a very welcome discovery when "Rabbi" Davidson set the facts on which we have been dwelling at the very forefront of his *Theology of the Old Testament,* published posthumously in 1904. "On the subject of *God*," he wrote, "the ideas of the ancient world are in many respects different from our own. And the ideas of the Old Testament have, in these points of difference, naturally greater affinity with those of the ancient world in general than with ours. One such point of difference is this, that it never occurred to any prophet or writer of the Old Testament to prove the existence of God. To do so might well have appeared an absurdity. . . . Scripture regards men as carrying with them, as part of their very thought, the conception of God. . . . This being the case, the Old Testament naturally has no occasion to speculate on how this knowledge that God *is* arises in the mind. Its position is far in front of this. It teaches how God who is, is known, and is known to be what He is. But it seems nowhere to contemplate men as ignorant of the existence of God, and therefore it nowhere depicts the rise or dawn of the idea of God's existence on men's minds. . . . The Old Testament as little thinks of arguing or proving that God may be known as it thinks of arguing that He exists. Its position here again is far in front of such an argument. How should men think of arguing that God could be known, when they were persuaded they knew Him, when they knew they were in fellowship with Him, when their consciousness and whole mind were filled and aglow with the thought of Him, and when through His Spirit He moved them and enlightened them, and guided their whole history?"[7]

What we have said about the Old Testament applies to

the New with but little variation. It is true that the concept of faith ($\pi\iota\sigma\tau\iota\varsigma$) now comes to have an altogether greater prominence and that the root of all evil is seen to lie precisely in unbelief. According to the teaching of our Lord what is wrong with the world is precisely that it *does not believe in God*. Yet it is clear that the unbelief which He so bitterly deplored was not an intellectual persuasion of God's non-existence but rather something that was wont to consort with the most undoubting intellectual persuasion of His reality. Those whom He rebuked for their lack of faith were not men who denied God with the top of their minds, but men who, while apparently incapable of doubting Him with the top of their minds, *lived* as though He did not exist. So far as our records show, He never had to deal with the kind of men to whom He would have to say, "You think you do not believe in God, yet in the bottom of your hearts you know that you are surrounded by His holiness and love." Rather had He to deal with men to whom He had to say, "You think you *do* believe in God, yet you refuse to trust Him in every hour and circumstance of need." Argument for God's existence was not at all what was needed in such a case, and it is not surprising that He did not offer any. When He bade men consider the flowers of the field, He was not—as has sometimes been supposed—using the argument from design to establish God's existence; He was using the argument *a fortiori* to make men put more trust in God's love.

What is true of the Gospels is true of the Epistles. Here again it is consistently taught that what is wrong with the world is its lack of faith or belief; yet again the belief that is lacking is of a kind that is quite compatible with the most unquestioned acceptance of God's existence. It is, of course, quite clear to us that saving faith in God the Father and in Jesus Christ His Son must include belief in God's existence as a necessary part and implication of it; but it is only rarely that the New Testament finds occasion to make this implication fully explicit. The most important passage is in the great chapter on faith in the Epistle to the Hebrews: "For he that cometh to God must believe that he is, and that he is a rewarder of them that diligently seek him." I remember hearing one of the most distinguished of living Biblical scholars remark that those two little words, ὅτι ἔστιν— "that he is," always struck him as less Hebrew in their emphasis, and more Greek, than almost anything else in the New Testament. And Dr. Moffatt comments on them that they "would appeal specially to those of the readers who had been born outside Judaism."[9] There is also the passage already quoted from the Epistle of James: "Thou believest that there is one God, thou doest well: the devils also believe and tremble. But wilt thou know, O vain man, that faith without works is dead?"[10] Though the reference is here not merely to the existence of God but also (in the true Hebrew fashion) to His unity, yet His existence does seem to be referred to explicitly. But such purely intellectual acceptance, though it must enter as a component part into a truly living faith, is held to be of little or no value in itself. There is plainly a touch of sarcasm in the words "Thou doest well: the devils also believe and tremble." The writer regards the intellectual recognition of God's existence as something that can be taken for granted in all men, and even in devils. Similarly, when St. Paul reminds the Gentile Ephesians that before their conversion to Christianity they were ἄθεοι, "without God," he cannot be taken to mean that they did not in those days believe in the existence of any kind of God.[11] Finally, there is the other statement of St. Paul, which was before us in our first chapter, to the effect that "ever since the creation of the world his unseen attributes, his eternal power and divinity, have been plainly seen in the things he has made."[12] St. Thomas Aquinas took this to be the argument from design, but such a reading of it is undoubtedly mistaken. What is said is not that the works of God's hands prove His existence but that they reveal certain aspects of His nature; and this, once again, is carefully pointed out by most modern commentators.

Thus for the New Testament, as for the Old, God is One who is directly known in His approach to the human soul. He is not an inference but a Presence. He is a Presence at once urgent and gracious. By all whom He seeks He is known as a Claimant; by all whom He finds, and who in Christ find Him, He is known as a Giver. The knowledge of

God of which the New Testament speaks is a knowledge for which the best argument were but a sorry substitute and to which it were but a superfluous addition. "He that hath seen me hath seen the Father; and how sayest thou then, Shew us the Father?"[13]

Non in dialectica, said St. Ambrose, *complacuit deo salvum facere populum suum* [It has not pleased God to save His people with arguments].

NOTES

[1] Section 10, pp. 119-126 (London: Oxford University Press; New York: Charles Scribner's Sons, 1939). Reprinted with permission.

[2] C. A. Briggs, *A Critical and Exegetical Commentary on the Book of Psalms,* vol. i, p. 77.

[3] Jeremiah 5:12.

[4] Jeremiah 5:21–3.

[5] *The Book of Isaiah,* vol. ii, p. 90.

[6] *Pensées,* ed. Brunschvicg, iv. 243.

[7] Davidson, pp. 30, 31, 34.

[8] Hebrews 17:6.

[9] *A Critical and Exegetical Commentary on the Epistle to the Hebrews,* p. 167.

[10] James 2:19–20.

[11] Ephesians ii. 12. "In Greek, however, it does not have the meaning of denying the existence of God. . . . The word must in this place to be taken to mean 'ignorant of God's true nature'."— E. F. Scott. *The Epistles of Paul to the Colossians, to Philemon and to the Ephesians* (The Moffatt Commentary), p. 169f.

[12] Romans 1:20.

[13] John 14:9.

A Religious Objection to Theistic Proofs

SÖREN KIERKEGAARD

Sören Kierkegaard (1813-1855), often called the father of modern Existentialism, rejected as irreligious the program, whose value was almost universally taken for granted in his own day, of demonstrating the existence of God. He saw the "proofs" as a tempting substitute for a living religious faith and commitment.

✳

The Absolute Paradox[1]

But what is this unknown something with which the Reason collides when inspired by its paradoxical passion, with the result of unsettling even man's knowledge of himself. It is the Unknown. It is not a human being, in so far as we know what man is; nor is it any other known thing. So let us call this unknown something: *God*. It is nothing more than a name we assign to it. The idea of demonstrating that this unknown something (God) exists, could scarcely suggest itself to the Reason. For if God does not exist it would of course be impossible to prove it; and if he does exist it would be folly to attempt it. For at the very outset, in beginning my proof, I will have presupposed it, not as doubtful but as certain (a presupposition is never doubtful, for the very reason that it is a presupposition), since otherwise I would not begin, readily understanding that the whole would be impossible if he did not exist. But if when I speak of proving God's existence I mean that I propose to prove that the Unknown, which exists, is God, then I express myself unfortunately. For in that case I do not prove anything, least of all an existence, but merely develop the content of a conception. Generally speaking, it is a difficult matter to prove that anything exists; and what is still worse for the intrepid souls who undertake the venture, the difficulty is such that fame scarcely awaits those who concern themselves with it. The entire demonstration always turns into something very different from what it assumes to be, and becomes an additional development of the consequences that flow from my having assumed that the object in question exists. Thus I always reason from existence, not toward existence, whether I move in the sphere of palpable sensible fact or in the realm of thought. I do not for example prove that a stone exists, but that some existing thing is a stone. The procedure in a court of justice does not prove that a criminal exists, but that the accused, whose existence is given, is a criminal. Whether we call existence an *accessorium* or the eternal *prius*, it is never subject to demonstration. Let us take ample time for consideration. We have no such reason for haste as have those who from concern for themselves or for God or for some other thing, must make haste to get its existence demonstrated. Under such circumstances there may indeed be need for haste, especially if the prover sincerely seeks to appreciate the danger that he himself, or the thing in question, may be non-existent unless the proof is finished; and does not surreptitiously entertain the thought that it exists whether he succeeds in proving it or not.

If it were proposed to prove Napoleon's existence from Napoleon's deeds, would it not be a most curious proceeding? His existence does indeed explain his deeds, but the deeds do not prove *his* existence, unless I have already understood the word "his" so as thereby to have assumed his existence. But Napoleon is only an individual, and in so far there exists no absolute relationship between him and his deeds; some other person might have performed the same deeds. Perhaps this is the reason why I cannot pass from the deeds to existence. If I call these deeds the deeds of Napoleon the proof becomes superfluous, since I have already named him; if I ignore this, I can never prove from the deeds that they are Napoleon's, but only in a purely ideal manner that such deeds are the deeds of a great general, and so forth. But between God and his works there exists an absolute relationship; God is not a name but a concept. Is this perhaps the reason that his *essentia involvit existentiam*? The works of God are such that only God can perform them. Just so, but where then are the works of God? The works from which I would deduce his existence are not immediately given. The wisdom of God in nature, his goodness, his wisdom in the governance of the world—are all these manifest, perhaps, upon the very face of things? Are we not here confronted with the most terrible temptations to doubt, and is it not impossible finally to dispose of all these doubts? But from such an order to things I will surely not attempt to prove God's existence; and even if I began I would never finish, and would in addition have to live constantly in suspense, lest something so terrible should suddenly happen that my bit of proof would be demolished. From what works then do I propose to derive the proof? From the works as apprehended through an ideal interpretation, i.e., such as they do not immediately reveal themselves. But in that case it is not from the works that I prove God's existence. I merely develop the ideality I have presupposed, and because of my confidence in *this* I make so bold as to defy all objections, even those that have not yet been made. In beginning my proof I presuppose the ideal interpretation, and also that I will be successful in carrying it through; but what else is this but to presuppose that God exists, so that I really begin by virtue of confidence in him?

And how does God's existence emerge from the proof? Does it follow straightway, without any breach of continuity? Or have we not here an analogy to the behavior of these toys, the little Cartesian dolls? As soon as I let go of the doll it stands on its head. As soon as I let it go—I must therefore let it go. So also with the proof for God's existence. As long as I keep my hold on the proof, i.e., continue to demonstrate, the existence does not come out, if for no other reason than that I am engaged in proving it; but when I let the proof go, the existence is there. But this act of letting go is surely also something; it is indeed a contribution of mine. Must not this also be taken into the account, this little moment, brief as it may be—it need not be long, for it is a *leap*. However brief this moment, if only an instantaneous now, this "now" must be included in the reckoning. If anyone wishes to have it ignored, I will use it to tell a little anecdote, in order to show that it really does exist. Chrysippus was experimenting with a sorites to see if he could not bring about a break in its quality, either progressively or retrogressively. But Carneades could not get it in his head when the new quality actually emerged. Then Chrysippus told him to try making a little pause in the reckoning, and so—so it would be easier to understand. Carneades replied: With the greatest pleasure, please do not hesitate on my account; you may not only pause, but even lie down to sleep, and it will help you just as little; for when you awake we will begin again where you left off. Just so; it boots as little to try to get rid of something by sleeping as to try to come into the possession of something in the same manner.

Whoever therefore attempts to demonstrate the existence of God (except in the sense of clarifying the concept, and without the *reservatio finalis* noted above, that the existence emerges from the demonstration by a leap) proves in lieu thereof something else, something which at times perhaps does not need a proof, and in any case needs none better; for the fool says in his heart that there is no God, but whoever says in his heart or to men: Wait just a little and I will prove it—what a rare man of wisdom is he![2] If in the moment of beginning his proof it is not absolutely undetermined whether God exists or not, he does not prove it; and if it is thus undetermined in the beginning he will never come to begin, partly from fear of failure, since God perhaps does not exist, and partly because he has nothing with which to begin. A project of this kind would scarcely have been undertaken by the ancients. Socrates at least, who is credited with having put forth the physico-teleological proof for God's existence, did not go about it in any such manner. He always presupposes God's existence, and under this presupposition seeks to interpenetrate nature with the idea of purpose. Had he been asked why he pursued this method, he would doubtless have explained that he lacked the courage to venture out upon so perilous a voyage of discovery without having made sure of God's existence behind him. At the word of God he casts his net as if to catch the idea of purpose; for nature herself finds many means of frightening the inquirer, and distracts him by many a digression.

NOTES

[1] *Philosophical Fragments,* translated by David F. Swenson (Princeton: Princeton University Press, 1936), Chapter III, pp. 31-35.

[2] What an excellent subject for a comedy of the higher lunacy! —Kierkegaard.

III

Contemporary
Problems

THE QUESTION OF
VERIFICATION AND
FALSIFICATION

Theology as Meaningless

A. J. AYER

A. J. Ayer (1910-), Wykeham Professor of Logic in the University of Oxford, introduced the doctrines of Logical Positivism into Britain in his now classic *Language, Truth and Logic* (first edition, 1936, second edition, 1946). In its earlier forms the verification principle—the rule that statements other than tautologies shall only be deemed to have meaning if they are verifiable or falsifiable in sense experience—brands all metaphysics, including theology, as meaningless. This is the position expounded in the selection dealing with theology which follows.

Ayer's other works are *The Foundations of Empirical Knowledge* (1940), *Philosophical Essays* (1954), *The Problem of Knowledge* (1956) and *The Concept of a Person* (1963). Ayer's general position in *Language, Truth and Logic* has been criticized by many writers. There is a good critique of classical Logical Positivism in its bearing upon religious statements by H. J. Paton in *The Modern Predicament* (London: Allen & Unwin and New York: The Macmillan Company, 1955), ch. 2.

❋

FROM *Language, Truth and Logic*[1]

. . . This mention of God brings us to the question of the possibility of religious knowledge. We shall see that this possibility has already been ruled out by our treatment of metaphysics. But, as this is a point of considerable interest, we may be permitted to discuss it at some length.

It is now generally admitted, at any rate by philosophers, that the existence of a being having the attributes which define the god of any non-animistic religion cannot be demonstratively proved. To see that this is so, we have only to ask ourselves what are the premises from which the existence of such a god could be deduced. If the conclusion that a god exists is to be demonstratively certain, then these premises must be certain; for, as the conclusion of a deductive argument is already contained in the premises, any uncertainty there may be about the truth of the premises is necessarily shared by it. But we know that no empirical proposition can ever be anything more than probable. It is only *a priori* propositions that are logically certain. But we cannot deduce the existence of a god from an *a priori* proposition. For we know that the reason why *a priori* propositions are certain is that they are tautologies. And from a set of tautologies nothing but a further tautology can be validly deduced. It follows that there is no possibility of demonstrating the existence of a god.

What is not so generally recognized is that there can be no way of proving that the existence of a god, such as the God of Christianity, is even probable. Yet this also is easily shown. For if the existence of such a god were probable, then the proposition that he existed would be an empirical hypothesis. And in that case it would be possible to deduce from it, and other empirical hypotheses, certain experiential propositions which were not deducible from those other hypotheses alone. But in fact this is not possible. It is sometimes claimed, indeed, that the existence of a certain sort of regularity in nature constitutes sufficient evidence for the existence of a god. But if the sentence "God exists" entails no more than that certain types of phenomena occur in certain sequences, then to assert the existence of a god will be simply equivalent to asserting that there is the requisite regularity in nature; and no religious man would admit that this was all he intended to assert in asserting the existence of a god. He would say that in talking about God, he was talking about a transcendent being who might be known through certain empirical manifestations, but certainly could not be defined in terms of those manifestations. But in that case the term "god" is a metaphysical term. And if "god" is a metaphysical term, then it cannot be even probable that a god exists. For to say that "God exists" is to make a metaphysical utterance which cannot be either true or false. And by the same criterion, no sentence which purports to describe the nature of a transcendent god can possess any literal significance.

It is important not to confuse this view of religious assertions with the view that is adopted by atheists, or agnostics.[2] For it is characteristic of an agnostic to hold that the existence of a god is a possibility in which there is no good reason either to believe or disbelieve; and it is characteristic of an atheist to hold that it is at least probable that no god exists. And our view that all utterances about the nature of God are nonsensical, so far from being identical with, or even lending any support to, either of these familiar contentions, is actually incompatible with them. For if the assertion that there is a god is nonsensical, then the atheist's assertion that there is no god is equally nonsensical, since it is only a significant proposition that can be significantly contradicted. As for the agnostic, although he refrains from saying either that there is or that there is not a god, he does not deny that the question whether a transcendent god exists is a genuine question. He does not deny that the two sentences "There is a transcendent god" and "There is no transcendent god" express propositions one of which is actually true and the other false. All he says is that we have no means of telling which of them is true, and therefore ought not to commit ourselves to either. But we have seen that the sentences in question do not express propositions at all. And this means that agnosticism also is ruled out.

Thus we offer the theist the same comfort as we gave to the moralist. His assertions cannot possibly be valid, but they cannot be invalid either. As he says nothing at all about the world, he cannot justly be accused of saying anything false, or anything for which he has insufficient grounds. It is only when the theist claims that in asserting the existence of a transcendent god he is expressing a genuine proposition that we are entitled to disagree with him.

It is to be remarked that in cases where deities are identified with natural objects, assertions concerning them may be allowed to be significant. If, for example, a man tells me that the occurrence of thunder is alone both necessary and sufficient to establish the truth of the proposition that Jehovah is angry, I may conclude that, in his usage of words, the sentence "Jehovah is angry" is equivalent to "It is thundering." But in sophisticated religions, though they may be to some extent based on men's awe of natural process which they cannot sufficiently understand, the "person" who is supposed to control the empirical world is not himself located in it; he is held to be superior to the empirical world, and so outside it; and he is endowed with super-empirical attributes. But the notion of a person whose essential attributes are non-empirical is not an intelligible notion at all. We may have a word which is used as if it named this "person," but, unless the sentences in which it occurs express propositions which are empirically verifiable, it cannot be said to symbolize anything. And this is the case with regard to the word "god," in the usage in which it is intended to refer to a transcendent object. The mere existence of the noun is enough to foster the illusion that there is a real, or at any rate a possible entity corresponding to it. It is only when we enquire what God's attributes are that we discover that "God," in this usage, is not a genuine name.

It is common to find belief in a transcendent god conjoined with belief in an after-life. But, in the form which it usually takes, the content of this belief is not a genuine hypothesis. To say that men do not ever die, or that the state of death is merely a state of prolonged insensibility, is indeed to express a significant proposition, though all the available evidence goes to show that it is false. But to say that there is something imperceptible inside a man, which is his soul or his real self, and that it goes on living after he is dead, is to make a metaphysical assertion which has no more factual content than the assertion that there is a transcendent god.

It is worth mentioning that, according to the account which we have given of religious assertions, there is no logical ground for antagonism between religion and natural science. As far as the question of truth or falsehood is concerned, there is no opposition between the natural scientist and the theist who believes in a transcendent god. For since the religious utterances of the theist are not genuine propositions at all, they cannot stand in any logical relation to the propositions of science. Such antagonism as there is between religion and science appears to consist in the fact that science takes away one of the motives which make men religious. For it is acknowledged that one of the ultimate sources of religious feeling lies in the inability of men to determine their own destiny; and science tends to destroy the feeling of awe with which men regard an alien world, by making them believe that they can understand and anticipate the course of natural phenomena, and even to some extent control it. The fact that it has recently become fashionable for physicists themselves to be sympathetic towards religion is a point in favor of this hypothesis. For this sympathy towards religion marks the physicists' own lack of confidence in the validity of their hypotheses, which is a reaction on their part from the anti-religious dogmatism of nineteenth-century scientists, and a natural outcome of the crisis through which physics has just passed.

It is not within the scope of this enquiry to enter more deeply into the causes of religious feeling, or to discuss the probability of the continuance of religious belief. We are concerned only to answer those questions which arise out of our discussion of the possibility of religious knowledge. The point which we wish to establish is that there cannot be any transcendent truths of religion. For the sentences which the theist uses to express such "truths" are not literally significant.

An interesting feature of this conclusion is that it accords with what many theists are accustomed to say themselves. For we are often told that the nature of God is a mystery which transcends the human understanding. But to say that something transcends the human understanding is to say that it is unintelligible. And what is unintelligible cannot significantly be described. Again, we are told that God is not an object of reason but an object of faith. This may be nothing more than an admission that the existence of God must be taken on trust, since it cannot be proved. But it may also be an assertion that God is the object of a purely mystical intuition, and cannot therefore be defined in terms which are intelligible to the reason. And I think there are many theists who would assert this. But if one allows that it is impossible to define God in intelligible terms, then one is allowing that it is impossible for a sentence both to be significant and to be about God. If a mystic admits that the object of his vision is something which cannot be described, then he must also admit that he is bound to talk nonsense when he describes it.

For his part, the mystic may protest that his intuition does reveal truths to him, even though he cannot explain to others what these truths are; and that we who do not possess this faculty of intuition can have no ground for denying that it is a cognitive faculty. For we can hardly maintain *a priori* that there are no ways of discovering true propositions except those which we ourselves employ. The answer is that we set no limit to the number of ways in which one may come to formulate a true proposition. We do not in any way deny that a synthetic truth may be discovered by purely intuitive methods as well as by the rational method of induction. But we do say that every synthetic proposition, however it may have been arrived at, must be subject to the test of actual experience. We do not deny *a priori* that the mystic is able to discover truths by his own special methods. We wait to hear what are the propositions which embody his discoveries, in order to see whether they are verified or confuted by our empirical observations. But the mystic, so far from producing propositions which are empirically verified, is unable to produce any intelligible propositions at all. And therefore we say that his intuition has not revealed to him any facts. It is no use his saying that he has apprehended facts but is unable to express them. For we know that if he really had acquired any information, he would be able to express it.

He would be able to indicate in some way or other how the genuineness of his discovery might be empirically determined. The fact that he cannot reveal what he "knows," or even himself devise an empirical test to validate his "knowledge," shows that his state of mystical intuition is not a genuinely cognitive state. So that in describing his vision the mystic does not give us any information about the external world; he merely gives us indirect information about the condition of his own mind.

These considerations dispose of the argument from religious experience, which many philosophers still regard as a valid argument in favor of the existence of a god. They say that it is logically possible for men to be immediately acquainted with God, as they are immediately acquainted with a sense-content, and that there is no reason why one should be prepared to believe a man when he says that he is seeing a yellow patch, and refuse to believe him when he says that he is seeing God. The answer to this is that if the man who asserts that he is seeing God is merely asserting that he is experiencing a peculiar kind of sense-content, then we do not for a moment deny that his assertion may be true. But, ordinarily, the man who says that he is seeing God is saying not merely that he is experiencing a religious emotion, but also that there exists a transcendent being who is the object of this emotion; just as the man who says that he sees a yellow patch is ordinarily saying not merely that his visual sense-field contains a yellow sense-content, but also that there exists a yellow object to which the sense-content belongs. And it is not irrational to be prepared to believe a man when he asserts the existence of a yellow object, and to refuse to believe him when he asserts the existence of a transcendent god. For whereas the sentence "There exists here a yellow-colored material thing" expresses a genuine synthetic proposition which could be empirically verified, the sentence "There exists a transcendent god" has, as we have seen, no literal significance.

We conclude, therefore, that the argument from religious experience is altogether fallacious. The fact that people have religious experiences is interesting from the psychological point of view, but it does not in any way imply that there is such a thing as religious knowledge, any more than our having moral experiences implies that there is such a thing as moral knowledge. The theist, like the moralist, may believe that his experiences are cognitive experiences, but, unless he can formulate his "knowledge" in propositions that are empirically verifiable, we may be sure that he is deceiving himself. It follows that those philosophers who fill their books with assertions that they intuitively "know" this or that moral or religious "truth" are merely providing material for the psycho-analyst. For no act of intuition can be said to reveal a truth about any matter of fact unless it issues in verifiable propositions. And all such propositions are to be incorporated in the system of empirical propositions which constitutes science.

NOTES

[1] Dover Publications, Inc., New York, and Victor Gollancz, Ltd., London, 2nd ed., pp. 114-120.

[2] This point was suggested to me by Professor H. H. Price.

Theology and Falsification

ANTONY FLEW

In 1950, in a short article which has evoked considerable and continuing discussion, Anthony Flew (1923-), Professor of Philosophy in the University of Keele, England, reopened in a new way the problem of the verifiability of religious statements and in particular of the statement "God exists." His article, which originally appeared in a since defunct journal, *University*, published by Basil Blackwell of Oxford, England, was later reprinted in *New Essays in Philosophical Theology* edited by Antony Flew and Alasdair MacIntyre.

Professor Flew is also the author of *A New Approach to Psychical Research* (1953) and *Hume's Philosophy of*

Belief (1961), and editor of *Body, Mind, and* (Macmillan, 1964), another volume in the Problems of Philosophy Series.

✽

Theology and Falsification[1]

Let us begin with a parable. It is a parable developed from a tale told by John Wisdom in his haunting and revelatory article "Gods."[2] Once upon a time two explorers came upon a clearing in the jungle. In the clearing were growing many flowers and many weeds. One explorer says, "Some gardener must tend this plot." The other disagrees, "There is no gardener." So they pitch their tents and set a watch. No gardener is ever seen. "But perhaps he is an invisible gardener." So they set up a barbed-wire fence. They electrify it. They patrol with bloodhounds. (For they remember how H. G. Wells's "invisible man" could be both smelt and touched though he could not be seen.) But no shrieks ever suggest that some intruder has received a shock. No movements of the wire ever betray an invisible climber. The bloodhounds never give cry. Yet still the Believer is not convinced. "But there is a gardener, invisible, intangible, insensible to electric shocks, a gardener who has no scent and makes no sound, a gardener who comes secretly to look after the garden which he loves." At last the Sceptic despairs, "But what remains of your original assertion? Just how does what you call an invisible, intangible, eternally elusive gardener differ from an imaginary gardener or even from no gardener at all?"

In this parable we can see how what starts as an assertion, that something exists or that there is some analogy between certain complexes of phenomena, may be reduced step by step to an altogether different status, to an expression perhaps of a "picture preference."[3] The Sceptic says there is no gardener. The Believer says there is a gardener (but invisible, etc.). One man talks about sexual behavior. Another man prefers to talk of Aphrodite (but knows that there is not really a superhuman person additional to, and somehow responsible for, all sexual phenomena).[4] The process of qualification may be checked at any point before the original assertion is completely withdrawn and something of that first assertion will remain (Tautology). Mr. Wells's invisible man could not, admittedly, be seen, but in all other respects he was a man like the rest of us. But though the process of qualification may be, and of course usually is, checked in time, it is not always judiciously so halted. Someone may dissipate his assertion completely without noticing that he has done so. A fine brash hypothesis may thus be killed by inches, the death by a thousand qualifications.

And in this, it seems to me, lies the peculiar danger, the endemic evil, of theological utterance. Take such utterances as "God has a plan," "God created the world," "God loves us as a father loves his children." They look at first sight very much like assertions, vast cosmological assertions. Of course, this is no sure sign that they either are, or are intended to be, assertions. But let us confine ourselves to the cases where those who utter such sentences intend them to express assertions. (Merely remarking parenthetically that those who intend or interpret such utterances as crypto-commands, expressions of wishes, disguised ejaculations, concealed ethics, or as anything else but assertions, are unlikely to succeed in making them either properly orthodox or practically effective.)

Now to assert that such and such is the case is necessarily equivalent to denying that such and such is not the case.[5] Suppose then that we are in doubt as to what someone who gives vent to an utterance is asserting, or suppose that, more radically, we are sceptical as to whether he is really asserting anything at all, one way of trying to understand (or perhaps it will be to expose) his utterance is to attempt to find what he would regard as counting against, or as being incompatible with, its truth. For if the utterance is indeed an assertion, it will necessarily be equivalent to a denial of the negation of that assertion. And anything which would count against the assertion, or which would induce the speaker to withdraw it and to admit that it had been mistaken, must be part of (or the whole of) the meaning of the negation of that assertion. And to know the meaning of the negation of an assertion is, as near as makes no matter, to know the meaning of that assertion.[6] And if there is nothing which a putative assertion denies then there is nothing which it asserts either: and so it is not really an assertion. When the Sceptic in the parable asked the Believer, "Just how does what you call an invisible, intangible, eternally elusive gardener differ from an imaginary gardener or even from no gardener at all?" he was suggesting that the Believer's earlier statement had been so eroded by qualification that it was no longer an assertion at all.

Now it often seems to people who are not religious as if there was no conceivable event or series of events the occurrence of which would be admitted by sophisticated religious people to be a sufficient reason for conceding "There wasn't a God after all" or "God does not really love us then." Someone tells us that God loves us as a father loves his children. We are reassured. But then we see a child dying of inoperable cancer of the throat. His earthly father is driven frantic in his efforts to help, but his Heavenly Father reveals no obvious sign of concern. Some qualification is made— God's love is "not a merely human love" or it is "an inscrutable love," perhaps—and we realize that such sufferings are quite compatible with the truth of the assertion that "God loves us as a father (but, of course . . .)." We are reassured again. But then perhaps we ask: what is this assurance of God's (appropriately qualified) love worth, what is this apparent guarantee really a guarantee against? Just what would have to happen not merely (morally and wrongly) to tempt but also (logically and rightly) to entitle us to say "God does not love us" or even "God does not exist"? I therefore put to the succeeding symposiasts the simple central questions, "What would have to occur or to have occurred to constitute for you a disproof of the love of, or of the existence of, God?"

NOTES

[1] From *New Essays in Philosophical Theology*, edited by Antony Flew and Aladair MacIntyre (London: The Student Christian Movement Press; New York: The Macmillan Company).

[2] *Proceedings of the Aristotelian Society*, 1944–5, reprinted as

Ch. X of *Logic and Language,* Vol I (Blackwell, 1951), and in his *Philosophy and Psycho-Analysis* (Blackwell, 1953).
[3] Cf. J. Wisdom, "Other Minds," *Mind,* 1940; reprinted in his *Other Minds* (Blackwell, 1952).
[4] Cf. Lucretius, *De Rerum Natura,* II, 655-60.

> *Hic siquis mare Neptunum Cereremque vocare*
> *Constituet fruges et Bacchi nomine abuti*
> *Mavolat quam laticis proprium proferre vocamen*
> *Concedamus ut hic terrarum dictitet orbem*
> *Esse deum matrem dum vera re tamen ipse*
> *Religione animum turpi contingere parcat.*

[5] For those who prefer symbolism: $p \equiv \sim \sim p$.
[6] For by simply negating $\sim p$ we get $p : \sim \sim p \equiv p$.

Religious Language as Ethically but not Factually Significant

R. B. BRAITHWAITE

R. B. Braithwaite (1900-), Knightsbridge Professor of Moral Philosophy in the University of Cambridge, author of *Scientific Explanation* (1953), has discussed the meaning of the statement "God exists" in his Eddington Memorial Lecture, "An Empiricist's View of the Nature of Religious Belief." Braithwaite responds to the challenge posed by the verification principle, formulated here by Ayer and Flew, by granting that religious statements do not have the kind of meaning possessed either by statements of empirical fact, by scientific hypotheses, or by logically necessary statements. Religious statements do however, he points out, have a use and in this sense have a meaning. A religious assertion, he says, is used primarily as a moral assertion; and "the primary use of a moral assertion [is] that of expressing the intention of the asserter to act in a particular sort of way specified in the assertion" (p. 12).

Braithwaite's theory has been criticized by a number of writers, including A. C. Ewing, "Religious Assertions in the Light of Contemporary Philosophy" (*Philosophy*, July, 1957); E. L. Mascall, *Words and Images* (London and New York: Longmans, Green & Co., 1957), ch. 3; J. A. Passmore, "Christianity and Positivism" (*Australasian Journal of Philosophy*, August, 1957); H. J. N. Horsburgh, "Professor Braithwaite and Billy Brown" (*Australasian Journal of Philosophy*, December, 1958); John Hick, *Philosophy of Religion* (Englewood Cliffs, N. J.: Prentice-Hall, Inc., 1963), pp. 90-93.

✻

An Empiricist's View of the Nature of

Religious Belief[1]

"The meaning of a scientific statement is to be ascertained by reference to the steps which would be taken to verify it." Eddington wrote this in 1939. Unlike his heterodox views of the *a priori* and epistemological character of the ultimate laws of physics, this principle is in complete accord with contemporary philosophy of science; indeed it was Eddington's use of it in his expositions of relativity theory in the early 1920's that largely contributed to its becoming the orthodoxy. Eddington continued his passage by saying: "This [principle] will be recognized as a tenet of logical positivism —only it is there extended to all statements."[2] Just as the tone was set to the empiricist tradition in British philosophy —the tradition running from Locke through Berkeley, Hume, Mill to Russell in our own time—by Locke's close association with the scientific work of Boyle and the early Royal Society, so the contemporary development of empiricism popularly known as logical positivism has been greatly influenced by the revolutionary changes this century in physical theory and by the philosophy of science which physicists concerned with these changes—Einstein and Heisenberg as well as Eddington—have thought most consonant with relativity and quantum physics. It is therefore, I think, proper for me to take the verification principle of meaning, and a natural adaptation of it, as that aspect of contemporary scientific thought whose bearing upon the philosophy of religion I shall discuss this afternoon. Eddington, in the passage from which I have quoted, applied the verificational principle to the meaning of scientific statements only. But we shall see that it will be necessary, and concordant with an empiricist way of thinking, to modify the principle by allowing *use* as well as *verifiability* to be a criterion for meaning; so I believe that all I shall say will be in the spirit of a remark with which Eddington concluded an article published in 1926: "The scientist and the religious teacher may well be content to agree that the *value* of any hypothesis extends just so far as it is verified by actual experience."[3]

I will start with the verificational principle in the form in which it was originally propounded by logical positivists— that the meaning of any statement is given by its method of verification.[4]

The implication of this general principle for the problem of religious belief is that the primary question becomes, not whether a religious statement such as that a personal God created the world is true or is false, but how it could be known either to be true or to be false. Unless this latter question can be answered, the religious statement has no ascertainable meaning and there is nothing expressed by it to be either true or false. Moreover a religious statement cannot be believed without being understood, and it can only be understood by an understanding of the circumstances which would verify or falsify it. Meaning is not logically prior to the possibility of verification: we do not first learn the meaning of a statement, and afterwards consider what would make us call it true or false; the two understandings are one and indivisible.

It would not be correct to say that discussions of religious belief before this present century have always ignored the problem of meaning, but until recently the emphasis has been upon the question of the truth or the reasonableness of religious beliefs rather than upon the logically prior question as to the meaning of the statements expressing the beliefs. The argument usually proceeded as if we all knew what was meant by the statement that a personal God created the world; the point at issue was whether or not this statement was true, or whether there were good reasons for believing it. But if the meaning of a religious statement has to be found by discovering the steps which must be taken to ascertain its truth-value, an examination of the methods for testing the statement for truth-value is an essential preliminary to any discussion as to which of the truth-values —truth or falsity—holds of the statement.

There are three classes of statement whose method of truth-value testing is in general outline clear: statements about particular matters of empirical fact, scientific hypotheses and other general empirical statements, and the logically necessary statements of logic and mathematics (and their contradictories). Do religious statements fall into any of these three classes? If they do, the problem of their meaningfulnes will be solved: their truth-values will be testable by the methods appropriate to empirical statements, particular or general, or to mathematical statements. It seems to me clear that religious statements, as they are normally used, have no place in this trichotomy. I shall give my reasons very briefly, since I have little to add here to what other empiricist philosophers have said.

I. Statements about particular empirical facts are testable by direct observation. The only facts that can be directly known by observation are that the things observed have certain observable properties or stand in certain observable relations to one another. If it is maintained that the *existence* of God is known by observation, for example, in the "self-authenticating" experience of "meeting God," the term "God" is being used merely as part of the description of that particular experience. Any interesting theological proposition, e.g. that God is personal, will attribute a property to God which is not an observable one and so cannot be known by direct observation. Comparison with our knowledge of other people is an unreal comparison. I can get to know things about an intimate friend at a glance, but this knowledge is not self-authenticating; it is based upon a great deal of previous knowledge about the connection between facial and bodily expressions and states of mind.

II. The view that would class religious statements with

scientific hypotheses must be taken much more seriously. It would be very unplausible if a Baconian methodology of science had to be employed, and scientific hypotheses taken as simple generalizations from particular instances, for then there could be no understanding of a general theological proposition unless particular instances of it could be directly observed. But an advanced science has progressed far beyond its natural history stage; it makes use in its explanatory hypotheses of concepts of a high degree of abstractness and at a far remove from experience. These theoretical concepts are given a meaning by the place they occupy in a deductive system consisting of hypotheses of different degrees of generality in which the least general hypotheses, deducible from the more general ones, are generalizations of observable facts. So it is no valid criticism of the view that would treat God as an empirical concept entering into an explanatory hypothesis to say that God is not directly observable. No more is an electric field of force or a Schrödinger wave-function. There is no prima facie objection to regarding such a proposition as that there is a God who created and sustains the world as an explanatory scientific hypothesis.

But if a set of theological propositions are to be regarded as scientific explanations of facts in the empirical world, they must be refutable by experience. We must be willing to abandon them if the facts prove different from what we think they are. A hypothesis which is consistent with every possible empirical fact is not an empirical one. And though the theoretical concepts in a hypothesis need not be explicitly definable in terms of direct observation—indeed they must not be if the system is to be applicable to novel situations—yet they must be related to some and not to all of the possible facts in the world in order to have a non-vacuous significance. If there is a personal God, how would the world be different if there were not? Unless this question can be answered God's existence cannot be given an empirical meaning.

At earlier times in the history of religion God's personal existence has been treated as a scientific hypothesis subjectable to empirical test. Elijah's contest with the prophets of

Baal was an experiment to test the hypothesis that Jehovah and not Baal controlled the physical world. But most educated believers at the present time do not think of God as being detectable in this sort of way, and hence do not think of theological propositions as explanations of facts in the world of nature in the way in which established scientific hypotheses are.

It may be maintained, however, that theological propositions explain facts about the world in another way. Nor perhaps the physical world, for physical science has been so successful with its own explanations; but the facts of biological and psychological development. Now it is certainly the case that a great deal of traditional Christian language—phrases such as "original sin," "the old Adam," "the new man," "growth in holiness"—can be given meanings within statements expressing general hypotheses about human personality. Indeed it is hardly too much to say that almost all statements about God as immanent, as an indwelling spirit, can be interpreted as asserting psychological facts in metaphorical language. But would those interpreting religious statements in this way be prepared to abandon them if the empirical facts were found to be different? Or would they rather re-interpret them to fit the new facts? In the latter case the possibility of interpreting them to fit experience is not enough to give an empirical meaning to the statements. Mere consistency with experience without the possibility of inconsistency does not determine meaning. And a metaphorical description is not in itself an explanation. This criticism also holds against attempts to interpret theism as an explanation of the course of history, unless it is admitted (which few theists would be willing to admit) that, had the course of history been different in some specific way, God would not have existed.

Philosophers of religion who wish to make empirical facts relevant to the meaning of religious statements but at the same time desire to hold on to these statements whatever the empirical facts may be are indulging, I believe, in a sort of "double-think" attitude: they want to hold that religious statements both are about the actual world (i.e. are em-

pirical statements) and also are not refutable in any possible
world, the characteristic of statements which are logically
necessary.

III. The view that statements of natural theology resemble the propositions of logic and mathematics in being
logically necessary would have as a consequence that they
make no assertion of existence. Whatever exactly be the
status of logically necessary propositions, Hume and Kant
have conclusively shown that they are essentially hypothetical.
$2 + 3 = 5$ makes no assertion about there being any things
in the world; what it says is that, *if* there is a class of five
things in the world, *then* this class is the union of two
mutually exclusive sub-classes one comprising two and the
other comprising three things. The logical-positivist thesis,
due to Wittgenstein, that the truth of this hypothetical proposition is verified not by any logical fact about the world but
by the way in which we use numerical symbols in our thinking goes further than Kant did in displacing logic and mathematics from the world of reality. But it is not necessary to
accept this more radical thesis in order to agree with Kant
that no logically necessary proposition can assert existence;
and this excludes the possibility of regarding theological
propositions as logically necessary in the way in which the
hypothetical propositions of mathematics and logic are necessary.

The traditional arguments for a Necessary God—the
ontological and the cosmological—were elaborated by
Anselm and the scholastic philosophers before the concurrent
and inter-related development of natural science and of
mathematics had enabled necessity and contingency to be
clearly distinguished. The necessity attributed by these arguments to the being of God may perhaps be different from the
logical necessity of mathematical truths; but, if so, no method
has been provided for testing the truth-value of the statement
that God is necessary being, and consequently no way given
for assigning meaning to the terms "necessary being" and
"God."

If religious statements cannot be held to fall into any of
these three classes, their method of verification cannot be any

of the standard methods applicable to statements falling in these classes. Does this imply that religious statements are not verifiable, with the corollary, according to the verificational principle, that they have no meaning and, though they purport to say something, are in fact nonsensical sentences? The earlier logical positivists thought so: they would have echoed the demand of their precursor Hume that a volume ("of divinity or school metaphysics") which contains neither "any abstract reasoning concerning quantity or number" nor "any experimental reasoning concerning matter of fact and existence" should be committed to the flames; though their justification for the holocaust would be even more cogent than Hume's. The volume would not contain even "sophistry and illusion": it would contain nothing but meaningless marks of printer's ink.

Religious statements, however, are not the only statements which are unverifiable by standard methods; moral statements have the same peculiarity. A moral principle, like the utilitarian principle that a man ought to act so as to maximize happiness, does not seem to be either a logically necessary or a logically impossible proposition. But neither does it seem to be an empirical proposition, all the attempts of ethical empiricists to give naturalistic analyses having failed. Though a tough-minded logical positivist might be prepared to say that all religious statements are sound and fury, signifying nothing, he can hardly say that of all moral statements. For moral statements have a use in guiding conduct; and if they have a use they surely have a meaning—in some sense of meaning. So the verificational principle of meaning in the hands of empiricist philosophers in the 1930's became modified either by a glossing of the term "verification" or by a change of the verification principle into the use principle: the meaning of any statement is given by the way in which it is used.[5]

Since I wish to continue to employ verification in the restricted sense of ascertaining truth-value, I shall take the principle of meaning in this new form in which the word "verification" has disappeared. But in removing this term from the statement of the principle, there is no desertion from the spirit of empiricism. The older verificational principle is subsumed under the new use principle: the use of an empirical statement derives from the fact that the statement is empirically verifiable, and the logical-positivist thesis of the "linguistic" character of logical and mathematical statements can be equally well, if not better, expressed in terms of their use than of their method of verification. Moreover the only way of discovering how a statement is used is by an empirical enquiry; a statement need not itself be empirically verifiable, but that it is used in a particular way is always a straightforwardly empirical proposition.

The meaning of any statement, then, will be taken as being given by the way it is used. The kernel for an empiricist of the problem of the nature of religious belief is to explain, in empirical terms, how a religious statement is used by a man who asserts it in order to express his religious conviction.

Since I shall argue that the primary element in this use is that the religious assertion is used as a moral assertion, I must first consider how moral assertions are used. According to the view developed by various moral philosophers since the impossibility of regarding moral statements as verifiable propositions was recognized, a moral assertion is used to express an *attitude* of the man making the assertion. It is not used to assert the proposition that he has the attitude—a verifiable psychological proposition; it is used to show forth or evince his attitude. The attitude is concerned with the action which he asserts to be right or to be his duty, or the state of affairs which he asserts to be good; it is a highly complex state, and contains elements to which various degrees of importance have been attached by moral philosophers who have tried to work out an "ethics without propositions." One element in the attitude is a feeling of approval towards the action; this element was taken as the fundamental one in the first attempts, and views of ethics without propositions are frequently lumped together as "emotive" theories of ethics. But discussion of the subject during the last twenty years has made it clear, I think, that no emotion or feeling of approval is fundamental to the use of moral assertions; it may be the case that the moral asserter has some specific feeling directed on to the course of action said to be right, but this is not the most important element in his "pro-attitude" towards the course of action: what is primary is his intention to perform the action when the occasion for it arises.

The form of ethics without propositions which I shall adopt is therefore a conative rather than an emotive theory: it makes the primary use of a moral assertion that of expressing the intention of the asserter to act in a particular sort of way specified in the assertion. A utilitarian, for example, in asserting that he ought to act so as to maximize happiness, is thereby declaring his intention to act, to the best of his ability, in accordance with the policy of utilitarianism: he is not asserting any proposition, or necessarily evincing any feeling of approval; he is subscribing to a policy of action. There will doubtless be empirical propositions which he may give as reasons for his adherence to the policy (e.g. that happiness is what all, or what most people, desire), and his having the intention will include his understanding what is meant by pursuing the policy, another empirically verifiable proposition. But there will be no specifically moral proposition which he will be asserting when he declares his intention to pursue the policy. This account is fully in accord with the spirit of empiricism, for whether or not a man has the intention of pursuing a particular behavior policy can be empirically tested, both by observing what he does and by hearing what he replies when he is questioned about his intentions.

Not all expressions of intentions will be moral assertions: for the notion of morality to be applicable it is necessary either that the policy of action intended by the asserter should be a general policy (e.g. the policy of utilitarianism) or that it should be subsumable under a general policy which the asserter intends to follow and which he would give as the reason for his more specific intention. There are difficulties and vagueness in the notion of a general policy of action, but these need not concern us here. All that we require is that, when a man asserts that he ought to do so-and-so, he is using the assertion to declare that he resolves, to the best of his ability, to do so-and-so. And he will not necessarily be insincere in his assertion if he suspects, at the time of making it, that he will not have the strength of character to carry out his resolution.

The advantage this account of moral assertions has over all others, emotive non-propositional ones as well as cognitive propositional ones, is that it alone enables a satisfactory answer to be given to the question: What is the reason for my doing what I think I ought to do? The answer it gives is that, since my thinking that I ought to do the action is my intention to do it if possible, the reason why I do the action is simply that I intend to do it, if possible. On every other ethical view there will be a mysterious gap to be filled somehow between the moral judgment and the intention to act in accordance with it: there is no such gap if the primary use of a moral assertion is to declare such an intention.

Let us now consider what light this way of regarding moral assertions throws upon assertions of religious conviction. The idealist philosopher McTaggart described religion as "an emotion resting on a conviction of a harmony between ourselves and the universe at large,"[6] and many educated people at the present time would agree with him. If religion is essentially concerned with emotion, it is natural to explain the use of religious assertions on the lines of the original emotive theory of ethics and to regard them as primarily evincing religious feelings or emotions. The assertion, for example, that God is our Heavenly Father will be taken to express the asserter's feeling secure in the same way as he would feel secure in his father's presence. But explanations of religion in terms of feeling, and of religious assertions as expressions of such feelings, are usually propounded by people who stand outside any religious system; they rarely satisfy those who speak from inside. Few religious men would be prepared to admit that their religion was a matter merely of feeling: feelings—of joy, of consolation, of being at one with the universe—may enter into their religion, but to evince such feelings is certainly not the primary use of their religious assertions.

This objection, however, does not seem to me to apply to treating religious assertions in the conative way in which recent moral philosophers have treated moral statements— as being primarily declarations of adherence to a policy of action, declarations of commitment to a way of life. That the way of life led by the believer is highly relevant to the sincerity of his religious conviction has been insisted upon by all the moral religions, above all, perhaps, by Christianity. "By their fruits ye shall know them." The view which I put forward for your consideration is that the intention of a Christian to follow a Christian way of life is not only the criterion for the sincerity of his belief in the assertions of Christianity; it is the criterion for the meaningfulness of his assertions. Just as the meaning of a moral assertion is given by its use in expressing the asserter's intention to act, so far as in him lies, in accordance with the moral principle involved, so the meaning of a religious assertion is given by its use in expressing the asserter's intention to follow a specified policy of behavior. To say that it is belief in the dogmas of religion which is the cause of the believer's intending to behave as he does is to put the cart before the horse: it is the intention to behave which constitutes what is known as religious conviction.

But this assimilation of religious to moral assertions lays itself open to an immediate objection. When a moral assertion is taken as declaring the intention of following a policy, the form of the assertion itself makes it clear what the policy is with which the assertion is concerned. For a man to assert that a certain policy ought to be pursued, which on this view is for him to declare his intention of pursuing the policy, presupposes his understanding what it would be like for him to pursue the policy in question. I cannot resolve not to tell a lie without knowing what a lie is. But if a religious assertion is the declaration of an intention to carry out a certain policy, what policy does it specify? The religious statement itself will not explicitly refer to a policy, as does a moral statement; how then can the asserter of the statement know what is the policy concerned, and how can he intend to carry out a policy if he does not know what the policy is? I cannot intend to do something I know not what.

The reply to this criticism is that, if a religious assertion is regarded as representative of a large number of assertions of the same religious system, the body of assertions of which the particular one is a representative specimen is taken by the asserter as implicitly specifying a particular way of life. It is no more necessary for an empiricist philosopher to explain the use of a religious statement taken in isolation from other religious statements than it is for him to give a meaning to a scientific hypothesis in isolation from other scientific hypotheses. We understand scientific hypotheses, and the terms that occur in them, by virtue of the relation of the whole system of hypotheses to empirically observable facts; and it is the whole system of hypotheses, not one hypothesis in isolation, that is tested for its truth-value against experience. So there are good precedents, in the empiricist way of thinking, for considering a system of religious assertions as a whole, and for examining the way in which the whole system is used.

If we do this the fact that a system of religious assertions has a moral function can hardly be denied. For to deny it would require any passage from the assertion of a religious system to a policy of action to be mediated by a moral assertion. I cannot pass from asserting a fact, of whatever sort, to intending to perform an action, without having the hypothetical intention to intend to do the action if I assert the fact. This holds however widely the fact is understood—whether as an empirical fact or as a non-empirical fact about goodness or reality. Just as the intention-to-act view of moral assertions is the only view that requires no reason for my doing what I assert to be my duty, so the similar view of religious assertions is the only one which connects them to ways of life without requiring an additional premiss. Unless a Christian's assertion that God is love (*agape*)—which I take to epitomize the assertions of the Christian religion—be taken to declare his intention to follow an agapeistic way of life, he could be asked what is the connection between the assertion and the intention, between Christian belief and Christian practice. And this question can always be asked if religious assertions are separated from conduct. Unless religious principles are moral principles, it makes no sense to speak of putting them into practice.

The way to find out what are the intentions embodied in a set of religious assertions, and hence what is the meaning of the assertions, is by discovering what principles of conduct the asserter takes the assertions to involve. These may be ascertained both by asking him questions and by seeing how he behaves, each test being supplemental to the other. If what is wanted is not the meaning of the religious assertions made by a particular man but what the set of assertions would mean were they to be made by anyone of the same religion (which I will call their *typical* meaning), all that can be done is to specify the form of behavior which is in accordance with what one takes to be the fundamental moral principles of the religion in question. Since different people will take different views as to what these fundamental moral principles are, the typical meaning of religious assertions will be different for different people. I myself take the typical meaning of the body of Christian assertions as being given by their proclaiming intentions to follow an agapeistic way of life, and for a description of this way of life—a description in general and metaphorical terms, but an empirical description nevertheless—I should quote most of the thirteenth chapter of I Corinthians. Others may think that the Christian way of life should be described somewhat differently, and will therefore take the typical meaning of the assertions of Christianity to correspond to their different view of its fundamental moral teaching.

My contention then is that the primary use of religious assertions is to announce allegiance to a set of moral principles: without such allegiance there is no "true religion." This is borne out by all the accounts of what happens when an unbeliever becomes converted to a religion. The conversion is not only a change in the propositions believed—indeed there may be no specifically intellectual change at all; it is a change in the state of will. An excellent instance is C. S. Lewis's recently published account of his conversion from an idealist metaphysic—"a religion [as he says] that cost nothing"—to a theism where he faced (and he quotes George MacDonald's phrase) "something to be neither more nor less nor other than *done*." There was no intellectual change, for (as he says) "there had long been an ethic (theoretically) attached to my Idealism": it was the recognition that he had to do something about it, that "an attempt at complete virtue must be made."[7] His conversion was a re-orientation of the will.

In assimilating religious assertions to moral assertions I do not wish to deny that there are any important differences. One is the fact already noticed that usually the behavior policy intended is not specified by one religious assertion in isolation. Another difference is that the fundamental moral teaching of the religion is frequently given, not in abstract terms, but by means of concrete examples—of how to behave, for instance, if one meets a man set upon by thieves on the road to Jericho. A resolution to behave like the good Samaritan does not, in itself, specify the behavior to be resolved upon in quite different circumstances. However, absence of explicitly recognized general principles does not prevent a man from acting in accordance with such principles; it only makes it more difficult for a questioner to discover upon what principles he is acting. And the difficulty is not only one way round. If moral principles are stated in the most general form, as most moral philosophers have wished to state them, they tend to become so far removed from particular courses of conduct that it is difficult, if not impossible, to give them any precise content. It may be hard to find out what exactly is involved in the imitation of Christ; but it is not very easy to discover what exactly is meant by the pursuit of Aristotle's *eudaemonia* or of Mill's *happiness*. The tests for what it is to live agapeistically are as empirical as are those for living in quest of happiness; but in each case the tests can best be expounded in terms of examples of particular situations.

A more important difference between religious and purely moral principles is that, in the higher religions at least, the conduct preached by the religion concerns not only external but also internal behavior. The conversion involved in accepting a religion is a conversion, not only of the will, but of the heart. Christianity requires not only that you should behave towards your neighbor as if you loved him as yourself: it requires that you should love him as yourself. And though I have no doubt that the Christian concept of *agape* refers partly to external behavior—the agapeistic behavior for which there are external criteria—yet being filled with *agape* includes more than behaving agapeistically externally: it also includes an agapeistic frame of mind. I have said that I cannot regard the expression of a feeling of any sort as the primary element in religious assertion; but this does not imply that intention to feel in a certain way is not a primary element, nor that it cannot be used to discriminate religious declarations of policy from declarations which are merely moral. Those who say that Confucianism is a code of morals and not, properly speaking, a religion are, I think, making this discrimination.

The resolution proclaimed by a religious assertion may then be taken as referring to inner life as well as to outward conduct. And the superiority of religious conviction over the mere adoption of a moral code in securing conformity to the code arises from a religious conviction changing what the religious man wants. It may be hard enough to love your enemy, but once you have succeeded in doing so it is easy to behave lovingly towards him. But if you continue to hate him, it requires a heroic perseverance continually to behave as if you loved him. Resolutions to feel, even if they are only partly fulfilled, are powerful reinforcements of resolutions to act.

But though these qualifications may be adequate for distinguishing religious assertions from purely moral ones, they are not sufficient to discriminate between assertions belonging to one religious system and those belonging to another system in the case in which the behavior policies, both of inner life and of outward conduct, inculcated by the two systems are identical. For instance, I have said that I take the fundamental moral teaching of Christianity to be the preaching of an agapeistic way of life. But a Jew or a

Buddhist may, with considerable plausibility, maintain that
the fundamental moral teaching of his religion is to recommend exactly the same way of life. How then can religious
assertions be distinguished into those which are Christian,
those which are Jewish, those which are Buddhist, by the
policies of life which they respectively recommend if, on
examination, these policies turn out to be the same?

Many Christians will, no doubt, behave in a specifically
Christian manner in that they will follow ritual practices
which are Christian and neither Jewish nor Buddhist. But
though following certain practices may well be the proper
test for membership of a particular religious society, a
church, not even the most ecclesiastically-minded Christian
will regard participation in a ritual as the fundamental characteristic of a Christian way of life. There must be some
more important difference between an agapeistically policied
Christian and an agapeistically policied Jew than that the
former attends a church and the latter a synagogue.

The really important difference, I think, is to be found in
the fact that the intentions to pursue the behavior policies,
which may be the same for different religions, are associated
with thinking of different *stories* (or sets of stories). By a
story I shall here mean a proposition or set of propositions
which are straightforwardly empirical propositions capable
of empirical test and which are thought of by the religious
man in connection with his resolution to follow the way of
life advocated by his religion. On the assumption that the
ways of life advocated by Christianity and by Buddhism are
essentially the same, it will be the fact that the intention
to follow this way of life is associated in the mind of a
Christian with thinking of one set of stories (the Christian
stories) while it is associated in the mind of a Buddhist with
thinking of another set of stories (the Buddhist stories)
which enables a Christian assertion to be distinguished from
a Buddhist one.

A religious assertion will, therefore, have a propositional
element which is lacking in a purely moral assertion, in that
it will refer to a story as well as to an intention. The
reference to the story is not an assertion of the story taken
as a matter of empirical fact: it is a telling of the story, or

an alluding to the story, in the way in which one can tell, or allude to, the story of a novel with which one is acquainted. To assert the whole set of assertions of the Christian religion is both to tell the Christian doctrinal story and to confess allegiance to the Christian way of life.

The story, I have said, is a set of empirical propositions, and the language expressing the story is given a meaning by the standard method of understanding how the story-statements can be verified. The empirical story-statements will vary from Christian to Christian; the doctrines of Christianity are capable of different empirical interpretations, and Christians will differ in the interpretations they put upon the doctrines. But the interpretations will all be in terms of empirical propositions. Take, for example, the doctrine of Justification by means of the Atonement. Matthew Arnold imagined it in terms of

. . . a sort of infinitely magnified and improved Lord Shaftesbury, with a race of vile offenders to deal with, whom his natural goodness would incline him to let off, only his sense of justice will not allow it; then a younger Lord Shaftesbury, on the scale of his father and very dear to him, who might live in grandeur and splendour if he liked, but who prefers to leave his home, to go and live among the race of offenders, and to be put to an ignominious death, on condition that his merits shall be counted against their demerits, and that his father's goodness shall be restrained no longer from taking effect, but any offender shall be admitted to the benefit of it on simply pleading the satisfaction made by the son;—and then, finally, a third Lord Shaftesbury, still on the same high scale, who keeps very much in the background, and works in a very occult manner, but very efficaciously nevertheless, and who is busy in applying everywhere the benefits of the son's satisfaction and the father's goodness.[8]

Arnold's "parable of the three Lord Shaftesburys" got him into a lot of trouble: he was "indignantly censured" (as he says) for wounding "the feelings of the religious community by turning into ridicule an august doctrine, the object of their solemn faith."[9] But there is no other account of the Anselmian doctrine of the Atonement that I have read which puts it in so morally favorable a light. Be that as it may, the only way in which the doctrine can be understood verificationally is in terms of human beings—mythological beings, it may be, who never existed, but who nevertheless would have been empirically observable had they existed.

For it is not necessary, on my view, for the asserter of a religious assertion to believe in the truth of the story involved in the assertions: what is necessary is that the story should be entertained in thought, i.e. that the statement of the story should be understood as having a meaning. I have secured this by requiring that the story should consist of empirical propositions. Educated Christians of the present day who attach importance to the doctrine of the Atonement certainly do not believe an empirically testable story in Matthew Arnold's or any other form. But it is the fact that entertainment in thought of this and other Christian stories forms the context in which Christian resolutions are made which serves to distinguish Christian assertions from those made by adherents of another religion, or of no religion.

What I am calling a *story* Matthew Arnold called a *parable* and a *fairy-tale*. Other terms which might be used are *allegory, fable, tale, myth*. I have chosen the word "story" as being the most neutral term, implying neither that the story is believed nor that it is disbelieved. The Christian stories include straightforward historical statements about the life and death of Jesus of Nazareth; a Christian (unless he accepts the unplausible Christ-myth theory) will naturally believe some or all of these. Stories about the beginning of the world and of the Last Judgment as facts of past or of future history are believed by many unsophisticated Christians. But my contention is that belief in the truth of the Christian stories is not the proper criterion for deciding whether or not an assertion is a Christian one. A man is not, I think, a professing Christian unless he both proposes to live according to Christian moral principles and associates his intention with thinking of Christian stories; but he need not believe that the empirical propositions presented by the stories correspond to empirical fact.

But if the religious stories need not be believed, what function do they fulfill in the complex state of mind and behavior known as having a religious belief? How is entertaining the story related to resolving to pursue a certain way of life? My answer is that the relation is a psychological and causal one. It is an empirical psychological fact that many people find it easier to resolve upon and to carry through a course of action which is contrary to their natural inclinations if this policy is associated in their minds with certain stories. And in many people the psychological link is not appreciably weakened by the fact that the story associated with the behavior policy is not believed. Next to the Bible and the Prayer Book the most influential work in English Christian religious life has been a book whose stories are frankly recognized as fictitious—Bunyan's *Pilgrim's Progress*; and some of the most influential works in setting the moral tone of my generation were the novels of Dostoevsky. It is completely untrue, as a matter of psychological fact, to think that the only intellectual considerations which affect action are beliefs: it is *all* the thoughts of a man that determine his behavior; and these include his phantasies, imaginations, ideas of what he would wish to be and do, as well as the propositions which he believes to be true.

This important psychological fact, a commonplace to all students of the influence of literature upon life, has not been given sufficient weight by theologians and philosophers of religion. It has not been altogether ignored; for instance, the report of the official Commission on Doctrine in the Church of England, published in 1938, in a section entitled "On the application to the Creeds of the conception of symbolic truth" says: "Statements affirming particular facts may be found to have value as pictorial expressions of spiritual truths, even though the supposed facts themselves did not actually happen. . . . It is not therefore of necessity illegitimate to accept and affirm particular clauses of the Creeds while understanding them in this symbolic sense."[10] But the patron saint whom I claim for my way of thinking is that great but neglected Christian thinker Matthew Arnold, whose parable of the three Lord Shaftesburys is a perfect example of what I take a religious story to be. Arnold's philosophy of religion has suffered from his striking remarks being lifted from their context: his description of religion as *morality touched by emotion* does not adequately express his view of the part played by imagination in religion. Arnold's main purpose in his religious writings was that of "cementing the alliance between the imagination and conduct"[11] by regarding the propositional element in Christianity as "literature" rather than as "dogma." Arnold was not prepared to carry through his programme completely; he regarded *the Eternal not ourselves that makes for righteousness* more dogmatically than fictionally. But his keen insight into the imaginative and poetic element in religious belief as well as his insistence that religion is primarily concerned with guiding conduct make him a profound philosopher of religion as well as a Christian teacher full of the "sweet reasonableness" he attributed to Christ.

> *God's wisdom and God's goodness!*—Ay, but fools
> Mis-define these till God knows them no more.
> *Wisdom and goodness, they are God!*—what schools
> Have yet so much as heard this simpler lore?[12]

To return to our philosophizing. My contention that the propositional element in religious assertions consists of stories interpreted as straightforwardly empirical propositions which are not, generally speaking, believed to be true has the great advantage of imposing no restriction whatever upon the empirical interpretation which can be put upon the stories. The religious man may interpret the stories in the way which assists him best in carrying out the behavior policies of his religion. He can, for example, think of the three persons of the Trinity in visual terms, as did the great Christian painters, or as talking to one another, as in the poems of St. John of the Cross. And since he need not believe the stories he can interpret them in ways which are not consistent with one another. It is disastrous for anyone to try to believe empirical propositions which are mutually inconsistent, for the courses of action appropriate to inconsistent beliefs are not compatible. The needs of practical life require that the body of believed propositions should be purged of inconsistency. But there is no action which is appropriate to thinking of a proposition without believing it; thinking of it may, as I have said, produce a state of mind in which it is easier to carry out a particular course of action, but the connection is causal: there is no intrinsic connection between the thought and the action. Indeed a story may provide better support for a long range policy of action if it contains inconsistencies. The Christian set of stories, for example, contains both a pantheistic sub-set of stories in which everything is a part of God and a dualistic Manichaean sub-set of stories well represented by St. Ignatius Loyola's allegory of a conflict between the forces of righteousness under the banner of Christ and the forces of darkness under Lucifer's banner. And the Marxist religion's set of stories contains both stories about an inevitable perfect society and stories about a class war. In the case of both religions the first sub-set of stories provides confidence, the second spurs to action.

There is one story common to all the moral theistic religions which has proved of great psychological value in enabling religious men to persevere in carrying out their religious behavior policies—the story that in so doing they are doing the will of God. And here it may look as if there is an intrinsic connection between the story and the policy of conduct. But even when the story is literally believed, when it is believed that there is a magnified Lord Shaftesbury who commands or desires the carrying out of the behavior policy, that in itself is no reason for carrying out the policy: it is necessary also to have the intention of doing what the magnified Lord Shaftesbury commands or desires. But the intention to do what a person commands or desires, irrespective of what this command or desire may be, is no part of a higher religion; it is when the religious man finds that what the magnified Lord Shaftesbury commands or desires accords with his own moral judgment that he decides to obey or to accede to it. But this is no new decision, for his own moral judgment is a decision to carry out a behavior policy; all that is happening is that he is describing his old decision in a new way. In religious conviction the resolution to follow a way of life is primary; it is not derived from believing, still less from thinking of, any empirical story. The story may psychologically support the resolution, but it does not logically justify it.

In this lecture I have been sparing in my use of the term "religious belief" (although it occurs in the title), preferring instead to speak of religious assertions and of religious conviction. This was because for me the fundamental problem is that of the meaning of statements used to make religious assertions, and I have accordingly taken my task to be that of explaining the use of such assertions, in accordance with the principle that meaning is to be found by ascertaining use. In disentangling the elements of this use I have discovered nothing which can be called "belief" in the senses of this word applicable either to an empirical or to a logically necessary proposition. A religious assertion, for me, is the assertion of an intention to carry out a certain behavior policy, subsumable under a sufficiently general principle to be a moral one, together with the implicit or explicit statement, but not the assertion, of certain stories. Neither the assertion of the intention nor the reference to the stories includes belief in its ordinary senses. But in avoiding the term "belief" I have had to widen the term "assertion," since I do not pretend that either the behavior policy intended or the stories entertained are adequately specified by the sentences used in making isolated religious assertions. So assertion has been extended to include elements not explicitly expressed in the verbal form of the assertion. If we drop the linguistic expression of the assertion altogether the remainder is what may be called religious belief. Like moral belief, it is not a species of ordinary belief, of belief in a proposition. A moral belief is an intention to behave in a certain way: a religious belief is an intention to behave in a certain way (a moral belief) together with the entertainment of certain stories associated with the intention in the mind of the believer. This solution of the problem of religious belief seems to me to do justice both to the empiricist's demand that meaning must be tied to empirical use and to the religious man's claim for his religious beliefs to be taken seriously.

Seriously, it will be retorted, but not objectively. If a man's religion is all a matter of following the way of life he sets before himself and of strengthening his determination to follow it by imagining exemplary fairytales, it is purely subjective: his religion is all in terms of his own private ideals and of his own private imaginations. How can he even try to convert others to his religion if there is nothing objective to convert them to? How can he argue in its defence if there is no religious proposition which he believes, nothing which he takes to be the fundamental truth about the universe? And is it of any public interest what mental techniques he uses to bolster up his will? Discussion about religion must be more than the exchange of autobiographies.

But we are all social animals; we are all members one of another. What is profitable to one man in helping him to persevere in the way of life he has decided upon may well be profitable to another man who is trying to follow a similar way of life; and to pass on information that might prove useful would be approved by almost every morality. The autobiography of one man may well have an influence upon the life of another, if their basic wants are similar.

But suppose that these are dissimilar, and that the two men propose to conduct their lives on quite different fundamental principles. Can there be any reasonable discussion between them? This is the problem that has faced the many moral philosophers recently who have been forced, by their examination of the nature of thinking, into holding non-propositional theories of ethics. All I will here say is that to hold that the adoption of a set of moral principles is a matter of the personal decision to live according to these principles does not imply that beliefs as to what are the practical consequences of following such principles are not relevant to the decision. An intention, it is true, cannot be logically based upon anything except another intention. But in considering what conduct to intend to practice, it is highly relevant whether or not the consequences of practicing that conduct are such as one would intend to secure. As R. M. Hare has well said, an ultimate decision to accept a way of life, "far from being arbitrary, . . . would be the most well-founded of decisions, because it would be based upon a consideration of everything upon which it could possibly be founded."[13] And in this consideration there is a place for every kind of rational argument.

Whatever may be the case with other religions Christianity

has always been a personal religion demanding personal commitment to a personal way of life. In the words of another Oxford philosopher, "the questions 'What shall I do?' and 'What moral principles should I adopt?' must be answered by each man for himself."[14] Nowell-Smith takes this as part of the meaning of morality: whether or not this is so, I am certain that it is of the very essence of the Christian religion.

NOTES

[1] Cambridge, England, and New York: Cambridge University Press, 1955.

[2] A. S. Eddington, *The Philosophy of Physical Science* (1939), p. 189.

[3] *Science, Religion and Reality,* ed. by J. Needham (1926), p. 218 (my italics).—Braithwaite.

[4] The principle was first explicitly stated by F. Waismann, in *Erkenntnis,* vol. 1 (1930), p. 229.—Braithwaite.

[5] See L. Wittgenstein, *Philosophical Investigations* (1953), especially sections 340, 353, 559, 560.

[6] J. M. E. McTaggart, *Some Dogmas of Religion* (1906), p. 3.

[7] C. S. Lewis, *Surprised by Joy* (1955), pp. 198, 212-13.

[8] Matthew Arnold, *Literature and Dogma* (1873), pp. 306-7.

[9] Matthew Arnold, *God and the Bible* (1875), pp. 18-19.

[10] *Doctrine in the Church of England* (1938), pp. 37-8.

[11] Matthew Arnold, *God and the Bible* (1875), p. xiii.

[12] From Matthew Arnold's sonnet "The Divinity" (1867).

[13] R. M. Hare, *The Language of Morals* (1952), p. 69.

[14] P. H. Nowell-Smith, *Ethics* (1954), p. 320.

Religious Statements as Factually Significant

JOHN HICK

John Hick (1922-   ), H. G. Wood Professor of Theology at the University of Birmingham, has attempted a different response from that of Braithwaite to the verificationist challenge. He accepts the verification principle in a modified form and tries to show that "God exists" is (whether true or false) a genuinely factual assertion.

Doctor Hick is also the author of *Faith and Knowledge* (1957), and *Philosophy of Religion* (1962) and editor of *Classical and Contemporary Readings in the Philosophy of Religion* (1964) and *Faith and the Philosophers* (1964).

The notion of "eschatological verification," upon which the argument hinges, is also used by I. M. Crombie, "Theology and Falsification," *New Essays in Philosophical Theology*. The idea, in one or the other formulation, has been criticized by several writers, including Paul F. Schmidt, *Religious Knowledge* (The Free Press of Glencoe, Inc., 1961), pp. 58f; Basil Mitchell, "The Justification of Religious Belief" (*Philosophical Quarterly*, July, 1961); D. R. Duff-Forbes, "Theology and Falsification Again" (*Australasian Journal of Philosophy*, August, 1961); and Kai Nielsen, "Eschatological Verification," (*The Canadian Journal of Theology*, October, 1963).

❈

Theology and Verification[1]

To ask "Is the existence of God verifiable?" is to pose a question which is too imprecise to be capable of being answered. There are many different concepts of God, and it may be that statements employing some of them are open to verification or falsification while statements employing others of them are not. Again, the notion of verifying is itself by no means perfectly clear and fixed; and it may be that on some views of the nature of verification the existence of God is verifiable whereas on other views it is not.

Instead of seeking to compile a list of the various different concepts of God and the various possible senses of "verify," I wish to argue with regard to one particular concept of deity, namely the Christian concept, that divine existence is in principle verifiable; and as the first stage of this argument I must indicate what I mean by "verifiable."

I

The central core of the concept of verification, I suggest, is the removal of ignorance or uncertainty concerning the truth of some proposition. That *p* is verified (whether *p* embodies a theory, hypothesis, prediction, or straightforward assertion) means that something happens which makes it clear that *p* is true. A question is settled so that there is no longer room for rational doubt concerning it. The way in which grounds for rational doubt are excluded varies of course with the subject matter. But the general feature common to all cases of verification is the ascertaining of truth by the removal of grounds for rational doubt. Where such grounds are removed, we rightly speak of verification having taken place.

To characterize verification in this way is to raise the question whether the notion of verification is purely logical or is both logical and psychological. Is the statement that *p* is verified simply the statement that a certain state of affairs exists (or has existed), or is it the statement also that someone is aware that this state of affairs exists (or has existed) and notes that its existence establishes the truth of *p*? A geologist predicts that the earth's surface will be covered with ice in 15 million years time. Suppose that in 15 million years time the earth's surface *is* covered with ice, but that in the meantime the human race has perished, so that no one is left to observe the event or to draw any conclusion concerning the accuracy of the geologist's prediction. Do we now wish to say that his prediction has been verified, or shall we deny that it has been verified on the ground that there is no one left to do the verifying?

The use of "verify" and its cognates is sufficiently various to permit us to speak in either way. But the only sort of verification of theological propositions which is likely to interest us is one in which human beings participate. We may therefore, for our present purpose, treat verification as a logico-psychological rather than as a purely logical concept. I suggest then that "verify" be construed as a verb which has its primary uses in the active voice: I verify, you verify, we verify, they verify or have verified. The impersonal passive, it is verified, now becomes logically secondary. To say that *p* has been verified is to say that (at least) someone has verified it, often with the implication that his or their report to this effect is generally accepted. But it is impossible, on this usage, for *p* to have been verified without someone having verified it. "Verification" is thus primarily the name for an event which takes place in human consciousness.[2] It refers to an experience, the experience of ascertaining that a given proposition or set of propositions is true. To this extent verification is a psychological notion. But of course it is also a logical notion. For needless to say, not *any* experience is rightly called an experience of verifying *p*. Both logical and psychological conditions must be fulfilled in order for verification to have taken place. In this respect, "verify" is like "know." Knowing is an experience which someone has or undergoes, or perhaps a dispositional state in which someone is, and it cannot take place without someone having or undergoing it or being in it; but not by any means every experience which people have, or every dispositional state in which they are, is rightly called knowing.

With regard to this logico-psychological concept of verification, such questions as the following arise. When *A*, but nobody else, has ascertained that *p* is true, can *p* be said to have been verified; or is it required that others also have undergone the same ascertainment? How public, in other words, must verification be? Is it necessary that *p* could in principle be verified by anyone without restriction even though perhaps only *A* has in fact verified it? If so, what is meant here by "in principle"; does it signify, for example, that *p* must be verifiable by anyone who performs a certain operation; and does it imply that to do this is within everyone's power?

These questions cannot, I believe, be given any general answer applicable to all instances of the exclusion of rational doubt. The answers must be derived in each case from an investigation of the particular subject matter. It will be the object of subsequent sections of this article to undertake such an investigation in relation to the Christian concept of God.

Verification is often construed as the verification of a prediction. However verification, as the exclusion of grounds for rational doubt, does not necessarily consist in the proving correct of a prediction; a verifying experience does not al-

ways need to have been predicted in order to have the effect
of excluding rational doubt. But when we are interested in
the verifiability of propositions as the criterion for their having factual meaning, the notion of prediction becomes central.
If a proposition contains or entails predictions which can
be verified or falsified, its character as an assertion (though
not of course its character as a true assertion) is thereby
guaranteed.

Such predictions may be and often are conditional. For
example, statements about the features of the dark side of the
moon are rendered meaningful by the conditional predictions which they entail to the effect that if an observer comes
to be in such a position in space, he will make such-and-such
observations. It would in fact be more accurate to say that
the prediction is always conditional, but that sometimes the
conditions are so obvious and so likely to be fulfilled in any
case that they require no special mention, while sometimes
they require for their fulfillment some unusual expedition or
operation. A prediction, for example, that the sun will rise
within twenty-four hours is intended unconditionally, at
least as concerns conditions to be fulfilled by the observer;
he is not required by the terms of the prediction to perform
any special operation. Even in this case however there is an
implied negative condition that he shall not put himself in
a situation (such as immuring himself in the depths of a
coal mine) from which a sunrise would not be perceptible.
Other predictions however are explicitly conditional. In these
cases it is true for any particular individual that in order to
verify the statement in question he must go through some
specified course of action. The prediction is to the effect that
if you conduct such an experiment you will obtain such a
result; for example, if you go into the next room you will
have such-and-such visual experiences, and if you then touch
the table which you see you will have such-and-such tactual
experiences, and so on. The content of the "if" clause is
always determined by the particular subject matter. The logic
of "table" determines what you must do to verify statements
about tables; the logic of "molecule" determines what you
must do to verify statements about molecules; and the logic

of "God" determines what you must do to verify statements about God.

In those cases in which the individual who is to verify a proposition must himself first perform some operation, it clearly cannot follow from the circumstances that the proposition is true that everybody has in fact verified it, or that everybody will at some future time verify it. For whether or not any particular person performs the requisite operation is a contingent matter.

II

What is the relation between verification and falsification? We are all familiar today with the phrase, "theology and falsification." Antony Flew[3] and others have raised instead of the question, "What possible experiences would verify 'God exists'?" the matching question "What possible experiences would falsify 'God exists'? What conceivable state of affairs would be incompatible with the existence of God?" In posing the question in this way it was apparently assumed that verification and falsification are symmetrically related, and that the latter is apt to be the more accessible of the two.

In the most common cases, certainly, verification and falsification are symmetrically related. The logically simplest case of verification is provided by the crucial instance. Here it is integral to a given hypothesis that if, in specified circumstances, A occurs, the hypothesis is thereby shown to be true, whereas if B occurs the hypothesis is thereby shown to be false. Verification and falsification are also symmetrically related in the testing of such a proposition as "There is a table in the next room." The verifying experiences in this case are experiences of seeing and touching, predictions of which are entailed by the proposition in question, under the proviso that one goes into the next room; and the absence of such experiences in those circumstances serves to falsify the proposition.

But it would be rash to assume, on this basis, that verification and falsification must always be related in this symmetrical fashion. They do not necessarily stand to one another as do the two sides of a coin, so that once the coin is spun it must fall on one side or the other. There are cases in which verification and falsification each correspond to a side on a different coin, so that one can fail to verify without this failure constituting falsification.

Consider, for example, the proposition that "there are three successive sevens in the decimal determination of π." So far as the value of π has been worked out, it does not contain a series of three sevens, but it will always be true that such a series may occur at a point not yet reached in anyone's calculations. Accordingly, the proposition may one day be verified if it is true, but can never be falsified if it is false.

The hypothesis of continued conscious existence after bodily death provides an instance of a different kind of such asymmetry, and one which has a direct bearing upon the theistic problem. This hypothesis has built into it a prediction that one will after the date of one's bodily death have conscious experiences, including the experience of remembering that death. This is a prediction which will be verified in one's own experience if it is true, but which cannot be falsified if it is false. That is to say, it can be false, but *that* it is false can never be a fact which anyone has experientially verified. But this circumstance does not undermine the meaningfulness of the hypothesis, since it is also such that if it be true, it will be known to be true.

It is important to remember that we do not speak of verifying logically necessary truths, but only propositions concerning matters of fact. Accordingly verification is not to be identified with the concept of logical certification or proof. The exclusion of rational doubt concerning some matter of fact is not equivalent to the exclusion of the logical possibility of error or illusion. For truths concerning fact are not logically necessary. Their contrary is never self-contradictory. But at the same time the bare logical possibility of error does not constitute ground for rational doubt as to the veracity of our experience. If it did, no empirical proposition could ever be verified, and indeed the notion of empirical verification would be without use and therefore without sense. What we rightly seek, when we desire the verification of a factual proposition, is not a demonstration of the logical impossibility of the proposition being false (for this would be a self-contradictory demand), but such kind and degree of evidence as suffices, in the type of case in question, to exclude rational doubt.

III

These features of the concept of verification—that verification consists in the exclusion of grounds for rational doubt concerning the truth of some proposition; that this means its exclusion from particular minds; that the nature of the experience which serves to exclude grounds for rational doubt depends upon the particular subject matter; that verification is often related to predictions and that such predictions are often conditional; that verification and falsification may be asymmetrically related; and finally, that the verification of a factual proposition is not equivalent to logical certification —are all relevant to the verification of the central religious claim, "God exists." I wish now to apply these discriminations to the notion of eschatological verification, which has been briefly employed by Ian Crombie in his contribution to *New Essays in Philosophical Theology*,[4] and by myself in *Faith and Knowledge*.[5] This suggestion has on each occasion been greeted with disapproval by both philosophers and theologians. I am, however, still of the opinion that the notion of eschatological verification is sound; and further, that no viable alternative to it has been offered to establish the factual character of theism.

The strength of the notion of eschatological verification is that it is not an *ad hoc* invention but is based upon an actually operative religious concept of God. In the language of Christian faith, the word "God" stands at the center of a system of terms, such as Spirit, grace, Logos, incarnation, Kingdom of God, and many more; and the distinctly Christian conception of God can only be fully grasped in its connection with these related terms.[6] It belongs to a complex of notions which together constitute a picture of the universe in which we live, of man's place therein, of a comprehensive divine purpose interacting with human purposes, and of the general nature of the eventual fulfillment of that divine purpose. This Christian picture of the universe, entailing as it does certain distinctive expectations concerning the future, is a very different picture from any that can be accepted by one who does not believe that the God of the New Testament exists. Further, these differences are such as to show themselves in human experience. The possibility of experiential confirmation is thus built into the Christian concept of God; and the notion of eschatological verification seeks to relate this fact to the problem of theological meaning.

Let me first give a general theological indication of this suggestion, by repeating a parable which I have related elsewhere,[7] and then try to make it more precise and eligible for discussion. Here, first, is the parable.

Two men are travelling together along a road. One of them believes that it leads to a Celestial City, the other that it leads nowhere; but since this is the only road there is, both must travel it. Neither has been this way before, and therefore neither is able to say what they will find around each next corner. During their journey they meet both with moments of refreshment and delight, and with moments of hardship and danger. All the time one of them thinks of his journey as a pilgrimage to the Celestial City and interprets the pleasant parts as encouragements and the obstacles as trials of his purpose and lessons in endurance, prepared by the king of that city and designed to make of him a worthy citizen of the place when at last he arrives there. The other, however, believes none of this and sees their journey as an unavoidable and aimless ramble. Since he has no choice in the matter, he enjoys the good and endures the bad. But for him there is no Celestial City to be reached, no all-encompassing purpose ordaining their journey; only the road itself and the luck of the road in good weather and in bad.

During the course of the journey the issue between them is not an experimental one. They do not entertain different expectations about the coming details of the road, but only about its ultimate destination. And yet when they do turn the last corner it will be apparent that one of them has been right all the time and the other wrong. Thus although the issue between them has not been experimental, it has nevertheless from the start been a real issue. They have not merely felt differently about the road; for one was feeling appropriately and the other inappropriately in relation to the actual state of affairs. Their opposed interpretations of the road constituted genuinely rival assertions, though assertions whose assertion-status has the peculiar characteristic of being guaranteed retrospectively by a future crux.

This parable has of course (like all parables) strict limitations. It is designed to make only one point: that Christian doctrine postulates an ultimate unambiguous state of existence *in patria* as well as our present ambiguous existence *in via*. There is a state of having arrived as well as a state of journeying, an eternal heavenly life as well as an earthly pilgrimage. The alleged future experience of this state cannot, of course, be appealed to as evidence for theism as a present interpretation of our experience; but it does suffice to render the choice between theism and atheism a real and not a merely empty or verbal choice. And although this does not affect the logic of the situation, it should be added that the alternative interpretations are more than theoretical, for they render different practical plans and policies appropriate now.

The universe as envisaged by the theist, then, differs as a totality from the universe as envisaged by the atheist. This difference does not, however, from our present standpoint within the universe, involve a difference in the objective content of each or even any of its passing moments. The theist and the atheist do not (or need not) expect different events to occur in the successive details of the temporal process. They do not (or need not) entertain divergent expectations of the course of history viewed from within. But the theist does and the atheist does not expect that when history is completed it will be seen to have led to a particular end-state and to have fulfilled a specific purpose, namely that of creating "children of God."

IV

The idea of an eschatological verification of theism can make sense, however, only if the logically prior idea of continued personal existence after death is intelligible. A desultory debate on this topic has been going on for several years in some of the philosophical periodicals. C. I. Lewis has contended that the hypothesis of immortality "is an hypothesis about our own future experience. And our understanding of what would verify it has no lack of clarity."[8] And Morris Schlick agreed, adding, "We must conclude that immortality, in the sense defined [i.e. 'survival after death,' rather than 'never-ending life'], should not be regarded as a 'metaphysical problem,' but is an empirical hypothesis, because it possesses logical verifiability. It could be verified by following the prescription: 'Wait until you die!' "[9] However, others have challenged this conclusion, either on the ground that the phrase "surviving death" is self-contradictory in ordinary language or, more substantially, on the ground that the traditional distinction between soul and body cannot be sustained.[10] I should like to address myself to this latter view. The only self of which we know, it is said, is the empirical self, the walking, talking, acting, sleeping individual who lives, it may be, for some sixty to eighty years and then dies. Mental events and mental characteristics are analyzed into the modes of behavior and behavioral dispositions of this empirical self. The human being is described as an organism capable of acting in the "high-level" ways which we characterize as intelligent, thoughtful, humorous, calculating, and the like. The concept of mind or soul is thus not the concept of a "ghost in the machine" (to use Gilbert Ryle's loaded phrase[11]) but of the more flexible and sophisticated ways in which human beings behave and have it in them to behave. On this view there is no room for the notion of soul in distinction from body; and if there is no soul in distinction from body there can be no question of the soul surviving the death of the body. Against this philosophical background the specifically Christian (and also Jewish) belief in the resurrection of the flesh or body, in contrast to the Hellenic notion of the survival of a disembodied soul, might be expected to have attracted more attention than it has. For it is consonant with the conception of man as an indissoluble psycho-physical unity, and yet it also offers the possibility of an empirical meaning for the idea of "life after death."

Paul is the chief Biblical expositor of the idea of the resurrection of the body.[12] His view, as I understand it, is this. When someone has died he is, apart from any special divine action, extinct. A human being is by nature mortal and subject to annihilation by death. But in fact God, by an act of sovereign power, either sometimes or always resurrects or (better) reconstitutes or recreates him—not, however, as the identical physical organism that he was before death, but as a *soma pneumatikon* ("spiritual body") embodying the dispositional characteristics and memory traces of the deceased physical organism, and inhabiting an environment with which the *soma pneumatikon* is continuous as the ante-mortem body was continuous with our present world. In discussing this notion we may well abandon the word "spiritual," as lacking today any precise established usage, and speak of "resurrection bodies" and of "the resurrection world." The principal questions to be asked concern the relation between the physical world and the resurrection world, and the criteria of personal identity which are operating when it is alleged that a certain inhabitant of the resurrection world is the same person as an individual who once inhabited this present world. The first of these questions turns out on investigation to be the more difficult of the two, and I shall take the easier one first.

Let me sketch a very odd possibility (concerning which, however, I wish to emphasize not so much its oddness as its possibility!), and then see how far it can be stretched in the direction of the notion of the resurrection body. In the process of stretching it will become even more odd than it was before; but my aim will be to show that, however odd, it remains within the bounds of the logically possible. This progression will be presented in three pictures, arranged in a self-explanatory order.

First picture: Suppose that at some learned gathering in this country one of the company were suddenly and inexplicably to disappear, and that at the same moment an exact replica of him were suddenly and inexplicably to appear at some comparable meeting in Australia. The person who appears in Australia is exactly similar, as to both bodily and mental characteristics, with the person who disappears in America. There is continuity of memory, complete similarity of bodily features, including even fingerprints, hair and eye coloration and stomach contents, and also of beliefs, habits, and mental propensities. In fact there is everything that would lead us to identify the one who appeared with the one who disappeared, except continuity of occupancy of space. We may suppose, for example, that a deputation of the colleagues of the man who disappeared fly to Australia to interview the replica of him which is reported there, and find that he is in all respects but one exactly as though he had traveled from say, Princeton to Melbourne, by conventional means. The only difference is that he describes how, as he was sitting listening to Dr. Z. reading a paper, on blinking his eyes he suddenly found himself sitting in a different room listening to a different paper by an Australian scholar. He asks his colleagues how the meeting had gone after he ceased to be there, and what they had made of his disappearance, and so on. He clearly thinks of himself as the one who was present with them at their meeting in the United States. I suggest that faced with all these circumstances his colleagues would soon, if not immediately, find themselves thinking of him and treating him as the individual who had so inexplicably disappeared from their midst. We should be extending our normal use of "same person" in a way which the postulated facts would both demand and justify if we said that the one who appears in Australia is the same person as the one who disappears in America. The factors inclining us to identify them would far outweigh the factors disinclining us to do this. We should have no reasonable alternative but to extend our usage of "the same person" to cover the strange new case.

Second picture: Now let us suppose that the event in America is not a sudden and inexplicable disappearance, and indeed not a disappearance at all, but a sudden death. Only, at the moment when the individual dies, a replica of him as he was at the moment before his death, complete with memory up to that instant, appears in Australia. Even with the corpse on our hands, it would still, I suggest, be an

JOHN HICK 265

extension of "same person" required and warranted by the postulated facts, to say that the same person who died has been miraculously recreated in Australia. The case would be considerably odder than in the previous picture, because of the existence of the corpse in America contemporaneously with the existence of the living person in Australia. But I submit that, although the oddness of this circumstance may be stated as strongly as you please, and can indeed hardly be overstated, yet it does not exceed the bounds of the logically possible. Once again we must imagine some of the deceased's colleagues going to Australia to interview the person who has suddenly appeared there. He would perfectly remember them and their meeting, be interested in what had happened, and be as amazed and dumb-founded about it as anyone else; and he would perhaps be worried about the possible legal complications if he should return to America to claim his property; and so on. Once again, I believe, they would soon find themselves thinking of him and treating him as the same person as the dead Princetonian. Once again the factors inclining us to say that the one who died and the one who appeared are the same person would outweigh the factors inclining us to say that they are different people. Once again we should have to extend our usage of "the same person" to cover this new case.

Third picture: My third supposal is that the replica, complete with memory, etc., appears, not in Australia, but as a resurrection replica in a different world altogether, a resurrection world inhabited by resurrected persons. This world occupies its own space, distinct from the space with which we are now familiar.[13] That is to say, an object in the resurrection world is not situated at any distance or in any direction from an object in our present world, although each object in either world is spatially related to each other object in the same world.

Mr. X, then, dies. A Mr. X replica, complete with the set of memory traces which Mr. X had at the last moment before his death, comes into existence. It is composed of other material than physical matter, and is located in a resurrection world which does not stand in any spatial re-

lationship with the physical world. Let us leave out of consideration St. Paul's hint that the resurrection body may be
as unlike the physical body as is a full grain of wheat from
the wheat seed, and consider the simpler picture in which
the resurrection body has the same shape as the physical
body.[14]

In these circumstances, how does Mr. X know that he
has been resurrected or recreated? He remembers dying; or
rather he remembers being on what he took to be his
death-bed, and becoming progressively weaker until, presumably, he lost consciousness. But how does he know that
(to put it Irishly) his "dying" proved fatal; and that he did
not, after losing consciousness, begin to recover strength,
and has now simply waked up?

The picture is readily enough elaborated to answer this
question. Mr. X meets and recognizes a number of relatives
and friends and historical personages whom he knows to have
died; and from the fact of their presence, and also from
their testimony that he has only just now appeared in their
world, he is convinced that he has died. Evidences of this
kind could mount up to the point at which they are quite
as strong as the evidence which, in pictures one and two,
convince the individual in question that he has been miraculously translated to Australia. Resurrected persons would be
individually no more in doubt about their own identity than
we are now, and would be able to identify one another in
the same kinds of ways, and with a like degree of assurance,
as we do now.

If it be granted that resurrected persons might be able to
arrive at a rationally founded conviction that their existence
is *post-mortem,* how could they know that the world in which
they find themselves is in a different space from that in
which their physical bodies were? How could such a one
know that he is not in a like situation with the person in
picture number two, who dies in America and appears as a
full-blooded replica in Australia, leaving his corpse in the
U.S.A.—except that now the replica is situated, not in
Australia, but on a planet of some other star?

It is of course conceivable that the space of the resurrection world should have properties which are manifestly incompatible with its being a region of physical space. But on the other hand, it is not of the essence of the notion of a resurrection world that its space should have properties different from those of physical space. And supposing it not to have different properties, it is not evident that a resurrected individual could learn from any direct observations that he was not on a planet of some sun which is at so great a distance from our own sun that the stellar scenery visible from it is quite unlike that which we can now see. The grounds that a resurrected person would have for believing that he is in a different space from physical space (supposing there to be no discernible difference in spatial properties) would be the same as the grounds that any of us may have now for believing this concerning resurrected individuals. These grounds are indirect and consist in all those considerations (*e.g.,* Luke 16:26) which lead most of those who consider the question to reject as absurd the possibility of, for example, radio communication or rocket travel between earth and heaven.

v

In the present context my only concern is to claim that this doctrine of the divine creation of bodies, composed of a material other than that of physical matter, which bodies are endowed with sufficient correspondence of characteristics with our present bodies, and sufficient continuity of memory with our present consciousness, for us to speak of the same person being raised up again to life in a new environment, is not self-contradictory. If, then, it cannot be ruled out *ab initio* as meaningless, we may go on to consider whether and how it is related to the possible verification of Christian theism.

So far I have argued that a survival prediction such as is contained in the *corpus* of Christian belief is in principle subject to future verification. But this does not take the argument by any means as far as it must go if it is to succeed. For survival, simply as such, would not serve to verify theism. It would not necessarily be a state of affairs which is manifestly incompatible with the non-existence of God. It might be taken just as a surprising natural fact. The atheist, in his resurrection body, and able to remember his life on earth, might say that the universe has turned out to be more complex, and perhaps more to be approved of, than he had realized. But the mere fact of survival, with a new body in a new environment, would not demonstrate to him that there is a God. It is fully compatible with the notion of survival that the life to come be, so far as the theistic problem is concerned, essentially a continuation of the present life, and religiously no less ambiguous. And in this event, survival after bodily death would not in the least constitute a final verification of theistic faith.

I shall not spend time in trying to draw a picture of a resurrection existence which would merely prolong the religious ambiguity of our present life. The important question, for our purpose, is not whether one can conceive of after-life experiences which would *not* verify theism (and in point of fact one can fairly easily conceive them), but whether one can conceive of after-life experiences which *would* serve to verify theism.

I think that we can. In trying to do so I shall not appeal to the traditional doctrine, which figures especially in Catholic and mystical theology, of the Beatific Vision of God. The difficulty presented by this doctrine is not so much that of deciding whether there are grounds for believing it, as of deciding what it means. I shall not, however, elaborate this difficulty, but pass directly to the investigation of a different and, as it seems to me, more intelligible possibility. This is the possibility not of a direct vision of God, whatever that might mean, but of a *situation* which points unambiguously to the existence of a loving God. This would be a situation which, so far as its religious significance is concerned, contrasts in a certain important respect with our present situation. Our present situation is one which in some ways seems to confirm and in other ways to contradict the truth of theism. Some events around us suggest the presence of an unseen benevolent intelligence and others suggest that no such intelligence is at work. Our situation is religiously ambiguous. But in order for us to be aware of this fact we must already have some idea, however vague, of what it would be for our situation to be not ambiguous, but on the contrary wholly evidential of God. I therefore want to try to make clearer this presupposed concept of a religiously unambiguous situation.

There are, I suggest, two possible developments of our experience such that, if they occurred in conjunction with one another (whether in this life or in another life to come), they would assure us beyond rational doubt of the reality of God, as conceived in the Christian faith. These are, *first*, an experience of the fulfillment of God's purpose for ourselves, as this has been disclosed in the Christian revelation; in conjunction, *second*, with an experience of communion with God as he has revealed himself in the person of Christ.

The divine purpose for human life, as this is depicted in the New Testament documents, is the bringing of the human person, in society with his fellows, to enjoy a certain valuable quality of personal life, the content of which is given in the character of Christ—which quality of life (*i.e.* life in relationship with God, described in the Fourth Gospel as eternal life) is said to be the proper destiny of human nature and the source of man's final self-fulfillment and happiness. The verification situation with regard to such a fulfillment is asymmetrical. On the one hand, so long as the divine purpose remains unfulfilled, we cannot know that it never will be fulfilled in the future; hence no final falsification is possible of the claim that this fulfillment will occur—unless, of course, the prediction contains a specific time clause which, in Christian teaching, it does not. But on the other hand, if and when the divine purpose *is* fulfilled in our own experience, we must be able to recognize and rejoice in that fulfillment. For the fulfillment would not be for us the promised fulfillment without our own conscious participation in it.

It is important to note that one can say this much without being cognizant in advance of the concrete form which such fulfillment will take. The before-and-after situation is analogous to that of a small child looking forward to adult life and then, having grown to adulthood, looking back upon childhood. The child possesses and can use correctly in various contexts the concept of "being grown-up," although he does not know, concretely, what it is like to be grown-up. But when he reaches adulthood he is nevertheless able to know that he has reached it; he is able to recognize the experience of living a grown-up life even though he did not know in advance just what to expect. For his understanding of adult maturity grows as he himself matures. Something similar may be supposed to happen in the case of the fulfillment of the divine purpose for human life. That fulfillment may be as far removed from our present condition as is mature adulthood from the mind of a little child; nevertheless, we possess already a comparatively vague notion of this final fulfillment, and as we move towards it our concept will itself become more adequate; and if and when we finally reach that fulfillment, the problem of recognizing it will have disappeared in the process.

The other feature that must, I suggest, be present in a state of affairs that would verify theism, is that the fulfillment of God's purpose be apprehended *as* the fulfillment of God's purpose and not simply as a natural state of affairs. To this end it must be accompanied by an experience of communion with God as he has made himself known to men in Christ.

The specifically Christian clause, "as he has made himself known to men in Christ," is essential, for it provides a solution to the problem of recognition in the awareness of God. Several writers have pointed out the logical difficulty involved in any claim to have encountered God.[15] How could one know that it was *God* whom one had encountered? God is described in Christian theology in terms of various absolute qualities, such as omnipotence, omnipresence, perfect goodness, infinite love, etc., which cannot as such be observed by us, as can their finite analogues, limited power, local presence, finite goodness, and human love. One can recognize that a being whom one "encounters" has a given finite degree of power, but how does one recognize that he has *un*limited power? How does one observe that an encountered being is *omni*present? How does one perceive that his goodness and love, which one can perhaps see to exceed any human goodness and love, are actually infinite? Such qualities cannot be given in human experience. One might claim, then, to have encountered a Being whom one presumes, or trusts, or hopes to be God; but one cannot claim to have encountered a Being whom one recognized to be the infinite, almighty, eternal Creator.

This difficulty is met in Christianity by the doctrine of the Incarnation—although this was not among the considerations which led to the formulation of that doctrine. The idea of incarnation provides answers to the two related questions: "How do we know that God has certain absolute qualities which, by their very nature, transcend human experience?" and "How can there be an eschatological verification of theism which is based upon a recognition of the presence of God in his Kingdom?"

In Christianity God is known as "the God and Father of our Lord Jesus Christ."[16] God is the Being about whom Jesus taught; the Being in relation to whom Jesus lived, and into a relationship with whom he brought his disciples; the Being whose *agape* toward men was seen on earth in the life of Jesus. In short, God is the transcendent Creator who has revealed himself in Christ. Now Jesus' teaching about the Father is a part of that self-disclosure, and it is from this teaching (together with that of the prophets who preceded him) that the Christian knowledge of God's transcendent being is derived. Only God himself knows his own infinite nature; and our human belief about that nature is based upon his self-revelation to men in Christ. As Karl Barth expresses it, "Jesus Christ is the knowability of God."[17] Our beliefs about God's infinite being are not capable of observational verification, being beyond the scope of human experience, but they are susceptible of indirect verification by the removal of rational doubt concerning the authority of Christ. An experience of the reign of the Son in the Kingdom of the Father would confirm that authority, and therewith, indirectly, the validity of Jesus' teaching concerning the character of God in his infinite transcendent nature.

The further question as to how an eschatological experience of the Kingdom of God could be known to be such has already been answered by implication. It is God's union with man in Christ that makes possible man's recognition of the fulfillment of God's purpose for man as being indeed the fulfillment of *God's* purpose for him. The presence of Christ in his Kingdom marks this as being beyond doubt the Kingdom of the God and Father of the Lord Jesus Christ.

It is true that even the experience of the realization of the promised Kingdom of God, with Christ reigning as Lord of the New Aeon, would not constitute a logical certification of his claims nor, accordingly, of the reality of God. But this will not seem remarkable to any philosopher in the empiricist tradition, who knows that it is only a confusion to demand that a factual proposition be an analytic truth. A set of expectations based upon faith in the historic Jesus as the incarnation of God, and in his teaching as being divinely authoritative, could be so fully confirmed in *post-mortem* experience as to leave no grounds for rational doubt as to the validity of that faith.

VI

There remains of course the problem (which falls to the New Testament scholar rather than to the philosopher) whether Christian tradition, and in particular the New Testament, provides a sufficiently authentic "picture" of the mind and character of Christ to make such recognition possible. I cannot here attempt to enter into the vast field of Biblical criticism, and shall confine myself to the logical point, which only emphasizes the importance of the historical question, that a verification of theism made possible by the Incarnation is dependent upon the Christian's having a genuine contact with the person of Christ, even though this is mediated through the life and tradition of the Church.

One further point remains to be considered. When we ask the question, "*To whom* is theism verified?" one is initially inclined to assume that the answer must be, "To everyone." We are inclined to assume that, as in my parable of the journey, the believer must be confirmed in his belief, and the unbeliever converted from his unbelief. But this assumption is neither demanded by the nature of verification nor by any means unequivocally supported by our Christian sources.

We have already noted that a verifiable prediction may be

conditional. "There is a table in the next room" entails conditional predictions of the form: if someone goes into the next room he will will see, etc. But no one is compelled to go into the next room. Now it may be that the predictions concerning human experience which are entailed by the proposition that God exists are conditional predictions and that no one is compelled to fulfill those conditions. Indeed we stress in much of our theology that the manner of the divine self-disclosure to men is such that our human status as free and responsible beings is respected, and an awareness of God is never forced upon us. It may then be a condition of *post-mortem* verification that we be already in some degree conscious of God by an uncompelled response to his modes of revelation in this world. It may be that such a voluntary consciousness of God is an essential element in the fulfillment of the divine purpose for human nature, so that the verification of theism which consists in an experience of the final fulfillment of that purpose can only be experienced by those who have already entered upon an awareness of God by the religious mode of apperception which we call faith.

If this be so, it has the consequence that only the theistic believer can find the vindication of his belief. This circumstance would not of course set any restriction upon who can become a believer, but it would involve that while theistic faith can be verified—found by one who holds it to be beyond rational doubt—yet it cannot be proved to the nonbeliever. Such an asymmetry would connect with that strand of New Testament teaching which speaks of a division of mankind even in the world to come.

Having noted this possibility I will only express my personal opinion that the logic of the New Testament as a whole, though admittedly not always its explicit content, leads to a belief in ultimate universal salvation. However, my concern here is not to seek to establish the religious facts, but rather to establish that there are such things as religious facts, and in particular that the existence or nonexistence of the God of the New Testament is a matter of fact, and claims as such eventual experiential verification.

NOTES

[1] *Theology Today*, XVII, 1, April 1960.

[2] This suggestion is closely related to Carnap's insistence that, in contrast to "true," "confirmed" is time-dependent. To say that a statement is confirmed, or verified, is to say that it has been confirmed at a particular time—and, I would add, by a particular person. *See* Rudolf Carnap, "Truth and Confirmation," Feigl and Sellars, *Readings in Philosophical Analysis*, 1949, pp. 119 f.

[3] Antony Flew, "Theology and Falsification," reprinted above, pp. 224f. On the philosophical antecedents of this change from the notion of verification to that of falsification, *see* Karl R. Popper, *The Logic of Scientific Discovery* (1934; E.T., 1959).

[4] *Op. cit.*, p. 126.

[5] Ithaca: Cornell University Press and London: Oxford University Press. 1957, pp. 150-62.

[6] Its clear recognition of this fact, with regard not only to Christianity but to any religion, is one of the valuable features of Ninian Smart's *Reasons and Faiths* (1958). He remarks, for example, that "the claim that God exists can only be understood by reference to many, if not all, other propositions in the doctrinal scheme from which it is extrapolated" (p. 12).

[7] *Faith and Knowledge*, pp. 150f.

[8] "Experience and Meaning," *Philosophical Review*, 1934, reprinted in Feigl and Sellars, *Readings in Philosophical Analysis*, 1949, p. 142.

[9] "Meaning and Verification," *Philosophical Review*, 1936, reprinted in Feigl and Sellars, *op. cit.*, p 160.

[10] *See* e.g., A. G. N. Flew, "Death," *New Essays in Philosophical Theology*; "Can a Man Witness his own Funeral?" *Hibbert Journal*, 1956.

[11] *The Concept of Mind*, 1949, which contains an important exposition of the interpretation of "mental" qualities as characteristics of behavior.

[12] I Cor. 15.

[13] On this possibility, *see* Anthony Quinton "Spaces and Times," *Philosophy*, XXXVII, No. 140 (April, 1962).

[14] As would seem to be assumed, for example, by Irenaeus (*Adversus Haereses*, Bk. II, Ch. 34, Sec. 1).

[15] For example, H. W. Hepburn, *Christianity and Paradox*, 1958, pp. 56f.

[16] II Cor. 11:31.

[17] *Church Dogmatics*, Vol. II, Pt. I, p. 150.

THE "LOGIC OF 'GOD'"

John Wisdom

John Wisdom (1904-), Professor of Philosophy in Cambridge University, and author of *Problems of Mind and Matter* (1934); *Other Minds* (1952); *Philosophy and Psycho-Analysis* (1953), was deeply influenced by Ludwig Wittgenstein, who taught at Cambridge between 1930 and 1947. Wisdom's essay "Gods" (1944, reprinted in his *Philosophy and Psycho-Analysis,* Oxford: Blackwell, 1953) initiated the revival of interest among British philosophers in the problems of religion which has been evident since World War II. The paper printed here was first broadcast by the British Broadcasting Corporation in 1950, and is published for the first time in this volume.

❊

The Modes of Thought and the Logic of God

I

I should like to say what I aim to do in these lectures and then do it. But there are difficulties about this. I have nothing to say—nothing except what everybody knows. People sometimes ask me what I do. Philosophy I say and I watch their faces very closely. "Ah—they say—that's a very deep subject isn't it?" I don't like this at all. I don't like their tone. I don't like the change in their faces. Either they are frightfully solemn. Or they have to manage not to smile. And I don't like either. Now scientists don't have to feel like this. They tell us what we don't know until they tell us—how very fast germs in the blood breed and that this stuff will stop them, what will or at least what won't take the stain out of the carpet. Even if I were a historian it would be better. Maybe you don't want to know just how the Abbey at Bury St.

Edmunds was run in the time of Abbot Samson, but at least you probably don't know and if only I did I could tell you. But as it is I haven't anything to say except what everybody knows already. And this instantly puts into my head a thought which I try not to but can't help but think namely "Have I anything to say at all worth saying"—a question which I fear is by now in your mind even if it wasn't before I started. Fortunately this brings me to what I want to do. For I want to urge that one who has nothing to say except what everybody knows already may yet say something worth saying and I want to bring out a little how this happens. This is itself something which everybody knows so if I succeed I succeed twice over rather like one who proves that someone in this room is whispering by pointing to someone who is whispering and saying, in a whisper, He is whispering. On the other hand even if I fail to demonstrate that what I claim is true it may still be true. Of course—for as everybody knows, one who says "Someone is whispering" may be right although in attempting to support this statement he points to the wrong person. And everybody knows that a child *may* get the right answer to a sum although he has made at least one mistake in his calculations. Everybody knows this. But don't we sometimes become unduly confident that what a man says is false because his argument is invalid or his premises false? And if we do then there are occasions on which it is worth saying to us "A man may be right in what he says although his argument is invalid and/or his premises false"—a thing which everybody knows.

Perhaps you now hope that satisfied with these antics I will say no more. But no. I am not satisfied. For I am not content to show that it is sometimes worth saying what everybody knows—that seems to me hardly worth saying. I want if I can to bring out a little of how, when, and why it is sometimes worth saying what everybody knows. I want to bring out the several ways of doing this and also how it is connected with informing people of what they do not know—Unlike philosophers, scientists need feel no embarrassment about accepting the salaries they are paid. Motor vans hurry with the late editions. And very properly. For we want to know what won. But how does anyone ever say to another anything worth saying when he doesn't know anything the other doesn't know?

And yet of course there are those who manage this. They say "You look *lovely* in that hat" to people who know this already. But this instance isn't a very clear one. For those to whom such things are said sometimes know not merely that what is said is so but are also very well aware of how what is said is so. Imagine something different. Imagine someone is trying on a hat. She is studying the reflection in a mirror like a judge considering a case. There's a pause and then a friend says in tones too clear, "My dear, it's the Taj Mahal." Instantly the look of indecision leaves the face in the mirror. All along she has felt there was about the hat something that wouldn't quite do. Now she sees what it is. And all this happens in spite of the fact that the hat could be seen perfectly clearly and completely before the words "The Taj Mahal" were uttered. And the words were not effective because they referred to something hidden like a mouse in a cupboard, like germs in the blood, like a wolf in sheeps' clothing. To one about to buy false diamonds the expert friend murmurs "Glass," to one terrified by what he takes to be a snake the good host whispers "Stuffed." But that's different, that *is* to tell somebody something he doesn't know—that that snake won't bite, that cock won't fight. But to call a hat the Taj Mahal is not to inform someone that it has mice in it or will cost a fortune. It is more like saying to someone "Snakes" of snakes in the grass but *not* concealed by the grass but still so well camouflaged that one can't see what's before one's eyes. Even this case is different from that of the hat and the woman. For in the case of the snakes the element of warning, the element of predictive warning, is still there mixed, intimately mixed, with the element of revealing what is already visible. This last element is there unmixed when someone says of a hat which is plainly and completely visible "It's the Taj Mahal." And there is another difference. There's nothing preposterous about calling a snake a snake, but to call a hat the Taj Mahal —well, it involves poetic license.

At this point someone protests. In philosophy there's always someone who protests. And here he says, "I don't know what you're making all this fuss about. In the first place a woman who says of a hat 'It's the Taj Mahal' just means 'It is like the Taj Mahal' or 'It is in some respects like the Taj Mahal.' By saying this she makes her friend feel that the hat is impossible. Well what of it? What has all this got to do with what you say is your main point, namely, that one person may show something to another without telling him anything he doesn't know. In this case nobody shows anybody anything—All that happens is that somebody is persuaded not to buy a hat. The hat you say was seen perfectly clearly from the first. Now it isn't seen any more clearly at the finish. The change is a change in feeling. It may be expressed in the words 'I see now' or 'It's impossible' but that is just an expression of a different attitude to the hat.

"And by the way may I ask what all this has got to do with philosophy. Here is mankind bewildered in a bewildering world. And what do you offer? Talk, talk about a hat."

My answer is this: In the first place it isn't true that the words about the hat only influence the hearer's feelings to the hat. They alter her apprehension of the hat just as the word "A hare" makes what did look like a clump of earth *look* like an animal, a hare in fact; just as the word "A cobra" may change the look of something in the corner by the bed. It is just because in these instances words change the apprehension of what is already before one that I refer to them.

Again it isn't true that the words "It's the Taj Mahal" meant "It is like the Taj Mahal." This more sober phrase is an inadequate substitute. This reformulation is a failure. It's feebler than the original and yet it's still too strong. For the hat isn't like the Taj Mahal, it's much smaller and the shape is very different. And the still more sober substitute "It is in some respects like the Taj Mahal" is still more inadequate. It's *much* too feeble. Everything is like everything in some respects—a man like a monkey, a monkey like a mongoose, a mongoose like a mouse, a mouse like a microorganism, and a man after all is an organism too. Heaven forbid that we should say there are no contexts in which it is worth while to remark this sort of thing. But it is not what the woman in the hat shop remarked. What she said wasn't the literal truth like "It's a cobra" said of what is, unfortunately, a cobra. But what she said revealed the truth. Speaking soberly what she said was false but then thank heaven we don't always speak soberly. Someone has said "The best of life is but intoxication" and that goes for conversation. People sometimes speak wildly but if we tame their words what we get are words which are tame and very often words which don't do anything near what the wild ones did. "My dear, that hat is Paris. . . . yet it's you" is not well translated by "That hat is in some respects like you." If for "It's the Taj Mahal" we put "It is in some respects like the Taj Mahal" we get the sort of negligible stuff that so often results from trying to put poetry into prose, from submission to the muddled metaphysics which pretends that a metaphor is no more than an emotive flourish unless and until we happen to have the words and the wits to translate it into a set of similes.

"But," says the protesting voice, "what she said about the hat wasn't poetry."

"All right, all right it wasn't poetry. And the bread in the upper room wasn't the body of Christ that later hung upon the Cross. Nor of course are there three incorruptibles and yet but one incorruptible, three persons yet one God. But sometimes one is less concerned with whether what one says is true, literally true, than one is to press past illusion to the apprehension of reality, its unity and its diversity."

"Well let that pass," says the sober voice, "since it agitates you so much, let it pass. It all seems rather vague to me and I don't know what you mean about the judge and his judgments. Could anything be further from poetry, more sober? However let it pass, let it pass and come to my second point. What has this conversation about a hat got to do with philosophy, this rather bizarre conversation about a hat?"

My answer is this: Is conversation about the nature and reality of goodness and beauty philosophical, metaphysical conversation? Is conversation about the reality and ultimate nature of the soul philosophical, metaphysical conversation? Is conversation about the reality and ultimate nature of matter philosophical, metaphysical conversation? Is conversation about the reality and ultimate nature of philosophical, metaphysical discussion philosophical, metaphysical conversation? It is. Well, the conversation about the hat throws light on all that—and more immediately conversation about conversation about the hat is a bit of metaphysics and bears on other bits. It *is* a member of the family of metaphysical conversations and its character throws a light on the other members of that family; and the conversation about the hat itself is a member of the family of *Attempts to come at the truth* and its character throws light on the character of the other members of that vast family. The character of any one human being whether Anna Karenina or Mrs. Flood, the plumber's wife, throws light on the characters of all the rest and they on it. For what is the character of a woman, of a man, of anything at all but the way she, he, it is like and unlike men, monkeys, microbes, the dust, the angels high in heaven, God on his throne—all that is and all that might have been.

"Hold on, hold on," says the voice. "This sounds rather like church. It's so obscure."

This makes me want to mutter "Thank heaven for the church." It is often obscurantist. But sometimes in those lecture halls we endeavor to substitute for it the light seems a thought too bright and on the brilliant plains of intellectual orthodoxy we half remember something lost in Lyonesse or something that was never found. Still—I must answer that voice of protest, that voice which somehow in spite of its anticlerical bias is also the voice of honesty, order, law, conscience saying "Let's get this clear. How can consideration of a conversation about a hat make metaphysics more manageable? Even if the conversation about the hat does a little illuminate the hat, isn't it a far cry to philosophy which professes to illuminate reality?"

II

At the end of the last discussion I was left facing the question "Why all this about a hat and the Taj Mahal?" If you want to bring out the fact that we sometimes use words not to give information as when we say "That will be fifteen guineas" nor to express and evoke feeling as when we exclaim "*Fifteen* guineas!" but to give a greater apprehension of what is already before us then why don't you choose a better example? For instance why not take the case of an accountant who has before him the assets and liabilities of a firm and asks "Are they solvent?" or a statistician who has before him the records of births and deaths for the last 50 years and asks "Has the average man today a greater expectation of life than he had 20 years ago?" Here are questions which can be settled on the basis of facts already ascertained and which are yet definite questions which can be settled by an agreed, definite, mathematical, deductive procedure. Why choose as an example a statement so preposterous and loosely worded that the question "Is it true?" is hardly a question at all . . . it not only cannot be answered by collecting new data by observation but also cannot be answered by any definite deductive procedure whatever?

My answer is: That is why I chose it. We all know and, what is more, we all recognize that there are questions which though they don't call for further investigation but only for reflection are yet perfectly respectable because the reflection they call for may be carried out in a definite demonstrative procedure which gives results Yes or No. My point is that this isn't the only sort of reflection and that the other sorts are not poor relations. May be they tend to have deplorable associates but they themselves we cannot afford to ignore. For they too take us toward a better apprehension of reality and also help us to understand better the character of all reflection including the more normal members of the family.

We do not deny that vague and queer things are said and that people make some show of considering them. We do not say that drama, novels, poetry never show us anything of the truth. But we are apt to half-feel that what is said in poetry is always more a matter of fancy than of fact, that it is not within the scope of reason. I am urging that there is more of poetry in science and more of science in poetry than our philosophy permits us readily to grasp. "There is within the flame of love a sort of wick or snuff that doth abate it" is not so far from "There is within the central rail on the Inner Circle a sort of current that, etc." "There is between a rising tide and the rising moon a sort of bond that, etc." Newton with his doctrine of gravitation gave us a so much greater apprehension of nature not so much because he told us what we would or would not see, like Pasteur or one who predicts what will be first past the post, but because he enabled us to see anew a thousand familiar incidents. To hint that when we are concerned with questions which are still unanswered even when we have left no stone unturned, no skid mark unmeasured, then thinking is no use is to forget that when the facts are agreed upon we still must hear argument before we give judgment. To hint that, when argument cannot show that in the usual usage of language the correct answer is Yes or No it shows us nothing, is to forget that such argument is in such a case just as necessary and just as valuable for an apprehension of the case before us as it is in those cases when it happens that we can express that greater apprehension in a word—Guilty, Not Guilty, Mad, Not Mad, Negligent, Not Negligent, Cruel, Not Cruel. To hint that whenever, in our efforts to portray nature, we break the bonds of linguistic convention and say what is preposterous then counsel must throw up the case because we are no longer at the bar of reason—to say this is to denigrate the very modes of thought that we need most when most we need to think.

And yet, in one's efforts to think clearly it is easy to speak as if it were a waste of time to try to answer a question which hasn't an answer Yes or No, Right or Wrong, True or False. And when lately some people had the courage to say, "A statement hasn't really a meaning unless it can be settled either by observation or by the sort of definite procedure by which questions of mathematics or logic are settled, otherwise it isn't a real, meaningful, worthwhile question but verbal, emotive, or nonsensical" then we welcomed this bold pronouncement because it seemed to say what we had long felt but not had the courage to say.

It is easy to see that this principle as it stands won't do. Consider the question "Here are the records for births and deaths for the last fifty years. Does the average man live longer today than he did twenty years ago?" This is not itself a hypothetical, mathematical, question. It is not the question "*If* the figures were as follows what *would* the answer be?" It is the question "These being the figures what *is* the answer?" This is a question about what has actually happened.

However it is settled by a definite deductive procedure. So such a case leaves it open to us to reformulate our tempting principle as follows: A question is a real, meaningful question only if either it can be answered by observation or it can be answered by demonstration from premises which are either self-evident or obtained by describing what we have observed.

This unspoken formula frames I submit a prevalent, though often unspoken, habit of thought. We know the man who when we are vigorously discussing some point interposes with "Look—we must define our terms, mustn't we?" He has been educated; he has been taught. His intentions are of the best. He is an ally against fluffy and futile talk. And yet so often by the time he has finished it seems somehow as if the questions he has answered aren't the ones we were interested in and worse still we seem to be unable to say what we were interested in. For example, suppose a man says to his wife, "The children ought to clean their shoes before going to school." "Oh, don't be so fussy," she says. "I am not being fussy," he says, "I'm merely concerned that the children should learn the ordinary politeness of taking some care of their appearance and not arrive at school in a slovenly state." "*Slovenly*," she says but at this point the good friend intervenes. He addresses himself to the wife. "Look," he says with his pleasant smile, "we must define our terms, mustn't we? One can't begin to answer a question until one has defined one's terms." "In that case one can't begin," she says, "for when one defines a word one puts another in its place." "Yes," he says, "but you know I don't mean that we ought to define *every* word we use. I mean we need to define the *vague* ones." "By equally vague ones I suppose," she says. "No, no," he says, "by more precise ones." "But," she says, "if what you put in place of the vague is something not

vague then the new words can't have the same meaning as
the old ones had." "I see what you mean," he says, "but still,
what is the use of arguing about a question which hasn't a
definite answer? One must know what one means." "Certainly one must know or come to know what one means,"
she says, "but that doesn't mean that there is no use in arguing about questions which haven't definite answers. They
are just the ones which are most interesting—those and the
ones which can't mean what they seem to mean, because
they are so preposterous. For instance I said just now that
Jack was fussy. We both knew what I meant—I meant like
an old hen. I daresay there is something to be said for saying
he is not fussy. But if so I want to have it said and I want
to have my say too. Now you say that we can't discuss this
question until we have defined our terms. I suppose you mean
the terms 'fussy' or 'slovenly.' But we were discussing it
until you interposed—I mean interrupted, spoke." "Well,"
he says, "I interposed because it seemed to me that you
were discussing a question which couldn't be answered. You
said Jack was fussy, he said he wasn't. But this wasn't a real
dispute, it was a question of words."

SHE: It *wasn't* a question of words, it was a real question,
a very real question.

HE: Well of course it was a question you and he had strong
feelings about. Or rather the word "fussy" is an *emotive*
word because it expresses our feelings and when you said that
Jack was fussy because he said the children ought to clean
their shoes before going to school, you expressed how you
felt about their doing this and about Jack—and when he said
he was not fussy he expressed his feelings about this and
about you. But there wasn't any real question between you.

SHE: What d'you mean, no *real* question?

HE: Well, I mean "Is Jack fussy?" isn't a question like
"Has Jack diphtheria?" which can be settled by taking a
swab from his throat. Nor is it like "Has he the money for
the tickets? They cost 15/- and he has 10/-, one shilling,
three sixpences and half a crown. Now is that 15/-?" There
is a procedure for settling such a question.

SHE: You are not now saying that we can't answer a question unless we can define our terms. But what are you saying? Is it that questions which can't be settled by observation nor by deduction aren't really questions? But what do you mean "aren't really questions"? Do you mean that there is no definite procedure for answering them? But what d'you call a definite procedure? Is legal procedure when cases are quoted in order to show for example that in this case before the court there was negligence or that there was not—is this a definite procedure? And does it always lead to an answer? Whenever I get a glimpse of what you mean it seems preposterous and it only doesn't seem preposterous when I don't know what you mean. But I want to *come* to know what you mean. I want to know what's at the back of your saying that questions which seem to be real questions aren't really; I want to know what makes you say it, what reasons you have, whether you are right or wrong or neither. Or is this not a real question because it hasn't a definite answer so that it is futile to discuss it?

"Well," he says, "I think you know what I mean. I mean that there are lots of questions which seem as if they could be answered by observation or deduction when they can't be really because they are matters of words or matters of feeling."

SHE: We all know that this sometimes happens. For instance one person might say that a certain food is in short supply and another that it is not because the one means that people can't get as much of it as they want to buy and the other means that there is no less of this food on the market than usual. Or to take a more trivial but simpler instance: I remember I once said of two horses which had the same father that they were half-brothers and someone else said that they were not and it turned out that this was because he didn't call *horses* half-brothers unless they had the same *mother*.

HE: I don't mean just trivial instances like that. I mean that there are questions which seem important to us and seem to call for much thought because they seem difficult to answer when really they are difficult to answer only because there is no way of answering them so that they have no answers. For instance take an old question which has very much concerned people—the question "Did someone make the world?" "Is there Someone behind it all?" This seems as if it could be answered like "Who made this watch?" "Who laid out this garden?" "Is there a master mind behind all these seemingly disconnected crimes?" But it can't be answered in that way. It couldn't be. What I mean is this: when you are told that there is someone, God, who brings the young lions their prey and feeds the cattle upon a thousand hills, it is natural to think that if you watch, perhaps in the hush at dawn or at sunset, you will see something to confirm this statement. You watch. What d'you see? Antelopes feeding perhaps, or zebras come down to drink. A lion springs—with wonderful acceleration it is true—but still his own acceleration. And if anything saves that zebra its the way he comes round on his hocks and gets going. There are the stars and the flowers and the animals. But there's no one to be seen. And no one to be heard. There's the wind and there's the thunder but if you call there's no answer except the echo of your own voice. It is natural to infer that those who told us that there is someone who looks after it all are wrong. But that is a mistake we are told. No such inference is legitimate, they say, because God is invisible.

SHE: God is a spirit and cannot be seen nor heard. But the evidences of his existence lie in the order and arrangement of nature.

HE: Ah. That is what is so often said. But it suggests that in nature there are evidences of God as there are in a watch the evidences of a maker, in a cathedral, the evidences of an architect, in a garden, the evidences of a gardener. And this is to suggest that God *could* be seen. It then turns out that this is a mistake. A gardener may be elusive, an architect retiring, a watch maker hard to find, but we know what it would be to see them and so confirm the guesses that it is they who are responsible for what we see before us. Now what would it be like to see God? Suppose some seer were to see, imagine we all saw, move upwards from the ocean to the sky some prodigious figure which declared in dreadful

tones the moral law or prophesied most truly—our fate.
Would this be to see God?

Wouldn't it just be a phenomenon which later we were
able to explain or not able to explain but in neither case
the proof of a living God. The logic of God if there is such
a logic isn't like that.

SHE: Indeed, indeed. The way to knowledge of God is not
as simple as we might confusedly hope. An evil and adulter-
ous generation seeketh after a sign and there shall no sign
be given it save the sign of the prophet Jonah. And that is
not an arbitrary decree but one by which God himself is
bound. What you call "the logic of God" couldn't be simpler
than it is without his being less than he is, for the simpler
the possible proofs that something is so the simpler it is for
it to be so.

HE: What d'you mean?

SHE: Well, if we mean by "a rainbow" only a certain
appearance in the sky then it is easy to know at a glance
whether today there is a rainbow or not. But in that case a
rainbow is only an appearance in the sky. The moment it is
more, that moment it's harder to know. If one who says
"There's a rainbow" means not merely that there is a certain
appearance in the sky but that that appearance is linked with
water and the sun, then the appearance is no longer by itself
a proof that what he says is so. It may be a sign but it is
not one from which he can read off the answer to the question "Is there a rainbow?" as he could when by "a rainbow"
was meant no more than a certain appearance in the sky.
When a rainbow is more than the appearance of a rainbow
then that appearance is not a sign which makes it beside the
point to look for the rest of what makes a rainbow a rainbow.
The simplest people are sometimes very good at telling
whether a storm is coming but the full proof, the full confirmation of what they reckon is so, cannot be less complex
than all that makes a storm. Horses are quick to know
whether one is angry, babies to know whether one loves
them, but the full proof of what they feel is so cannot be
less complex than is anger or love itself—as you say it is
not merely that there *is* not some fool-proof proof of God.

There *couldn't* be. But that doesn't mean that there are no evidences of God's existence; it doesn't mean that there are no proofs of his existence; nor that these are not to be found in experience; nor even that they are not to be found in what we see and hear. One cannot see power but it's from what we see that we know that power is present when we watch the tubetrain mysteriously move towards the Marble Arch, and the more we watch, the more explicable the mystery becomes, the more, without limit, the proof approaches a demonstration. Each day a thousand incidents confirm the doctrine that energy is indestructible: and if the present proof is not a demonstration that is not because the conclusion calls for reasons of a kind we never get. It is because the doctrine is infinite in its implications so that beyond any conceivable evidence at any time there is still evidence beyond that time—evidence for or evidence against—until no wheels are turning and time stops. In the same way, as the scroll of nature unrolls the proof of an eternal God prevails—or fails—until on the day of judgment doctrine, like theory, must become a verdict and all be lost or won.

III

HE: I understand that you are now saying that the order and arrangement of nature proves the existence of God, not as the moving machinery of a mill indicates the flow of water beneath it, but as the behavior of an electrical machine proves the presence of electricity because electricity just is such behavior. The average man is invisible but we may know whether he is orderly or disorderly because his existence and nature are deducible from that of individual men. He is orderly if they are orderly because his being orderly just is their being orderly. But now if the existence of God is deducible from the fact that nature is orderly then one who says that God exists merely puts in theological words what others express in the words, "In nature nothing is inexplicable, there is always a reason why." And those who speak of God would not allow that this is all they mean. This is why I say that the question, "Does God exist?" cannot be answered by observation and also cannot be answered by deduction. And this is why I say that though it seems to be a question it is not. The statement "God's in his heaven" may express a feeling but it is not some thing that could be true or false, because nothing would make it false and therefore nothing would make it true.

SHE: You make too little of a move in thought which from a mass of data extracts and assembles what builds up into the proof of something which, though it doesn't go beyond that data, gives us an apprehension of reality which before we lacked. The move from the myriad transactions of the market to the conclusion that sterling is stronger isn't negligible. The move from the bewildering and apparently disorderly flux of nature to the doctrine that all that happens happens in order is one which called for our best efforts and gave us a very different apprehension of nature. Perhaps it took Spinoza a long way towards God.

Still it *is* very true that those who speak of God don't mean merely that nature is orderly. Nature would be orderly if it were nothing but an enormous clock slowly but inevitably running down. But then I am not saying that if there is order in Nature that proves that God exists. The fact that a machine is electrical is not deducible from the fact that its behavior is orderly. If there were no order in its behavior it couldn't be electrical but there could be order in its behavior without its being electrical. It might run by falling weights. It is the fact that the order in its behavior is of a certain character which makes the machine electrical. It doesn't need winding but from time to time it stops or goes more slowly just when the fire goes out—that's what makes it electrical. The mere fact that Nature is orderly would never prove that Energy is indestructible. What makes this true is the fact that the order in nature is of a certain character. It might have been of a different character but, as it is, each day confirms the doctrine of the conservation of energy.

The order of nature might have been of a character which would make it fair to say, "It is all in the hands of someone who made it and then fell asleep" or, "It's all in the hands of someone who arranges the little ironies of fate." For all I have said to the contrary it may be of this character. For I am not trying to prove that God does exist but only to prove that it is wrong to say that there could be no proof that he does or that he does not.

HE: But surely this comparison of the logic of God with the logic of Energy isn't a legitimate comparison.

SHE: I don't know whether it's legitimate or not. I am making it.

HE: Yes but—well, it's like this: I understand you when you say that just as those who speak of the existence and properties of Energy don't deduce all they say from the fact that the procession of events in nature is orderly but from the particular character of that procession of events, so those who speak of God don't deduce his existence and properties merely from the fact that the procession of events is orderly but from the particular character of that procession. But surely the question "Does God exist?" is very different from the question "Does Energy exist?". I don't mean merely that the questions are different like the question "Is there any milk?" is different from "Is there any wine?". Those questions are very unlike because milk is very unlike wine. But they are very like in the sort of procedure which settles them; that is, the logic of milk is like the logic of wine. But surely the way we know of the existence of energy is very different from the way, if any, in which we know of the existence of God. For one thing, people have spoken of knowing the presence of God not from looking around them but from their own hearts. The logic of God may be more like the logic of Energy or of Life than at first appears but surely it is very different.

SHE: It *is* different. One can't expect to bring out the idiosyncrasies in what you call "the logic of God" by a single comparison. The way in which we know God who has been called "the Soul of the World," "the Mind of the Universe," might also be compared with the way one knows the soul or mind of another creature. It is clear that one couldn't find the soul behind the face of one's neighbor or one's cat as one could find at last the elusive and even ghostly inhabitant of the house next door. Because of this people have said that when we speak of the consciousness of another this is a way of speaking of those sequences of bodily events which are the manifestations of consciousness, just as when we speak of energy that is a way of speaking of the manifestations of energy and when we speak of a procession that is just a way of speaking of what makes up the procession. Here again this comparison is dangerous unless it is accompanied by a warning. For it neglects the fact that though one who has never tasted what is bitter or sweet and has never felt pain may know very well the behavior characteristic of, for instance, pain, he yet cannot know pain nor even that another is in pain—not in the way he could had he himself felt pain. It is from looking round him that a man knows of the pain, of the love and of the hate in the world, but it is also from his own heart.

HE: Yes, but what I mean is this. Even though we couldn't see energy because it isn't the sort of thing which could be seen we know very well what to look for in order to know of its existence and where it flows, we can measure it and deduce the laws of its transmission and conservation. Even when we ask of someone, "Is he really pleased to see us?" we know what to look for to prove that the answer is "Yes," and what to look for to prove that the answer is "No." We may ask him and beg him to tell us the truth, and if we are not satisfied we may await developments, watch for further signs, and these may, in your words, approach more and more a demonstration. But with the questions "Does God exist?" "Is this what he approves or that?" there is no agreement as to what to look for, no agreement as to what the character of the order of events must be to count in favor of the answer "Yes" or in favor of the answer "No."

SHE: Not *no* agreement. If there were *no* agreement that *would* make the question meaningless. But it is not true that there is no agreement. One could describe a future for the world which were it to come would prove the triumph of the Devil. Hells, it is true, are more easily described than Heavens, and Paradise lost than Paradise regained. Descriptions of heaven are apt to be either extremely hazy or to involve too much music or too much hunting. And this isn't a joke, it may spell a contradiction in perfection. But it's not true that we haven't a clue about the kingdom of heaven. Every description of what appears to be Heaven and turns out to be Hell makes plainer the boundaries of Heaven. We don't know what would be Heaven and this shows itself in the fluctuating logic of Heaven, that is to say in our feeble grasp of what it is we do want to do with the words, "Will the kingdom of heaven come?" "Does God exist?" But this doesn't prove that there isn't anything we want to do with them. An artist may not know what he wants to do, and only come to know by doing first one thing which isn't what he wanted to do and then another which also isn't what he wanted to do. But this doesn't prove that there wasn't anything he wanted to do. On the contrary in finding what he didn't want to do he may find at last what he did. In the same way with words, finding out what one didn't mean, one may find out at last what one did mean.

Now with regard to God and the Devil and whether there is any meaning in asking whether they exist! Freud so far from thinking these questions meaningless says in the last of the New Introductory Lectures: "It seems not to be true that there is a power in the universe which watches over the well-being of every individual with parental care and brings all his concerns to a happy ending. On the contrary, the destinies of man are incompatible with a universal principle of benevolence or with—what is to some degree contradictory —a universal principle of justice. Earthquakes, floods and fires do not differentiate between the good and devout man and the sinner and unbeliever. And, even if we leave in-animate nature out of the account and consider the destinies of individual men in so far as they depend on their relations with others of their own kind, it is by no means the rule that virtue is rewarded and wickedness punished, but it happens often enough that the violent, the crafty and the unprincipled seize the desirable goods of the earth for themselves, while the pious go empty away. Dark, unfeeling and unloving powers determine human destiny . . ." Something about the facts, Freud feels, is brought out by saying not merely that

often men do evil things but by saying too that "dark, unfeeling and unloving powers determine human destiny."
It's preposterous but we know what he means—not clearly,
but obscurely. Others have spoken in the same way. St. Paul
says, "that which I do I allow not: for what I would that I
do not; but what I hate, that do I." Euripides makes Helen
say to Menelaus:

> ". . . And yet how strange it is!
> I ask not thee; I ask my own sad thought,
> What was there in my heart, that I forgot
> My home and land and all I loved, to fly
> With a strange man? Surely it was not I,
> But Cypris there!"

HE: It's all very well for her to say, "It was not I." The
fact is she did it.

SHE: There is evasion in such words as there has been
ever since Eve said, "The serpent beguiled me," ever since
Adam said, "The woman that thou gavest me she gave me
of the tree." There is evasion and confusion and inappropriate humility perhaps in one who says, "Yet not I but
the grace of God that dwelleth in me." And yet is it all
evasion and confusion? Is it for nothing that we speak of
someone as not having been himself, as never having been
able to be himself. We speak of compulsive acts, compulsive
thoughts, of having been possessed. Possessed by what? A
demon evil or good or both good and evil. And why do
we speak so? Because we come on something done by
Dr. Jekyll which is out of order, out of character, inexplicable, if it was Dr. Jekyll who was in control. It is in an
effort to understand, to bring order into the apparently
chaotic, that we find ourselves saying preposterously, "It
wasn't really Dr. Jekyll, it was Mr. Hyde—or the Devil
himself."

HE: But there is no need to speak of the Devil here. It is
just that there was more in Dr. Jekyll than appeared.

SHE: Not just that. There was more than there appeared
in the man who called about the gas meter and left with the
pearls. But that's different. *We* were taken aback when we

found he'd gone with the pearls, but *he* wasn't. It was all in
order as far as he was concerned. But in those cases of
multiple personality, for example in that case Dr. Moreton
Prince studied, the one personality, Miss Beauchamp, was
horrified to learn of the lies which Sally, the other personality, told. Miss Beauchamp couldn't have told such lies and
still be Miss Beauchamp.

HE: Yes, but Sally was just a part of Miss Beauchamp's
unconscious. There were in her desires and thoughts which
she didn't allow, as St. Paul says, which she didn't know, to
translate St. Paul's Greek still more literally.

SHE: I am not denying that we can explain the seemingly
inexplicable and grasp the order in what seems like chaos
with the help of the conceptions of the unconscious, of the
super ego, of the id, of internal objects, of ghosts that are
gone whenever we turn to see them, of currents hidden in the
depths of the soul. But if the logic of God and of the Devil
is more eccentric than it seems, so also is the logic of the
Super Ego and the Id and the Unconscious. Indeed what
makes us speak of the unconscious and the good and the evil
in it, the wine of life and the poison of death so mixed, is
closely connected with what makes us speak of a hidden
power for good—God—and a hidden power for evil—the
Devil. For when we speak of the thoughts and acts of Mr.
So-and-So as "coming out of his unconscious" we are often
inclined to say that they are not altogether his, that he is
compelled, driven, helped, possessed by something not himself. When we recognize the unconscious of the soul we no
longer find adequate the model of objects with definite shapes,
and we begin to think of the soul as the energy continually
flowing and transformed. For example Natasha in *War and
Peace* though she loves Prince André Bolkonsky is fascinated
by Prince Kouragine. His fast horses stand at the gate and
it is nothing in her that prevents her flying with him. It was
after Bolkonsky had heard of all this that his friend Peter
Bezukov visited him and told him that Natasha was very ill.
Bolkonsky replied that he was sorry to hear of her illness
and—Tolstoy says—an evil smile like his father's curled his
pinched lips. He said, "Then Prince Kouragine did not after

all consent to give her his hand." Peter replied, "He could not—he is already married." Prince André laughed evilly—again reminding one of his father.

Here I feel the presence of evil, evil that has flowed from the father to the son. Anger against Natasha was justified if you like. But that's not what I am now thinking about. Whether anger was or was not justified—in that laugh we feel evil, an evil that we can't place altogether in Prince André. We feel inclined to trace it also to his father. But then when we come to the father it doesn't seem to lie altogether in him either. He was the man who a little before he died accused the daughter who loved him of "endless imaginery crimes, loaded her with the bitterest reproaches, accused her of having poisoned his existence. . . . dismissed her from his presence, saying she might do whatever she pleased, that he would have nothing more to say to her, and that he never would set eyes on her again." And this was only the climax of what had gone on for years. This wasn't out of character. *Or was* it? For later he is dying. He makes a desperate effort to speak. "I'm always thinking of you" he says, and as she bows her head to hide her tears he strokes her hair and says, "I called you all night." "If I had but known," she says. Dark, unfeeling, and unloving powers determine human destiny.

Or is this going too far? Is it evil and unloving power only that determines human destiny and directs the course of nature? Or is there also at work a good and loving power? It has been said that once at least a higher gift than grace did flesh and blood refine, God's essence and his very self—in the body of Jesus. Whether this statement is true or false is not now the point but whether it's so obscure as to be senseless. Obscure undoubtedly it is but senseless it is not, beyond the scope of reason it is not. For to say that in Nero God was incarnate is not to utter a senseless string of words nor merely to express a surprising sentiment; it is to make a statement which is absurd because it is against all reason. If I say of a cat, "This cat is an abracadabra" I utter a senseless string of words, I don't make a statement at all and therefore don't make an absurd statement. But if I say of a cat which is plainly dead, "In this cat there is life" I make a statement which is absurd because it is against all reason. The cat is not hunting, eating, sleeping, breathing; it is stiff and cold. In the same way the words, "In Nero God was incarnate" are not without any meaning; one who utters them makes a statement, he makes a statement which is absurd and *against* all reason and therefore *not* beyond the scope of reason. Now if a statement is not beyond the scope of reason then any logically parallel statement is also not beyond the scope of reason. For example, the statement, "Your house is well designed" is not beyond the scope of reason. It may be obviously true or absurdly false or obviously neither true nor false, but it's not beyond the scope of reason. The statement, "My house is well designed" is logically parallel to the statement, "Your house is well designed." The statement, "My house is well designed" may be absurdly false or neither true nor false or obviously true. But like the parallel statement about your house it is not beyond the scope of reason. The statement "In Jesus God was incarnate" is logically parallel to "In Nero God was incarnate." The latter we noticed is not beyond the scope of reason. Therefore the statement "In Jesus God was incarnate" is not beyond the scope of reason.

And we may come at the same result more directly. Consider the words "Was there someone, Jesus, in whom God was incarnate?" These words call first for investigation. Was there such a person as Jesus is alleged to have been? Was there someone born of a virgin? Was there someone who rose from the dead? Was there someone who said all or some or most of the things Jesus is alleged to have said? Did someone speak as this man is said to have spoken? These things settled, we have only started. How far does the rest of experience show that what this man said was true? Did what Jesus said reveal what we hadn't known or what we had known but hadn't recognized? Was there someone, Jesus, who was God incarnate? The question calls for investigation but it also calls like every other question for thought, reflection, reason. He made himself the Son of God. "Preposterous presumption" the priests said, but was it the truth?

The facts agreed upon, still a question is before the bar of reason as when, the facts agreed upon, still a question comes before a Court. Was there negligence or was there not? Was there a later opportunity or was there not? To such a question may be the answer is "Yes," maybe the answer is "No," maybe the answer is neither "Yes" nor "No." But the question is not beyond the scope of reason. On the contrary it calls for very careful consideration and not the less when what's relevant is conflicting and not the less because what's relevant is not enumerable because there's not a separate name for every relevant feature of the case and an index to measure its weight. In a cat crouched to spring burns the flame of life. There are signs we can mention—nothing moves but very slightly the tail and there's something about the eyes but what? She springs. Still the proof of life eludes language but it's there, was there, and will be there, in the moving picture before us. Was Jesus God incarnate? The law in this matter is not as simple nor as definite nor as fully written out in statutes as we might wish it could be. The question is large, slippery, subtle. But it is not true that nothing is more relevant to it than another, so that nothing supports one answer more than it supports the other. On the contrary every incident in the life of Christ is relevant to this question as every incident in the life of Nero is relevant to the same question about him. To both much more is relevant. For an affirmative answer to either implies the existence of God. And to this question every incident in the history of the world is relevant—whether it is the fall of a sparrow or the coming of harvest, the passing of an empire or the fading of a smile.

Here ends this talk about how in the end questions about God and the Devil are to be answered.

The statement "There is someone who feeds the cattle upon a thousand hills, who can match the powers of evil and lift up the everlasting doors" is not one to which what is still hidden from us in Space and Time is all irrelevant. But it seems to me it is not only this that makes the question, "Is that statement true?" a hard one. It is also the fact that this question calls upon us to consider all that is already before us, in case it should happen that having eyes we see not, and having ears we hear not.

The consideration this question calls for cannot be conducted by a definite step by step procedure like that of one who calculates the height or weight or prospects of life of the average man or the Bengal Tiger. Nor is it a question which though it has no answer "Yes" or "No" may yet be considered on perfectly conventional lines like the question before the court, "Was there or was there not neglect of duty?" For the statement "There is one above who gives order and life amongst disorder and death" when taken on perfectly conventional lines is as preposterous as the statement that the sun doesn't move though we see it climb the sky. Nor are the new lines on which the statement is to be taken firmly fixed as they are with "We are turning to the sun at n m.p.h." And yet in spite of all this and whatever the answer may be the old questions "Does God exist?" "Does the Devil exist?" aren't senseless, aren't beyond the scope of thought and reason. On the contrary they call for new awareness of what has so long been about us, in case knowing nature so well we never know her.

Nothing in all this makes less of the call for critical attention whatever sort of statement we are considering. Nothing in all this makes less of the need to get clear about what we mean by a statement, to get clear as to what we are comparing with what. Just this is called for, just this is done, in that statement so obvious yet so preposterous, "My dear, it's the Taj Mahal."

A SELECTED AND ANNOTATED

BIBLIOGRAPHY

THE ONTOLOGICAL

ARGUMENT

Historically and theologically two of the most important writings on the ontological argument are a book by the Protestant theologian Karl Barth, *Anselm: Fides Quaerens Intellectum* (1931. E.T., London: Student Christian Movement Press; Richmond: John Knox Press, 1960) and a long article by the Roman Catholic lay theologian Étienne Gilson, "Sens et Nature de l'Argument de Saint Anselme" (*Archives d'Histoire Doctrinale et Litteraire du Moyen Age,* 1934). Barth presents the Anselmic argument, not as an attempted proof of God's existence, but as an unfolding of the significance of God's revelation of himself as One whom the believer is prohibited from thinking as less than the highest conceivable reality. Part I of Gilson's article argues that Anselm must be understood in relation to his own thought-world and that the key to his ontological argument is the epistemological realism of his *De Veritate* (of which there is an excellent English translation in Richard McKeon, *Selections from Medieval Philosophers,* Vol. I, New York: Charles Scribner's Sons, 1929). Part II of Gilson's article contains an important critique of Barth's book.

Some of the most interesting discussions by contemporary philosophers, in addition to the one by Norman Malcolm included in this volume, are: Gilbert Ryle, "Mr. Collingwood and the Ontological Argument" (*Mind,* 1935); Charles Hartshorne, *Man's Vision of God* (Chicago: Willett, Clark & Co., 1941), chapter X, and *The Logic of Perfection* (La Salle, Ill.: Open Court Publishing Co., 1962), chapter 2; Nicholas Rescher, "The Ontological Argument Revisited" (*The Australasian Journal of Philosophy,* 1959); and Jerome Shaffer, "Existence, Predication and the Ontological Argument" (*Mind,* July, 1962).

THE COSMOLOGICAL ARGUMENT

Two competent expositions and defenses of the cosmological argument by Roman Catholic theologians are: R. Garrigou-Lagrange, *God: His Existence and His Nature* (1914. E.T., St. Louis: B. Herder Book Co., 2 vols., 1934 & 1936), volume I, chapter 3; and R. P. Phillips, *Modern Thomistic Philosophy* (London: Burns, Oates & Washbourne, Ltd., 1935), volume II, Part III, chapters 2 and 3. The argument is also used by two leading Anglican neo-Thomist writers, Austin Farrer in *Finite and Infinite* (London: Dacre Press, 1943, second edition, 1960), Part III, and E. L. Mascall in *He Who Is* (London: Longmans, Green & Co., 1943), chapters 5 and 6. Another writer who has recently defended the argument is Samuel M. Thompson, *A Modern Philosophy of Religion* (Chicago: Henry Regnery Co., 1955), Part VI. There is a brilliant restatement of the cosmological argument in the last chapter of Richard Taylor's *Metaphysics* (Englewood Cliffs, N.J.: Prentice Hall, 1963).

A classic critique (in addition to Hume's, included in this volume) is that of Immanuel Kant, *Critique of Pure Reason*, Transcendental Dialectics, chapter III, section 5. Paul Edwards' "The Cosmological Argument," in *The Rationalist Annual*, 1959, is a careful criticism by a contemporary philosopher of the analytical school.

For a full discussion of Hume's treatment of religion, *see* Antony Flew, *Hume's Philosophy of Belief* (London: Routledge & Kegan Paul, 1961), ch. 9.

THE TELEOLOGICAL ARGUMENT

The design argument was elaborated in every possible way by a multitude of eighteenth and nineteenth century divines, but amongst this extensive literature Paley's *Natural Theology*, of which the opening chapter is included in this volume, stands out.

This has become available again as edited by Frederick Ferré in the Library of Liberal Arts, 1964. Treatments of the argument in the style of that period continue to be produced, examples being, at a more popular level, Arthur I. Brown, *Footprints of God* (Fundamental Truth Publishers, 1947), and at a more sophisticated level, Robert E. D. Clark, *The Universe: Plan or Accident?* (Philadelphia: Muhlenberg Press, 1961). A. E. Taylor in *Does God Exist?* (London: Macmillan & Co., 1945) is the last serious philosopher to have sponsored a form of design argument.

Kant's classic critique of what he called the Physico-theological argument occurs in his *Critique of Pure Reason,* Transcendental Dialectic, chapter 3, section 6. Some of Hume's main criticisms in the *Dialogues Concerning Natural Religion* (of which the modern scholarly edition is that by Norman Kemp Smith, Oxford, 1935) are also made by him in his *Enquiry Concerning the Human Understanding,* section XI. A direct and vigorous criticism of the Paley type of argument occurs in chapter 44 of Clarence Darrow's *The Story of My Life* (New York: Grossett & Dunlap, Inc., 1932). Arthur Pap has some interesting pages on the ideas of design and probability in *Elements of Analytic Philosophy* (New York: The Macmillan Company, 1949) chapter 9, section c.

Hume's *Dialogues* (parts X and XI) states the challenge to the design argument from the fact of evil. From the side of religious belief the literature of theodicy is enormous. St. Augustine's many-sided discussion of the problem can be found in his *Confessions,* Bk. VII, chapters 3-5, 12-16; *Enchiridion,* chapters 3-5, and *City of God,* Bk. XI, chapters 16-18 and Bk. XII, chapters 1-9. Austin Farrer provides a contemporary Augustinian discussion in *Love Almighty and Ills Unlimited* (New York: Doubleday, 1961). Leibniz's *Theodicy* (recently translated by E. M. Huggard, London: Routledge & Kegan Paul, 1952) is a major classic. R. A. Tsanoff's *The Nature of Evil* (New York: The Macmillan Co., 1931) is a valuable account of the history of man's attempts to grapple with this problem. Contemporary theological treatments include François Petit, *The Problem of Evil* (New York: Hawthorn Books, 1959), and Charles Journet, *The Meaning of Evil* (London: Geoffrey Chapman, 1963), from a Catholic standpoint, and Nels Ferré, *Evil and the Christian Faith* (New York: Harper, 1947) and J. S. Whale, *The Christian Answer to the Problem of Evil* (London: Student Christian Movement Press, 1939), from a Protestant standpoint.

Four important recent articles on the subject by contemporary philosophers are: Antony Flew, "Divine Omnipotence and Human Freedom" (Flew and MacIntyre, editors, *New Essays in Philosophical Theology,* New York: The Macmillan Company, 1955); J. L. Mackie, "Evil and Omnipotence" (*Mind,* April, 1955); Ninian Smart, "Omnipotence, Evil and Supermen" (*Philosophy,* April and July, 1961, with further discussions in January and

April, 1962), replying to the argument offered by Mackie and Flew; and H. D. Aiken, "God and Evil" (*Ethics*, January, 1958).

THE MORAL ARGUMENT

In addition to Hastings Rashdall's account of the argument another important exposition from the same period is W. R. Sorley's *Moral Values and the Idea of God* (Cambridge University Press, 1918). Two recent theologians who have used a moral argument are John Baillie, *The Interpretation of Religion* (Edinburgh: T. & T. Clark, 1929) chapters 5-7, and his brother D. M. Baillie, *Faith in God* (Edinburgh: T. & T. Clark, 1927), chapter 5. The distinguished Kantian scholar, H. J. Paton, discusses the argument sympathetically in *The Modern Predicament* (London: Allen & Unwin; New York: The Macmillan Company, 1955), chapter 21.

THE ARGUMENT FROM RELIGIOUS EXPERIENCE

This argument is used by David Elton Trueblood, *Philosophy of Religion* (New York: Harper Brothers, 1957), ch. 11, as well as by A. E. Taylor in the passage reprinted here. H. D. Lewis' *Our Experience of God* (London: Allen & Unwin; New York: The Macmillan Company, 1959) is a full-scale contemporary philosophical treatment of the subject of religious experience. Two classics in this field are Rudolf Otto's *The Idea of the Holy* (1917. E.T., 1923), and William James's *The Varieties of Religious Experience* (1902).

The main critical issue raised today concerning the cognitive value of religious experience is formulated by C. B. Martin, *Religious Belief* (Ithaca: Cornell University Press, 1959), ch. 5, and by Ronald Hepburn, *Christianity and Paradox* (London: Watts; New York: Humanities Press, 1958), chapters 3 and 4.

THE THEISTIC ARGUMENTS

IN GENERAL

A. E. Taylor's article on "Theism" in the *Encyclopaedia of Religion and Ethics*, edited by James Hastings (Edinburgh: T. & T. Clark; New York: Charles Scribner's Sons, 1908–1921) volume 12, is a valuable historical discussion of the theistic arguments. John Hospers, *An Introduction to Philosophical Analysis* (New York: Prentice-Hall, 1953; London: Routledge & Kegan Paul, 1959), pp. 322–374, provides a contemporary critique of the arguments. Almost any general work on the philosophy of religion discusses the arguments, some of the most recent such books being Samuel M. Thompson, *A Modern Philosophy of Religion* (Chicago: Henry Regnery, 1955), David Elton Trueblood, *Philosophy of Religion* (New York: Harper Brothers, 1957), Geddes MacGregor, *Introduction to Religious Philosophy* (Boston: Houghton Mifflin, 1959), and John Hick, *Philosophy of Religion* (Englewood Cliffs, N.J.: Prentice Hall, 1963). J. J. C. Smart's article "The Existence of God" (Flew and MacIntyre, editors, *New Essays in Philosophical Theology*) discusses most of the traditional arguments, as does Wallace I. Matson's *The Existence of God* (Ithaca, N.Y.: Cornell University Press, 1965).

DISCUSSIONS AND

QUESTIONINGS

Atheism and Agnosticism

The classics of modern atheism come from the nineteenth century—Ludwig Feuerbach's *The Essence of Christianity* (1841. E.T., 1853); Baron Holbach's *System of Nature*, Vol. II (1853), and *Good Sense* (1856); and Charles Bradlaugh's "A Plea for Atheism," which is reprinted in *Charles Bradlaugh—Champion of Liberty* (London: Watts & Co., 1933).

Two classic statements of the agnostic position are T. H. Huxley's essay "Agnosticism" (a term which Huxley invented), which appears in *Science and the Christian Tradition* (New York: Appleton & Co., 1894), and Sir Leslie Stephen's *An Agnostic's Apology* (New York: G. P. Putnam, 1903).

The nearest contemporary equivalents to this type of work are Bertrand Russell's *Why I Am Not a Christian* (London: Allen & Unwin; New York: Simon & Schuster, Inc., 1957); Julian Huxley's *Religion Without Revelation* (2nd ed., London: Max Parrish, 1957); Ronald Hepburn's *Christianity and Paradox* (London: Watts & Co.; New York: Humanities Press, 1958); and Walter Kaufmann's *Critique of Religion and Philosophy* (New York: Harper & Row, 1958) and *The Faith of a Heretic* (Garden City, N.Y.: Doubleday, 1962).

The Religious Rejection of the Theistic Proofs

Sören Kierkegaard is the main figure here. There are few passages in his books devoted explicitly to the theme, but many of the central positions developed in his *Philosophical Fragments* (1844), *Concluding Unscientific Postscript* (1846) and *Training in Christianity* (1850) have a direct bearing upon it. Martin Buber's *Eclipse of God* (New York: Harper & Brothers, 1952) represents in certain respects a similar point of view. For a classic statement of the psychological ineffectiveness of philosophic proofs *see* Cardinal Newman's "The Tamworth Reading Room" (1941), reprinted in *Essays and Sketches,* Vol. II.

Recent Religious Apologetics Not Based upon the Theistic Arguments

Some of the many works of this kind are John Baillie, *Our Knowledge of God* (London: Oxford University Press, 1939; New York: Charles Scribner's Sons, 1962) and *The Sense of the Presence of God* (London: Oxford University Press, 1963); Charles A. Bennett, *The Dilemma of Religious Knowledge* (New Haven: Yale University Press, 1931); Erich Frank, *Philosophical Understanding and Religious Truth* (London: Oxford University Press, 1945); John Hick, *Faith and Knowledge* (Ithaca, N.Y.: Cornell University Press; London: Oxford University Press, 1957); H. D. Lewis, *Our Experience of God* (London: Allen & Unwin; New

York: The Macmillan Company, 1959); H. Richard Niebuhr, *The Meaning of Revelation* (New York: The Macmillan Company, 1941).

CONTEMPORARY PROBLEMS

Frederick Ferré's *Language, Logic and God* (New York: Harper, 1961) provides a general introduction to the two types of contemporary problems treated here, as does William Blackstone's *The Problem of Religious Knowledge* (Englewood Cliffs, N.J.: Prentice Hall, 1963). John Wisdom's "Gods," reprinted in *Logic and Language,* I, edited by Antony Flew (Oxford: Basil Blackwell, 1951) and in John Wisdom's *Philosophy and Psycho-Analysis* (Oxford: Basil Blackwell, 1953), launched the discussion concerning the cognitive or noncognitive character of religious language. The essays by Antony Flew, R. M. Hare, Basil Mitchell and Ian Crombie in *New Essays in Philosophical Theology* (London: Student Christian Movement Press; New York: The Macmillan Company, 1955) continue it, as do some of the papers in *Faith and Logic,* edited by Basil Mitchell (London: Allen & Unwin, 1957). E. L. Mascall, *Words and Images* (London: Longmans, Green & Co.; New York: St. Martin's Press, Inc., 1958), and T. R. Miles, *Religion and the Scientific Outlook* (London: George Allen & Unwin, 1959) treat in part the same subject.

There are as yet few explorations of the nature of religious language, but amongst them is Ian Ramsey, *Religious Language* (London: Student Christian Movement Press, 1957); and as attempts to give a noncognitive analysis of religious statements, including affirmations of the existence of God, the lecture by R. B. Braithwaite reprinted in part in this book; the work just cited by T. R. Miles; and J. H. Randall, Jr., *The Role of Knowledge in Western Religion* (Boston: Starr King Press, 1958); Peter Munz, *Problems of Religious Knowledge* (London: Student Christian Movement Press, 1959); Paul F. Schmidt, *Religious Knowledge* (New York: The Free Press of Glencoe, 1961). These problems are also discussed in *Religious Experience & Truth,* edited by Sidney Hook (New York: New York University Press, 1961).